Scotland Reclaimed

THE INSIDE STORY OF SCOTLAND'S FIRST DEMOCRATIC PARLIAMENTARY ELECTION

Murray Ritchie

THE SALTIRE SOCIETY

Scotland Reclaimed
published 2000 by
The Saltire Society
9 Fountain Close,
22 High Street,
Edinburgh EH1 1TF

A catalogue record for this book is available
from the British Library.

ISBN 0 85411 077 1

Cover Design by James Hutcheson

Printed and bound in Scotland by Bell & Bain Limited

Foreword

Professor Tom Devine

1999 was an historic year for Scotland, probably the most historic of this century. The nation elected its first ever democratic parliament which was formally opened by Her Majesty the Queen on 1st July. Here, Murray Ritchie, the Scottish Political Editor of *The Herald*, gives an absorbing account of these momentous months. It is neither a narrative nor a description of what happened but rather a personal diary of the events, personalities and issues during the election written with verve and insight by one of Scotland's leading journalists. Murray Ritchie knows all the main players and reported on all the major developments in the campaign. He provides new information and background on the key elements: Labour's ruthlessly efficient electoral machine; the role of the press; the SNP's controversial policies on Kosovo and the performance of the party leaders.

Ritchie tells it as he saw and experienced the election as a skilled journalist at the heart of the action. I commend it to all who are keen to find out the real story behind the headlines.

T. M. Devine
October 1999

Preface

Harry Reid, Editor, The Herald

In 1997, one of my first acts as Editor of *The Herald* was to appoint the first Scottish Political Editor in the paper's 214 year history. For many years, *The Herald* had enjoyed the services of a series of distinguished Political Editors working in the Palace of Westminster. Now at last the time had come to complement our Westminster team of three journaliists with an equally strong team here in Scotland.

The appointment became urgent as it was increasingly clear that New Labour were going to win a watershed victory in the spring General Election, and that as a consequence, Scotland would soon be heading for a referendum on Devolution.

I decided to bring back Murray Ritchie, *The Herald*'s first European Editor, from Brussels. This was a difficult decision, made easier by the fact that we already had in place, in Robbie Dinwoodie, an outstanding Scottish Political Correspondent. I was confident that together they would spearhead the pre-eminent team of political and parliamentary writers in the New Scotland.

The third member of our Scottish political team, Frances Horsburgh, was appointed a short time later. Frances has been our Local Government Correspondent for quite a long period, and it was high time to spring her from the at times arcane and byzantine manoeuvrings in Scotland's various city halls. This book owes a great deal, as Murray Ritchie would be the first to acknowledge, to his two first-class colleagues in *The Herald's* Scottish political team.

Murray Ritchie himself is a genuine character, one of the few left in Scottish journalism. To write that might be sentimental but it also has the merit of being true. At times he can be carnaptious. He can overdo the role of the grizzled, abrasive hack. But beneath this hard shell there lurks an observer and writer of considerable sophistication and acumen. His journalistic stints in Brussels, and in an earlier life in East Africa, have given him a well-developed sense of context. He is Scottish through and through, a patriot in the best sense of the word, but in no way is he, in either his personality or his writing, parochial or provincial. One of my worries on recalling him from Brussels was that he was exchanging the macro politics of the European Union for the micro politics of a small, politically immature country. But that worry proved unfounded. He threw himself into chronicling the new politics of Scotland with an invigorating mixture of zest, scepticism and aggression.

The short book he has written belies its size, for it is a big book in both theme and treatment. It is an account, very much from the inside, of what were arguably the most exciting months in Scotland's modern history. There have undoubtedly been more dangerous times and more vital times. Scotland was and remains closely linked with England, as part of the United Kingdom. When the United Kingdom was fighting for its very existence in the dark days of 1940 and 1941, the events that unfolded were truly momentous and of far more significance than anything that happened in Scotland in 1999. Again, the slow but steady march towards universal suffrage, in which Scotland was to the fore, was of far greater constitutional and democratic import than devolution.

But what made the events in the first half of 1999 so special was that a new parliament was being elected. That may happen as a matter of course in new countries; but it does not often happen in countries as gnarled and as old as Scotland. Old is not a word that New Labour likes, but it remains true; Scotland is an old country. The performance of our new Parliament will be crucial; it will determine, in effect, whether we should remain as part of the Union or should contend for independence. These are very high stakes, and they extend beyond the merely political to all aspects of our national life - cultural, sociological, economic and even moral.

More years ago than I care to remember, I studied modern history as an undergraduate. I could never decide whether I preferred the sweep and force of narrative history, told with gusto, or the minute attention to detail relayed by the on-the-spot chronicler dealing with day-to-day events. Murray Ritchie's book is written in the form of a diary, but I reckon it does manage to blend the best of both *genres*. Murray is blessed with a crisp, sapid prose style and his book is a most useful and most readable account of what Professor Tom Devine calls 'the real story'. It is a book that can be read now for pleasure and enlightenment. I suspect that it will also be read, far into the future, by many people, historians and others, who want to know exactly what did happen in the months leading to the election of Scotland's first democratic parliament. It is thus a pleasure and a privilege for me to commend this book.

Harry Reid
Editor, The Herald
31 January 2000

Acknowledgements

This book owes its existence to many people who deserve my thanks, especially Harry Reid, Editor of *The Herald*, for his unstinting encouragement, Paul Scott of the Saltire Society for his advice; Robbie Dinwoodie and Frances Horsburgh, my colleagues on *The Herald*'s Scottish political desk, for their patience during its preparation; Ian Watson of *The Herald* library for help in selecting the cover picture; Bill McArthur for permission to use several of his cartoons from *The Herald*; and some politicians who should remain anonymous lest they be damned by association.

M.R.
Glasgow
January 2000

To Andree

Contents

Introduction

Home for Home Rule

In May, 1997, as Britain was assessing the effects of Labour's landmark General Election victory, the telephone rang in the flat in Brussels which had been my home for five years. It was Harry Reid, recently appointed Editor of *The Herald*, with the news that he was recalling me to Glasgow. My time as *The Herald*'s European Editor – so enjoyable and so instructive – was at an end and I was now to become Scottish Political Editor covering the progress of Tony Blair's new government towards Home Rule for Scotland.

Regret at leaving a fascinating job reporting the fast-moving affairs of the European Union was mixed with excitement at the prospect of going home to report and be part of a political event for which I had yearned over decades. All my life I had supported the establishment of a Scottish Parliament - most Scots had done the same – and here I was being given the opportunity to chronicle its birth. This was as daunting a journalistic prospect, as it was irresistible. In my time with *The Herald* – coming on for 30 years – I had always been something of a dilettante writer on Scottish politics, a columnist and occasional pundit, but never a full-time political correspondent. Now I was being pushed headlong into what promised to be the most turbulent and exhilarating two years in modern Scottish political history as the Scots prepared for a national debate on their future relationship with England. Their actions would decide the fate of Great Britain, no less, although the English were only then beginning to grasp the significance of what their northern neighbours and fellow Britons these past three centuries were up to.

This English puzzlement at Scotland and its people is nothing new. From the moment the two old nations had become one, those Scots suddenly flooding into London (the traffic was rather one way) were seen as curiosities. Even today there seems a lack of basic understanding in England about Scotland and perhaps the same applies to a lesser extent in reverse. To the English many Scots seem chippy or difficult. Yet hundreds of years have passed since the English showed hostility to Scotland. There is no reason, therefore, for Scottish Nationalism to thrive on external oppression. English cultural and political influence, even domination, of Scotland cannot be compared with the behaviour of former totalitarian regimes of Eastern Europe or with the persecution of racial minorities around the world. Sheer indifference to Scotland is the worst charge which could be levelled against the English. So what motivates Scottish Nationalism?

Opponents of the Scottish National Party who seek to portray it as racist or Anglophobic are being dishonest. Despite current concerns expressed in mainly English newspapers about creeping anti-Englishness in Scotland I can say, hand on heart, that I know no-one in Scotland who hates the English. Doubtless there are bigots among the Scots as among other peoples, but from my observation of the Scots among whom I have lived most of my life, bigotry is mainly confined to religious sectarianism, particularly in the west of Scotland. There are signs of nascent white racism, which common decency condemns, but the incidence is probably no greater than in most other European countries. Emerging concern about the Scots' evolving relationship with the English is the direct result of constitutional pressures and bears some examination.

Many Scots are saddened and alarmed by the ineluctable force of English political domination, or the slow Anglicisation of Scottish life. But hatred? No. If the Jacobite rebellions, opposed by many Scots particularly in the lowlands, are left in the mists of history and discounted because they were primarily religious as distinct from national conflicts, Scots have no equivalent in the past three centuries of Union to compare with Irish resistance to the English, or even with the fleeting Welsh practice of burning holiday homes of which there are many in Scotland. Nationalists in Scotland like to regard themselves as internationalists, not xenophobes. Cardinal Tom

Winning, the leader of Scotland's 750,000 Roman Catholics (most of whom are said to be Labour voters) made the point in a speech which dismayed Labour and provoked much debate, when he described Scottish Nationalism before the May, 1999, elections as "mature, respectful of democracy and international in outlook." His apparent endorsement of Nationalism, if not the SNP, was in marked contrast to the familiar charges made by Tony Blair at his party's Blackpool conference when he condemned Scottish Nationalists as separatists and wreckers. (The same Tony Blair has been known to praise the work of prominent Irish Nationalists who have blood on their hands, a contradiction which has not gone unnoticed in Scotland).

Two of the SNP's most prominent champions have offered individualistic definitions of Scottish Nationalism. When Winnie Ewing won a famous victory in the Hamilton Parliamentary by-election of 1967 she declared: "Stop the world – Scotland wants to get on." And when Sean Connery, the SNP-supporting actor, gave a pep talk (written by himself without the aid of spin-doctors) to the party during the Scottish elections, he explained his Nationalist credo in uncomplicated terms: "I just want my country to be like any other country." This is not the language of narrow separatism or cultural exclusiveness, but the exact opposite.

In the Thatcher and Major years this misunderstanding in England of the Scots and their aspirations was fuelled by the London press and reinforced by some Tory political mischief. Tabloids and Scot-baiters in the Commons from English Tory seats, who regularly disrupted Scottish Questions with provocative interventions, found some sport in labelling the Scots as subsidy junkies, wholly dependent on English generosity, and ungrateful with it. When Scots offered to resolve this difficulty by threatening independence, even limited autonomy, they were condemned as separatist wreckers. Such over-simplifications of Scottish thinking might be crude and useful on the hustings, and are probably confined to the English chattering classes, but they resonate north of the Border. Scots watched in some amusement after Tony Blair's victory as MPs in England jostled to question the need for so many Scots in the Labour Cabinet. One London newspaper campaigned indignantly against the presence of a Scottish politician at the head of the Department of Transport in England. Complaints were aired in London newspapers about television news presenters speaking in Scottish or Welsh accents. A former Tory Home Secretary, Kenneth Baker, called for Home Rule for England and warned of an English backlash to events in Scotland, quoting Chesterton:

> Smile at us, pay us, pass us
> But do not quite forget
> For we are the people of England
> Who have not spoken yet.

For good measure he made a claim which would have been jeered if it had come from a Scottish MP of any party: "The Union we have known for 300 years is over."

Sometimes this cross-Border debate descended into farce as when the so-called Tartan Army of Scottish football fans covered their faces with blue woad in the manner of Hollywood's bizarre portrayal of Sir William Wallace in the film, Braveheart. The Tartan Army makes a point of cheering on any team playing England in the World Cup, a mischievous provocation which, understandably, irritates the English – which is why, naturally, Scots persist with it. This practice has since been held partly responsible for the gradual reappearance of the Cross of St George at English national occasions. Slowly, the Scots do indeed appear to be encouraging the English to rediscover their own Nationalism. Until now the English have happily and habitually referred to Britain as England and waved the Union Jack as though it were the flag of England. Braveheart was an enjoyably ridiculous tartan Western which was remarkably successful around the world, but how the English hated it for disturbing the demons lurking deep down in their psyche. Most Scots merely laughed at it as hokum, just as they chuckle at the antics of the Tartan Army whose foot soldiers are regarded by their thinking compatriots as harmless lunatics.

Nationalism in Scotland has a long record of generating more heat than light because it questions the sentiment of Britishness among Scots themselves. This curious double identity is under threat, too, as Scots have been encouraged effectively to choose between being Scots, British or European. Indeed the Scottish Tories, the most Unionist of the Unionists, have formally adopted as party policy the proclamation – made in Hampden Park, no less – that they are Scots first and British second. Polls suggest that absolutists on both sides are ahead of themselves in this debate. While most Scots see themselves as Scottish first and British second, these same Scots show no immediate sign of wishing to abandon their Britishness – a paradox which, confusingly, should encourage both the SNP and its opponents like Kenneth Baker in equal measure. For the SNP this sentimental attachment to Britishness among Scots might be a hindrance but it is real, perhaps the most solid obstacle to independence. For those seeking to preserve the Union, these same polls suggest worryingly that the appeal of Britishness is on the wane among Scots. Surveys throw up all manner of optimistic signals to those who support independence, sometimes suggesting majorities for breaking the Union, sometimes a majority for the SNP. Voters, however, tend to confound pollsters. In simple terms there are more people in Scotland who want independence than vote for it, but the tide in attitudes appears to be running the SNP's way.

Nationalist economic arguments have tended to gain force in recent years among Scots who appear less impressed than previous generations with lectures from Unionist politicians about independence leading to ruination. The Irish Republic in its early years was always used by Unionists as an example of how the Scots would suffer, but that argument has since disappeared (for obvious reasons). Were the dismal science not so dismal, the economic debate in Scotland might be conducted at a more elevated level but in reality politicians merely toss claims, counter claims and statistics at each other. While the SNP has produced impressive research and won respectable endorsements for its conclusions, Labour has shown itself adept at discrediting it with fusillades of Treasury-driven figures and fact sheets. Given that the politicians will never agree on even the most basic economic arguments as they affect Scottish independence there is one option I would recommend to students of this subject: look around Western Europe for comparable small, independent EU member states (or even those outside the EU) and consider how many are better off than Scotland. Sometimes voters might close their ears and simply consider the evidence of their own eyes.

Other factors are also at work in Scotland, but not yet in England. In 1997 the SNP became the first significant British political party to flirt with republicanism, offering as party policy a referendum on the monarchy in an SNP-controlled Scottish Parliament. More significant than the mere consideration of that policy – which was seen as rather bold and was predictably condemned by enemies of Nationalism – was the fact that the SNP appeared to benefit, surging ahead in opinion polls. Other factors were probably at work but there is little doubt that this act of radicalism did the Nationalists no harm. Indeed it might have been a factor which persuaded the Prince of Wales famously to invite the leader of the SNP, Alex Salmond, to Balmoral for a private chat.

These factors and many more galvanised politics in the Scotland I had left in 1992 for Brussels. As I arrived home in the summer of 1997 I found the place in a political swirl, excited by the sudden and strong currents of constitutional debate, and the near certainty of change. Leaving Brussels was a wrench. My five years there, most of it spent travelling around Europe with the opportunity to observe many contrasting styles of government, had been a similarly exciting time for anyone interested in politics. The European Union was preparing to expand towards the east where Communism had collapsed and many small countries were hesitatingly embracing democracy, and preparing to launch the single currency. These were huge and journalistically fascinating issues. But the prospect of returning to Scotland to report the setting up of our first Parliament in Edinburgh since 1707 was not to be missed for anything. I was back home within days of Harry's summons, raring to go.

2

A Scot in Europe

The ending of exile on the Continent was cause for reflection. My arrival in Brussels had been the direct result of the 1992 General Election and the Conservatives' narrow return to power, yet again. It had also served to reinforce my belief that Scotland – without any individual identity in the European Union – could never thrive to its best advantage without its own Parliament. For Scottish Parliament campaigners the outcome of the 1992 contest had been a crushing if not greatly surprising disappointment. The victorious Tories had defied Scottish constitutional aspirations for decades and although heavily defeated in Scotland – as usual – they were again back in power where it mattered, in Westminster. John Major's success had offered Scotland's Home Rulers only the grim prospect of another five years of waiting and wanting and complaining.

Soon after his win John Major himself told me frankly and without a moment's hesitation that he had no intention of allowing the Tories to change their minds on the so-called Scottish Question. There would be no Home Rule and no U-turn on their long years of hostility to devolution because nothing mattered more than the strength of the Union which was the very foundation of Britain. The very thought of another prolonged spell of watching Scottish politics being conducted in a vacuum, with a small and unrepresentative minority of unpopular MPs running the country and continually thumbing their noses at Scottish electoral opinion was too much for me to bear. We were back in the old routine where the Scots voted overwhelmingly for parties which wanted a Scottish Parliament but where we kept getting the centralist Tories as our government, because of the numerical superiority of English votes.

My then Editor, Arnold Kemp, was anxious that *The Herald* should increase its European coverage as the Maastricht treaty came into force. He offered me the new post of European Editor and off I went to Brussels where politics were real and exciting and fast-moving, the perfect antidote to the frustration of trying to take Scottish politics seriously. Very soon I learned that while Europe and the ambitions of the fast-changing European Union were hot political topics in Scotland – mainly thanks to the SNP's catchy "Independence in Europe" slogan – the same did not apply in reverse. In busy workaday Brussels, Scotland simply did not register, being regarded as a mere region of the United Kingdom, a constitutional reality which goes to the heart of Scottish political attitudes and argument today. The Brussels machine tended to think of Scotland – when it thought of it at all – in much the same way as British governments, that is to say as little more than a sort of souped-up English county, a mere region.

True, Scotland is, in a sense a region of Britain, but it is also an ancient European nation which had been sovereign and independent for hundreds of years until 1707, and Edinburgh is one of Europe's longest-established and most beautiful capitals. Yet to the power brokers of Brussels, Scotland was no more constitutionally than just another anonymous tract of a member State. It was almost invisible, discernible only through the British prism. Indeed a source of constant irritation to me was a painting in the form of a stylised map of the European Union which adorned the press room of the European Commission. On that map the EU stopped at Carlisle.

One incident which rankled greatly with me at the time concerned my request for equal access with my British press colleagues to Foreign Office briefings which took the form of pleasant lunches in the splendour of the official residence of the British Ambassador to the European Union. Without this facility it was impossible for a British journalist to work on equal terms with the rest of the press corps in Brussels. When I asked why I was being excluded I was informed earnestly by a Foreign Office spokesman that the Ambassador did not like too many people around his table because it meant he might have to raise his voice. When I protested that the Foreign Office was giving my journalistic rivals and my employer's commercial competitors an unfair advantage, the temperature began to rise. The Foreign Office spokesman, by now deeply embarrassed (he was half Scottish himself) explained apologetically that another reason for my exclusion was that *The Herald* was not published in London. In one sense the absurdity of this was hilarious and the cause of some fun, but it was also a practical difficulty. The Ambassador's briefings were unmissable for any journalist wanting a grasp of British policy at a time of great tension between the UK and Brussels and anyone out of the loop was in trouble. Soon I was joined in Brussels by Chris McLaughlin, my opposite number from the *Scotsman*, who met with the same treatment. We had some sport asking for a formal and official Foreign Office explanation for this ridiculous discrimination and we were informed, solemnly that there were three reasons for *The Herald* and the *Scotsman* being barred from the lunchtime musings of Her Majesty's Ambassador. These proved to be collector's items: one, such briefings were by tradition "London-centric;" two, UK ministers did not read the Scottish papers; and three (my favourite), if people in Scotland wanted to find out what was happening in the European Union they could always buy the English papers.

Arnold Kemp and Magnus Linklater, who was then editing the *Scotsman*, had to be calmed down when we reported back to them. The two Editors decided to give diplomacy one more chance by asking the Foreign Office finally to have both newspapers treated equally with the rest of the British press in Brussels – or, they warned, we would publish full accounts of our treatment on our front pages on the same day. This was blackmail, or at least a crude demand with menaces, but it worked a treat. McLaughlin and I immediately enjoyed a slap-up lunch at the Foreign Office's expense and our relations with the government were from that moment on all sweetness and light. Of course, this sort of silliness should never have happened. But it did, not because of any institutionalised anti-Scottish sentiment or other malice – indeed the Ambassador himself was a Glaswegian who knew nothing of the house rules operated by his own staff until we drew them to his personal attention – but because of years of Whitehall custom and good old-fashioned London metropolitan myopia. I have dined out on that little spat ever since, happy in the knowledge that its repetition annoys the Foreign Office. Brussels did nothing to persuade me that Scotland (the same could be said of Wales) was as effectively represented as it might have been in the European Union. Where other small European nations enjoyed direct membership of the council of ministers and despatched large delegations to the European Parliament, Scotland's voice was muffled by the need to speak with a British accent. What was good for Scotland was good only if it suited the United Kingdom as a whole. Other "regions" of the EU's member states at least enjoyed the advantage of having autonomous Parliaments or governments represented in Brussels – for example, most of the German Lander, Spanish nations including Euskadi (the Basque Country), and Catalonia, the two main Belgian regions of Flanders and Wallonia - but Scotland had no diplomatic or political presence beyond a couple of middle-ranking Scottish Office civil servants on loan to the UK Permanent Representation.

This lack of political clout for Scotland had obvious practical disadvantages. Soon after my arrival in Brussels the council of industry ministers met to discuss steel plant closures across the EU, a subject which would have been of critical interest to Scotland had not the Ravenscraig integrated mill just been closed in Lanarkshire after years of nationwide campaigning to preserve it. Ravenscraig *was* the Scottish steel industry, a sort of national totem, a symbol of Scottish determination to sustain a significant manufacturing sector with steel as its base.

At that Brussels meeting the UK's minister agreed with his colleagues from across the community, without a vote, that the EU's small member states should be allowed to subsidise, if desired, and preserve single-plant steel production while the big member states were being forced to cut capacity. British support therefore, came from a senior minister in a government which had just refused to lift a finger to help Ravenscraig, which was rumoured to be profitable, after the privatisation of British Steel. How galling it was to watch a Westminster-based minister working happily on behalf of the Irish and Portuguese and Luxembourg steel industries while apparently oblivious to the plight of the steel industry in Scotland. Quite clearly if Scotland had enjoyed separate representation in Brussels or had at least had a Parliament to give a persuasive voice to the national interest there might still be a Scottish industry thriving in Ravenscraig today.

In that and many other areas it became obvious to me that Scotland was disadvantaged by being represented by a centralist, London-based Parliament and government. When the EU banned the export of British beef those producers who suffered acutely included farmers in Scotland and Northern Ireland where the incidence of BSE was lower than in the rest of the UK because their herds had been fed exclusively on grass. Yet all attempts to have "clean" producers in Northern Ireland and Scotland exempted early were resisted as Conservative ministers, with their Unionist preoccupations, insisted that the UK must be treated as one unit. The incoming Labour government took the same view, despite a willingness by the European Commission to consider lifting the embargo on an area-by-area basis. Without a government or a Parliament, Scotland's voice was quieted, if not silenced.

Admittedly, there is another side to the story. In fisheries – an industry important to Scotland's economy because 70% of the British catch goes into Scottish boats – the full voting weight of the United Kingdom proved useful in disputes where Scotland on its own would have carried less clout. Scottish Office ministers occasionally led UK government delegations to the fisheries council and cast British votes. But those occasions were exceptional.

As I prepared to come home I was struck by the number of Scots in Brussels, mostly in influential and therefore sensitive positions in the EU institutions, who privately expressed frustration with the way their country was represented at the heart of Europe. These people were by no means all Scottish Nationalists or supporters of independence (not necessarily the same, as I shall explain). Like most Scots they supported an autonomous Scotland with more influence at the heart of Europe. They were genuinely concerned expatriates with expert knowledge of the EU who fretted at the obvious failings of the system which was supposed to serve their nation's interests. They will be heartened now that the Scottish Parliament is to have its own office in Brussels where it can exert a measure of political and diplomatic influence in the United Kingdom representation. In strict constitutional terms the UK government will remain the single voice which speaks for Britain in the councils of the European Union but at least it will be a voice which must now routinely take account of a legislature beyond Westminster, even if Westminster has the last word. That at least is progress.

Back in Scotland I found that the old political order, once so seemingly immovable, had been swept away overnight in that incredible defeat of the Tories. Where Labour had cunningly embraced Home Rule – or devolution as they insist on calling it, so as not to sound like the Scottish Nationalists – the Tories had rejected it out of hand right to the bitter end. For their trouble the Tories were vaporised by the Scots (and Welsh) electorates. Not one Scottish Tory MP survived as Labour and the SNP made gains and, for a change, the Scots and English voted together for a new beginning after 18 years of Conservative rule. Suddenly, the prospect of a Scottish Parliament was alive again for only the second time in almost three centuries.

3

Unfinished Business

Scotland's quest for Home Rule had never really stopped, despite long periods of mute acceptance of the new order, particularly from around 1870, and was as old as the Treaty of Union itself. From the moment in 1707 when the Scottish Parliament (a plaything of noblemen and, therefore, hopelessly undemocratic) adjourned itself, surrendering the nation's independence, to form the new country of Britain, the Scots had complained and campaigned for its restoration. The last words spoken in that Parliament were those of the leading politician of the day, the Chancellor, Lord Seafield, who remarked that the adjournment was the "end of ane auld sang."

That phrase was to echo down the centuries until the moment on May 12, 1999, when the veteran Nationalist, Winnie Ewing, took the chair as the new Parliament's oldest member. She reminded the first democratically-elected Scottish Parliament that its predecessor in 1707 had not been abolished but adjourned, and she declared: "I want to start with the words I have always wanted to say, or hear somebody else say – the Scottish Parliament, adjourned on the twenty-fifth day of March, 1707, is hereby reconvened."

That historic moment was the culmination of hundreds of years of effort to have returned to Scotland a Parliament either devolved from Westminster but still within the Union – which is the constitutional status of the new legislature – or the Parliament of an independent State. It had taken some doing. In those 292 years there had been 33 Home Rule for Scotland Bills brought before the House of Commons and all had failed to win support from the English majority (and sometimes from the Scots themselves). It had taken more than a century for Labour to bring to fruition the sentiments of its Scottish founder, Keir Hardie. From its inception Labour had championed Home Rule but not outright independence although that,

"I'm voting YES! yes?"

too, had sympathisers in the party (and a few are still around even today). Keir Hardie expressed his sentiments in *Labour Leader* in 1889: "I believe the people of Scotland desire a Parliament of their own, and it will be for them to send to the next House of Commons a body of men pledged to obtain it." By then the Scottish Trades Union Congress had been established and it, too, lent support for Home Rule. Indeed, the STUC was to become at times a much stronger advocate than Labour, encouraging some of its admirers to refer to it as the political wing of the Scottish Labour Party.

More than 100 years on, the leader of the Scottish Labour Party, Donald Dewar, a scholarly and crafty and distinctively Scottish politician, rose in the Commons in his capacity as Secretary of State for Scotland to introduce the 34th Bill. Mr Dewar knew that this time it would not fail.

Scotland duly went to the polls in a Referendum on September 11, 1997, and voted overwhelmingly for a devolved Parliament with wide-ranging powers, including some control over British personal taxation. The people delivered their decision on a day which happened by coincidence to be the 700th anniversary of the battle of Stirling Bridge in which the Scottish folk hero and martyr, Sir William Wallace, vanquished an English force in the cause of independence. Even the Scots themselves, who had long become afflicted by national self-doubt and a talent for disagreement, seemed somewhat taken aback at their own ability to show some unity of purpose. "The people have seized the moment," Mr Dewar said. "This is a confident vote. We are a nation which believes in ourselves, believes we can and should take most of the important decisions that affect our lives, and we are right."

The people's decision meant that Britain would never be the same again – something which caused some belated indignation in England as the political implications dawned south of the Border. The way was now open for British constitutional change on a scale never experienced since Irish Partition. For some the arrival of a devolved Scottish Parliament was welcomed as a staging post on the journey to independence. Whether politicians such as Tam Dalyell, who believes the new legislature is "a Motorway to independence with no exits" are correct or whether, in the words of (Lord) George Robertson, the Scottish Parliament will "kill the Scottish National Party stone dead" remains to be seen. At the time of writing the SNP is certainly very much alive with 35 MSPs and is the official Opposition. This is a curious and probably prophetic constitutional arrangement. In how many "stateless nations" searching for autonomy is the democratically elected Opposition party separatist? As the SNP is fond of reminding its opponents, it has to win only once – and Opposition parties in Britain have a habit of eventually becoming governments. (This boast could yet turn out to be rash: even if it were to win a Scottish General Election one day, the SNP might still lose a referendum on independence.)

For Mr Dewar the success of the 1997 Referendum was a personal triumph. With SNP and Liberal Democrat support he had guided to overwhelming acceptance a constitutional formula which gave Scotland full control of domestic business, leaving Westminster in charge of foreign affairs and defence, both of which are responsibilities slowly leaking to Brussels, and a few other areas of national competence. Mr Dewar was a life-long Home Ruler but most certainly not a Nationalist or separatist. Like all senior Labour politicians he was and remains convinced of the advantages of the Union with England. He regarded as his mission in life the completion of what his old friend and fellow Home Ruler, John Smith, had famously called Scotland's "unfinished business" – the restoration of the nation's Parliament. John Smith had become leader of Labour Party only to die, on the point of becoming British Prime Minister, from a heart attack, before seeing his dream for Scotland come to reality.

When he introduced the new Bill, Mr Dewar, a bookworm and lover of language, showed his delight with the refreshingly plain and unlegalistic wording of the first clause: "There shall be a Scottish Parliament." The Bill's progress through the House of Commons was uncomplicated and swift because of Labour's huge majority, and brought to a happy conclusion a long history of Labour Party agitation in Scotland – not always determined or even approved of by the leadership, but never quite abandoned – for Home Rule. For most of the 20th century the Labour Party had argued the case for a Scottish Parliament, for a variety of compelling but, to outside eyes, sometimes opaque reasons. They say you have to be a Scot to understand Scotland and the forces which drive its sense of nationhood. Yet the imperatives driving the demand for Home Rule were real enough, reflecting a deep-seated feeling of discomfort among many Scots, admittedly not all, that their nation was not properly run inside the British constitutional arrangement and that change was essential. But what kind of change? Some wanted autonomy of the sort which devolution has provided. Others believed in complete independence, in or out of the European Union, others still wanted some system of federal status. But despite much argument about which of these offered the best solution, a clear majority of Scots united in the simple conviction that any one of them would be preferable to direct rule from London.

Hostility to the Union with England had risen and fallen and risen again over the years. When the Treaty of Union was signed without any reference to the people and in the complete absence of what we know as modern democracy, it was hated by the Scottish people who took to the streets across the country, rioting and protesting at the surrender of their independence by the privileged clique which controlled the State. But defiance was in vain. Against a background of English military threat (the English feared Scotland's alliance with the French), the raising of obstacles to Scottish trade and not least a parlous Scottish economy, the Scottish Parliament's members, many of whom had been bribed by the English government, voted for the Union. Across Scotland there was outrage and heartbreak at what was seen as a breathtaking betrayal. As ever, Robert Burns, Scotland's national bard, spoke for the nation:

O, would, or I had seen the day
That Treason thus could sell us,
My auld grey head had lien in clay,
Wi' Bruce and loyal Wallace!
But pith and power, till my last hour,
I'll mak this declaration:
"We're bought and sold for English gold"
Such a parcel of rogues in a nation!

Since the Union's inception Scots have argued about its advantages. Some, like Paul Scott, the respected Nationalist historian and diplomat, see little good in it and condemn it eloquently and convincingly for damaging Scotland's interests over three centuries. Others queue to praise it, citing the success of Great Britain – Scotland and England united under the Union flag – in building the greatest empire the world has ever seen, giving birth to the industrial revolution, and fighting in a partnership which emerged on the winning side in two World Wars and many lesser conflicts.

I take the view that both critics and champions have valid cases to argue. The Union has never been ideal for Scotland – how could it be so when the Treaty involved the abolition of an independent legislature and its absorption into a "British" Parliament which was in effect the English Parliament by another name? To describe the Union as a merger of two independent States is fanciful: it was not much more than a takeover of Scotland by England. But even a forced takeover can have some benefits.

Scots will argue to this day about whether the Enlightenment was the result of the Union. Undeniably, Scotland prospered intellectually to a phenomenal degree in the 18th century, offering more in proportion to its size to the common weal than any other country before or since. Adam Smith became widely recognised as the father figure of economics (and not, as some would claim, latter-day right-wing free-market forces). David Hume was established as a philosopher of world pre-eminence, and many more intellectual forces made an indelible impact on British and world affairs. Sir Walter Scott, the world's first great novelist, came soon after to re-invent Scotland in the image of a romantic, tartanised land of misty peaks and brooding lochs. Scott has been accused, perhaps unfairly, of inventing a phoney Scotland. Historians disagree about the truth of his responsibility for the music hall image of the Scot, a phenomenon which some find offensive and embarrassing while others, especially the tourist trade, find bankable.

Down the years of Union many ambitious and talented Scots found success in London and in the outposts of the British Empire. In the halcyon period of British imperialism, when Britannia ruled the waves, it was not surprising that Scottish resentment of the Union faded as careers and fortunes were made. But the Union's benefits were not the only cause of this gradual change of attitude. Acceptance of the Union had to be forced on much of Scotland, piledriven into the national psyche, as the Gaelic culture was crushed with excessive cruelty after Culloden. This military defeat of the Jacobites, the last battle on British soil, heralded convulsive socio-economic change which destroyed a way of life in the Highlands and led eventually to forced evictions from the land in the notorious Highland clearances of the 19th century. Those banished from the glens at bayonet point or burned out of their homes in a pioneering example of ethnic cleansing were the Union's victims – but they were no longer around to complain. Thus was much lingering resistance to the new constitutional order removed.

Gradually, Scotland's distinctive culture became ever more Anglicised but the nation did begin to escape some of its poverty, a process which accelerated with the success of the Empire. The mercantile elite of Scotland enjoyed a share of previously unimagined wealth and power gained through British trade advantages opened up by the industrial revolution. Unionism became established as Scots and English united as "Church and Queen" British Protestant subjects. Yet still the Scots remained distinctively Scottish, not the "North Britons" as the English called us (seldom referring to themselves as

"South Britons" for they, too, have never lost their sense of national identity).

The concept of Britishness was never stronger than when the Empire was at its zenith. As David Marquand neatly theorised: "Imperial Britain was Britain. Empire was not an optional extra for the British, it was their reason for being British as opposed to English or Scots or Welsh. Deprived of empire and plunged into Europe 'Britain' had no meaning." Slowly, it began to dawn on the Scots that there was another Union – the European Union – at a higher political level than Britishness. Most Scots, being internationalists and not a few of them nationalists, have taken more easily to the process of European integration than have their English neighbours. It was this nervousness, sometimes hostility, to the European adventure which helped to destroy John Major's government and continues to plague the Tory leadership of the Euro-sceptic William Hague by disrupting party unity today. Post-imperialism has never quite let the Conservative Party off the hook of nostalgia for a lost age of Britishness and even finds an echo with some British government attitudes under Labour today – the reluctance to remove border controls in the European single market, deep suspicion of the EU's single currency, the alarming wish of the rest of the EU to integrate defence capabilities and foreign affairs, both areas where Britannia was once answerable to no-one. All this is too much for some in the United Kingdom but for many Scots – not all, but probably a majority – there is little to fear from joining the single currency (we're in one already with England and have been for a couple of centuries); we have no army to speak off beyond the Scottish regiments and no need for one beyond the capacity to support international efforts by such as Nato or the UN.

Scots have been quicker to recognise the pressures on Britain since the end of the Second World War when today's European Union was invented specifically for the purpose of preserving a permanent peace. With European political and economic integration has come a new questioning in Scotland of the benefits of remaining inside the United

Kingdom. So far those who wish to break the Treaty of Union and settle for independence have been in a minority, despite the findings of occasional opinion polls. Scots like it both ways: they want to be closer to Europe, taking the so-called Westminster by-pass to Brussels, but they also have a lingering and sentimental, but strong, attachment to Britishness. For this reason the SNP has made significant progress but not yet made the breakthrough of which it dreams.

Post-war Scottish Nationalism surfaced as a threat to the constitutional order in 1945 when Dr Robert McIntyre won a Westminster by-election in Motherwell and Wishaw for the SNP. This undreamed of result sent shockwaves through Britain's Establishment but they quickly subsided as the SNP's arrival as a force in Scottish politics was written off as an entertaining aberration. Behind the scenes, however, strategists and thinkers in the two big Unionist parties, Labour and the Conservatives (the federally-minded Liberals were by now marginalised) sensed trouble looming. Unionists of all sorts were to learn that Scottish nationalism tends to move in waves, perhaps 20 years apart, with each one leaving a higher tide mark than the one before. The next came in 1967 when Winnie Ewing won Hamilton in a sensational by-election. I was much amused in researching the Hamilton result to see how *The Glasgow Herald*'s political correspondent of the day predicted the outcome. "At Westminster only a belief in the incredible allows a win for Mrs Ewing, the nationalist candidate, though she is expected to beat the Conservative for second place." Well, the incredible did allow a win and Mrs Ewing exploded on to the political scene, again sending the Unionists scurrying for ideas on how to halt the return of Nationalism. Hamilton in 1967 was a much bigger shock than Motherwell and Wishaw, by then consigned to Nationalist folk memory. Although Mrs Ewing, like McIntyre before her, lost the seat in the subsequent General Election, she had done enough to revive the debate about a Scottish Parliament. Labour was traumatised and forced to rediscover its half-forgotten commitment to Home Rule. Some Labour forces were opposed to giving Scotland a Parliament because they saw it merely as a monument to the appeasement of Nationalism – which, of course, is exactly what it is. The SNP was now shaping as a real threat to Labour in Scotland, forcing Harold Wilson's government to question whether constitutional change should be offered as a sop. And then in 1973 the personable and talented Margo MacDonald defied all expectations by taking Glasgow Govan, a run-down inner-city Labour fiefdom. The Nationalists followed this a year later by reaching new heights of success in a General Election when they took a record 11 seats in Westminster. Jim Sillars, an eloquent left-wing Nationalist, who had grown impatient with Labour's reluctance to force Home Rule, and who was to become Margo MacDonald's husband, returned to the scene of her triumph to take Govan for the SNP in 1988. Again, he was to surrender it in the following General Election. This pattern of by-election victories followed by General Election defeats was not broken until 1995 when Roseanna Cunningham, an avowed republican, shocked the Scottish Establishment by capturing the safe Tory seat of Perth and Kinross and followed this by becoming two years later the first SNP MP to hold on in a General Election.

After the drama of 1974, Labour could no longer dodge or ignore the pressures of Scottish nationalism. Yet it seemed reluctant to take the plunge into constitutional reform. A streak of Unionism still ran strongly through the Scottish party, not least because many on the left detested Nationalism, refusing to equate it with anything other than the type of xenophobia which had disfigured Europe in the Second World War. While this was patently unjust – the SNP has an unblemished record of peaceful and democratic campaigning – it was a useful slander in the heat of political battle. The same Scottish Labour Party which now proclaims its fidelity to Home Rule had to be led by the nose to adopt it as a priority. Labour's Scottish executive rejected the idea at first and had to be ordered by an angry Harold Wilson to call a special conference for the express purpose of embracing what we learned at that time to call devolution. The Scottish Party duly did as it was bidden, passing a call for a Scottish Parliament with no real legislative or tax-varying power. Willie Ross, Secretary of State for Scotland, and one of the great opponents of Home Rule, stood blinking in a watery sun in Dalintober Street, Glasgow, after the decision and proclaimed without a hint of embarrassment but to general hilarity: "I have always been a devolutionist."

Labour called a Referendum in 1979 on its proposals for a so-called Scottish Assembly. For Home Rulers the result was a catastrophe, a memory which was to haunt campaigners for a Scottish Parliament for 20 years until it was exorcised in the success of May, 1997. Although the Yes campaign succeeded in 1979, the outcome was not exactly a shining democratic triumph. A tiny majority of those who voted did so for devolution but the whole exercise collapsed because the winning side failed to muster 40% of the electorate. This requirement – or brazen fiddle in the eyes of the Yes campaign – had been slipped in by George Cunningham, a backbench Labour MP in Westminster (and a Scot), at the last minute. In broad terms one third of the Scottish people voted Yes, another one-third No, and the rest did not bother to vote at all. Either the Scots were bored or, more likely, unimpressed with what had been on offer. They seemed to want a more powerful legislature – a Parliament rather than a talking shop. Either way, the result was a disaster and as a means of scuttling Home Rule for a generation the 40% rule proved devastating, leading to long years of acrimony fuelled by constant accusations from the Nationalists that Labour had betrayed the cause. Labour, for its part, responded by attacking the Nationalists for voting to bring down the Labour government of James Callaghan and ushering in the era of Margaret Thatcher whose resistance to Scottish constitutional aspiration was characteristically total.

For the SNP the 1979 result was no less a disaster as it saw its poll ratings collapse to a point where they bumped along the bottom for a decade. Given the SNP's role as the constant maker of waves in Scottish politics, a long political winter dawned as Nationalism's appeal faded. A mood of sullen frustration settled on the country for years. Thatcher and her hardline Cabinet set about killing off all ideas

Donald's diminishing game plan.

about decentralising the power of Westminster, a policy which John Major continued without a moment's hesitation.

Major was the Tory Prime Minister who paid the greatest price when Scotland spurned his party, sweeping all of its MPs into oblivion. The Nationalists moved into the vacuum created by the Tory slaughter and proclaimed themselves the Opposition in Scotland, at least in terms of public perception and share of votes, if not in numbers of MPs (the SNP had only six to the Liberal Democrats' 10). Now the political mood of Scotland had changed radically again, to the great alarm of the SNP's Unionist opponents in the other parties. In 1998 the Nationalists continued their surge, attacking Labour with relish as the new government, with 56 Scottish seats in Westminster, suffered a series of internal scandals and damaging headlines.

On Referendum night Calum MacDonald, a Scottish Office Labour minister, sought to dismiss the threat of Nationalism when he remarked in a television interview: "The Nats are like midges – they are always there." To which a Nationalist promptly replied: "Yes, but midges make big men run." Which is undoubtedly true of politics in Scotland where Labour's big men had to move at full tilt to fend off the SNP in their rush to deliver a Scottish Parliament. SNP leader Alex Salmond has often argued that "Labour's car runs on SNP petrol."

In early 1998 Labour began to see its support melting in the Scottish opinion polls, of which the most respected and longest established is System Three in *The Herald*. This trend became a crisis for Labour in April of that year when System Three showed the Nationalists drawing level with Labour on 40%. To Labour's consternation the SNP then moved steadily ahead until it broke all popularity records in June where it claimed a 14-point lead. In London there was bafflement because in the rest of the United Kingdom Labour was still basking in record popularity ratings. Donald Dewar's leadership was called into question as the Tories and much of the London-based press complained that Labour's pursuit of devolution was inviting a separatist putsch in Edinburgh.

a sudden attempt to overth political rivolt

Some of the wilder SNP optimism of that period was misplaced, as my diary of events will attempt to show. As before, the Scottish voters showed themselves skilled at using the Nationalists as a fork with which to prod Labour down the road of constitutional radicalism. But in fairness to Mr Dewar, he was as good as his word in reforming – if not abandoning – the old and discredited first-past-the-post electoral system for the Scottish Parliament. He and Labour's Liberal Democrat partners in the Scottish Constitutional Convention, which was the engine room for devolution for more than a decade, opted for the Additional Member System of voting. This gave Labour the best of both worlds because it preserved first-past-the-post in its entirety – providing Labour with a huge inbuilt advantage – but it also went a considerable way towards ensuring proportionality by means of a second vote which electors cast for MSPs from party lists. This important – and brave – reform was designed to allow Labour's opponents, especially the stricken Tories, to make their presence felt in the new Parliament. Mr Dewar knew that by sticking to the old voting system he would have been accused of promoting just another Glasgow-style Scottish Labour Soviet in Edinburgh. Even Labour had grave misgivings about that and Mr Dewar and Labour deserve credit for respecting the democratic expression of the Scottish voters. Although the Tories still scored a duck in constituency voting in the Scottish Parliament elections they made a parliamentary comeback of sorts by winning 18 seats through votes for list candidates.

Although the SNP failed to make the breakthrough to power it had hoped for, it made yet another advance. With 35 MSPs the Nationalists emerged as the official Opposition in Scotland, much better able than ever before to punch their electoral weight. For Alex Salmond the months leading to the campaign had been a mixture of personal success – he is a deadly television debater, much feared by his opponents – and considerable danger. First he had to persuade his party, whose raison d'etre is independence, to accept for the moment Labour's policy of devolution and to make it work. To some fundamentalist Nationalists this was an act of disloyalty but Mr Salmond carried his party easily, moving on to lend SNP support to Labour and the LibDems in the Yes campaign in the Referendum, taking credit for providing 500,000 votes. "I'll take votes from anyone," Mr Dewar said defensively, when his critics questioned the wisdom of a Labour-SNP joint campaigning platform. In Mr Salmond's view the temporary alliance with Labour was no more than the means of providing building blocks for independence. "If the Scots get a devolved Parliament and see how constitutional change works to their benefit, they'll obviously want more of it," he reasoned.

Will Scottish Home Rule lead to Scottish independence? That is now the new Scottish Question. My own guess – there can be no certainties – is that it will, eventually, unless Labour and the other Unionists can force the genie of Scottish Nationalism back into its bottle. And there is no sign of that happening. Scotland's Tories remain scorned by the electorate, showing no signs of revival and thus allowing space for Nationalism to thrive. More than two years into government, traditionally a troublesome time for parties in power, Labour has never been more popular. Plainly, the Tony Blair phenomenon has not yet burned itself out, a remarkable achievement for the British Prime Minister. But no party lasts in democratically elected government in perpetuity.

Plainly, things did go wrong for Labour in Scotland in May, 1999. Not, perhaps, as wrong as they threatened to do a year earlier, but wrong. The Parliament is still stuffed with Nationalist MSPs just waiting for the chance to pounce. The very people whom Labour promised to kill "stone dead" enjoy unprecedented prominence, a bigger threat than ever before to the Union. This was never in Labour's script which, though allowing for a power-sharing deal with the LibDems, had predicted a ragbag of mainly Tories and a few Nationalists as the Opposition – nothing which would seriously challenge the Union. When the blueprint for running Scotland in coalition was drawn in the Constitutional Convention, the Tories were off running the government and the SNP had absented itself permanently from negotiations. Come the Scottish Parliament elections and the wipeout of the Tories, everything changed, leaving the Nationalists in a stronger position than ever in their history. For this reason a new and unpredictable chapter in the story of Home Rule for Scotland is now being written. Home Rule for Scotland means that after 292 years of the Treaty of Union, Britain will never be the same again. What follows is a flavour of the forces which brought about this critical turn of events.

The birth of a nation?

The Diary

1

Too Close to Call

21st January - 9th March

January 21, 1999

Harry Reid and I take Tasmina Ahmed-Sheikh, the Tory candidate in Govan to lunch. She is the startlingly attractive daughter of a Pakistani father and Welsh-speaking, half-English, white mother who was an actress with the Royal Shakespeare Company. She tells us how her father arranged her marriage and how, like a good Muslim girl, she meekly obeyed – failing to let him know she was already madly in love with her intended. Quite a convenient conjunction of events.

Tasmina is presented to us by Conservative Central Office as typical of the new breed of Scottish Tory, young, talented and determined, the type on whom the party's future depends after the slaughter of the General Election. She certainly makes a change from tweedy old colonels.

She predicts a major upset in Govan, believing privately and not for attribution that the SNP will win and that she can push Labour into third place behind her which would, indeed, be a sensation. Her secret weapon appears to be the disillusionment of Govan's immigrant community who are mainly Pakistani Moslems with the local MP, Mohammad Sarwar, the millionaire businessman and former Glasgow councillor. He won the constituency at the General Election after a brutal selection battle with Mike (now Lord) Watson, another Glasgow Labour MP who lost his seat and his power base when the constituency was redrawn.

Sarwar is about to go on trial in the High Court at Edinburgh next week charged with electoral fraud and attempting to pervert the course of justice. There is a widespread assumption that all of Labour's notorious internal feuding in Govan has been caused by Sarwar's heavy-handed but successful attempts to flood the constituency with his own supporters. If this is true it would amount to entryism on a grand scale and is deeply resented by many Labour old-timers. But little of this can be discussed in detail because, of course, it could prejudice his trial.

One of the problems in dealing with the Sarwar saga is that he is such a personable man, whatever he may or may not have done. He once told me that when he arrived in Glasgow as a poor immigrant from Pakistan in 1971 having seen nothing but old photographs of the place. Thus he turned up expecting to find a city of grand Victorian palaces like the City Chambers and Kelvingrove museum and the university on Gilmorehill. No-one had told him about the garret in Maryhill which was to become his home. He started life in Glasgow selling eggs and went on to make a fortune in the wholesale trade, selling to Asians all over the United Kingdom. He is a gentle and smiling man and extremely influential in his own community but there is a suspicion that he is clueless about the niceties of political life. Now he stands accused of trying to behave in Glasgow as some politicians do in Pakistan.

When Sarwar was elected in 1997 his success was publicised around the world. He was invariably described as "Britain's first Moslem MP" but his arrest and the scandal which exploded around him have caused huge embarrassment and resentment in the Moslem world, not least in Glasgow. Tasmina describes a very plausible scenario. She suspects that the Moslems of Govan, who account for about one eighth of the electorate, will vote for her in large numbers and not for a Labour candidate who was put there under Sarwar's influence.

Good old Govan. It is every Scottish political journalist's favourite constituency after the epic battles between Labour and the Nationalists in the 1970s and 1980s which have become part of folklore. This is where Margo MacDonald emerged as an SNP force – Margo, Queen of Scots, as she was known – when she took the seat from Labour in the early 1970s. When Labour won it back they did so with a candidate called Harry Selby, a local barber, who was selected in the classic Govan Old Labour style. The story goes around that his adoption meeting was attended by 13 people and seven of them were called Selby.

In the late 1980s Margo's husband, Jim Sillars, regained Govan for the SNP after another famous and bruising contest but he lost it again at the following General Election, taking his farewell from public life with a memorably bitter denunciation of the Scots as "90-minute patriots." Sillars was a great politician, the best performer in Scotland by far, but he had a headstrong style which was both his strength and weakness. If he could have worked more harmoniously with people he might have become the first Prime Minister of Scotland. Throughout his political life he was always tipped as "a future Scottish premier" but his disillusionment appears irreparable. What a shame.

Gordon Jackson, one of Scotland's most eminent QCs, who is reputed to earn £250,000 a year, is Labour's candidate. He is by far the party's best choice since Bruce Millan, the MP who became Secretary of State for Scotland before leaving Govan for Brussels to become a UK European commissioner, thus paving the way for Jim Sillars's historic win. There is still a belief in Govan that if Millan had died, Labour would have won the by-election. But the voters did not like their loyalty to Labour being taken for granted when their MP abandoned them for a plum job in Brussels.

Gordon Jackson is personable and very New Labour, a favourite with the leadership, and was the runaway winner at his selection meeting when all sorts of ghastly and blatant malpractices were alleged. One "member" was seen filling in five ballot papers while others, who spoke no English and had never been seen at Labour meetings before, were able only to say the word "Jackson" when asked questions. Gordon is, of course, quite innocent in all of this and plainly embarrassed.

Having evidently become bored with practising law he is now seeking a job which pays perhaps a tenth of his current income. As each day passes he appears more and more concerned by what he has let himself in for. As the *Daily Record* said this morning, following up my story in *The Herald* on the latest ballot-rigging row: "Welcome to Govan politics, Gordon."

Govan is, therefore, by far the most interesting constituency in Scotland. It is also the SNP's number one target seat in its battle with Labour.

January 22nd
Nicola Sturgeon of the SNP is still only in her twenties and, like Tasmina Ahmed-Sheikh and Gordon Jackson, she is a lawyer. She is also tipped as a future party leader but for the moment is the Nationalists' education spokeswoman. She tells me she is confident but not certain of taking Govan and predicts that the Moslems won't all vote for Tasmina because they know the Tories have no hope of winning. I suspect she is right. If they – and others too, for that matter – want revenge on Labour for all the embarrassments and ignominy caused by the Sarwar fuss then they will turn to the Nats as the obvious force for change. Govan was reduced to the status of Labour marginal in the General Election and it will be the most closely watched result on May 6 because if the SNP and Nicola don't take it from Labour, the Nationalists can forget the whole election.

I introduce Harry to Nicola. He has wanted to meet her for some time to discuss education (he was education correspondent of the *Scotsman* in a former life) and the two of them become involved in a series of spirited exchanges, with Harry, in mischievous mood none too subtly testing her knowledge and debating skills. Nicola emerges unscathed and Harry pronounces himself greatly impressed. She permits herself just the hint of a smile of satisfaction as we say goodbye.

January 29th

William Hague is in Glasgow to lend his support to the Scottish Tories in what amounts to a bizarre campaign relaunch. The poor old Tories. Wiped out at the General Election they have been going round in ever diminishing circles for 18 months trying to figure out how to win back support. Predictably, their coverage so far has been unsympathetic. Their latest wheeze is to hire Hampden Park, of all places, for a gathering of Tory candidates for Holyrood and the local elections. Hague makes the mistake of leaving the safety of the hospitality suite for a photo-call in the stand where he and the party's Scottish leader, David McLetchie, are booed by workmen putting the finishing touches to the refurbished stadium. This, of course, delights the television crews and clearly annoys Hague who responds rather lamely that workmen "always give leaders a hard time." The papers are full of reworkings of the Scotland-Argentina football theme and mickey-taking about Willie's Tartan Army. Sometimes politicians who rely so heavily on the bright ideas of PR advisers deserve exactly what they get.

Journalists are invited to lunch with Hague and McLetchie at Yes, a new restaurant which someone suggested to the leader might more appropriately be called No, given the Tories usual response to Scottish opinion over the years. Hague laughs excessively at such a mild joke. He seems nervous at being in Scotland which he plainly regards, with some justification, as a hostile outpost.

Hague tells us he is convinced that Scottish nationalism is by no means such a threat to the United Kingdom as English nationalism. He launches into a tale of how the flag of St George is becoming evident at political meetings all over the south of England – not so much in his native Yorkshire, more in the South East where most people in England live. This, he tells us, symbolises a reawakening of English nationalism which deserves attention and respect. Something must be done, he insists, to answer the needs of England in the Commons where Scottish devolution is belatedly causing the English to consider their own constitutional status.

"Have you noticed the numerical resonance between
Scottish Tories and hen's teeth?"

Hague believes that eventually but inevitably an important vote will be taken in the Commons – one which affects the English only – when the balance will be tipped by the large number of MPs from Scotland. This will cause resentment and division, he predicts. "And what happens then?" he asks us. None of us around the lunch table has the nerve to point out that for 18 years the Tories, with their English majority at Westminster, rammed unpopular decisions down the throats of Scots while telling us we must accept their constitutional legitimacy. The poll tax is the abiding example.

After this lecture we were given a talk on the new and rather sudden Scottishness of the Tories, despite their continued loyalty to the Treaty of Union. They will from now on be Scottish and British, not British and Scottish – and they must be better Europeans. I ask Hague if that means the Scottish Tories will be allowed to admit publicly what many say in private – that Scotland's need of the European single currency is greater than that of the rest of Britain and that perhaps we should be in sooner rather than later, against the wishes of the English Tories. He gives us a sermon about the British economy, including Scotland's, being unsuited to entry now, or even soon. Plainly, he is out of touch with business opinion in Scotland, which is warming to the euro, and with public opinion, too, which is now turning in Scotland in favour of British membership.

Pressed, Hague admits that this generous new autonomy for the Tories in Scotland extends only to policy areas which reflect the powers of the Scottish Parliament. In other words the Scottish Tories won't be allowed a say in Europe and will remain bound to the party line from London. Nor will they be changing their name from the Scottish Conservative and Unionist Association.

In *The Herald* I describe McLetchie's speech as the "Hampden Declaration." It was written by Michael Fry, one of those oddball Tories who would prefer to see Scotland independent rather than devolved, which is a point of view verging nowadays on heresy for our Conservatives. Michael is proud of giving first expression to the new Scottishness of McLetchie's policies and insists that the new

Tory freedom north of the Border will be genuine and demonstrable. Unfortunately, he let slip that publication of the speech had been delayed slightly – because it had first to be approved by Hague. I cut that gem out of my story, reluctantly, after being persuaded that clearing a major policy speech with a party leader is routine when the leader himself is expected on the platform with the speaker.

From today the Tories will be fighting an election while riding two horses. They will seek to tartanise themselves as never before while proclaiming the sanctity of the Union. When I suggest to Hague that this lacks credibility I am howled down by Hague himself, McLetchie and Raymond Robertson, the party chairman. They protest too much. It will take more than this to convince the Scots that the Tories really have changed.

February 5th

What a contrast there is between Tony Blair, who is in Glasgow today to launch Labour's election campaign, and previous Labour Prime Ministers. Harold Wilson always chose Glasgow audiences when he was starting General Election tour of the UK, probably because Glasgow always gave him a warm welcome and the audiences were prepared to put up with long speeches in which he covered every conceivable topic so that he could say later: "As I made clear in my Glasgow speech..."

Blair turns up with his ever-expanding entourage of press handlers and speaks to an invited audience in the Royal Scottish Academy of Music and Drama. It is all very happy-clappy New Labour. A student jazz band belts out a deafening American convention-style entrance. Donald Dewar picks the questioners from an audience of party members, school children and business leaders, some of whom are well known as hostile to independence. (They were also anti-devolution at one time and have simply seen the future.) The questions are hardly armour-piercing. One of the businessmen congratulates Blair on Labour's efforts to pass laws enforcing early payment to suppliers. Another questioner who somehow avoids Labour's vetting efforts asks Blair if he will make sure Cherie does not change the colour of the toilet paper in 10 Downing Street. The Prime Minister responds that he wonders if he might be missing something significant, and he speaks for all of us.

A couple of questioners win applause for expressing hostility to tuition fees and Labour's treatment of single mothers but for the most part Blair is given an easy ride. Over the years I have seen several gatherings where Prime Ministers fielded questions from Glasgow audiences but never one quite like this. The idea, of course, is to let Blair get his message across without the media getting in the way. To this end all access to Blair by the print media on this occasion is blocked. He does some one-to-one interviews with television and radio, which he can control. This has become routine. Alastair Campbell, his press secretary, briefs journalists the night before and then Blair delivers the words, taking care to stick reasonably faithfully to the script. This way there can be no awkward questions from the Scottish press which he once famously denounced as "unreconstructed wankers."

Blair's speech includes a long passage of unrestrained Nat-bashing and a plea to electors to avoid Scottish patriotism masquerading as policy. He champions the Union with England which, he argues, will offer Scotland and Britain strength while independence would weaken both countries. Devolution or divorce, is how he puts it.

How odd it is to some Scottish eyes that Blair in one breath praises Irish Nationalists because they are joining in a peace-process after 30 years of murder and terrorism, but vilifies Scottish nationalists who have a perfect record of democratic and peaceful campaigning. Ireland is different, obviously, but it is plain that Blair and Labour are in some difficulty dealing with nationalism in Scotland because of its overlap with patriotism.

On a previous visit to Glasgow Blair fell into the trap of preaching British patriotism, giving the impression it was somehow superior to Scottish patriotism. This is a dangerous area for him and for Labour as the SNP seeks to play up his middle-England image. Yet it must be said that he has so far managed to avoid becoming identified as Son of Thatcher as the Nationalists and the Scottish Socialist Party portray him. Blair's personal popularity is something Labour in Scotland frets about constantly, privately briefing that its polls show he is more popular in Scotland than in England. This appears to be untrue if the published polls are to be believed. System Three in *The Herald* recently found that only 42% thought he was sympathetic to Scotland, which is pretty good, all things considered. But the dangers are there. If he continues to portray Scottish nationalism/patriotism as narrow and economically suicidal then he risks talking Scotland itself down – and that would be just what the SNP would love.

February 8th

The polls continue to show the election is too close to call. There is a wonderful irony in this. It was Labour which described Scottish devolution as the "settled will" of the Scottish people. When he was Shadow Scottish Secretary George Robertson predicted that devolution would "kill the SNP stone dead." If these assertions are true, why are the Prime Minister and his Cabinet colleagues running around Scotland beseeching us to shun separatism? This election is becoming a referendum on independence, exactly what Labour did not want, far less envisage. What is more, this appears likely to be the pattern of every Scottish general election until the SNP wins one. After all, the Nationalists need to win only once – and Britain as we know it would probably cease to exist soon after. The enormity of this is something which still fails to register with most people south of the Border where the media still seem oblivious to the significance of events in Scotland. Our poll today by System Three in *The Herald* shows Labour two points ahead of the SNP in the first vote for Holyrood and level-pegging with Labour on the second vote. This is in line with other recent polls but miles out of kilter with ICM in the *Scotsman* where Labour has a comfortable lead. No-one I know believes ICM, especially after the mess it made of the North-East of Scotland Euro by-election where it suggested a four-point lead for the SNP just before the Nats romped home with a 30-point lead. But ICM did get the General Election result spot on after being all over the place during the campaign. System Three on the other hand appeared to be consistent during the campaign right up to their final poll when it went rather awry. With opinion polling for the Scottish Parliament elections we are in uncharted territory. It will be interesting to see who comes closest to the result.

February 18th
To dinner with the SNP and almost 300 businessmen and women. I never thought I would see the day when a posh hotel was crammed with £200-a-head corporate movers and shakers in dinner suits queuing up to pour funds into the separatists' cause. This is the second of the SNP's big dinners for big business. The first was in Edinburgh last year and attracted about 80 interested businessmen at £40 a head. So tonight's bash is big progress and must worry Labour's election machine which has been trying tirelessly to discredit the SNP in the eyes of the Scottish business sector. But no-one will be more depressed than the wretched Tories who were once the beneficiaries of this kind of expense sheet benevolence and whose corporate support has reportedly dried up.

Alex Salmond looks slightly uncomfortable in his dinner jacket and trews – he refuses to wear the kilt for reasons I must discover some day – and his speech is suitably dull for an audience sitting with hands on wallets. But he knows exactly what he is doing as he drones on about taxation levels, replacements for private finance initiatives and the rest. Difficult to say how it will be received but no-one appears hostile. I calculate on the back of an envelope that the Nats must have pulled in almost £50,000 before costs. This could simply never have happened before in Scotland. Some Scots still look askance at the SNP which is struggling to shake off its image as a party of single issue fanatics in tartan. But this sort of event suggests that as the Nationalists rise in the polls – and they are certain already of being at least the Opposition in the Scottish Parliament – they are

Eck's little local difficulty.

being taken seriously. Now they are beginning to grow up and it is a sight to see – all those captains of Scottish and British industry politely applauding the deadly secessionist menace.

February 21st
The Nats are having fun with CNN's website today which shows that only six of Labour's approved candidates for Holyrood have bothered to reply to a circular asking their views on the future of Trident nuclear missiles on the Clyde – and not one of them has supported Labour policy to keep the Royal Navy's nuclear fleet in Scottish waters. But 55 of their SNP rivals have responded, saying unanimously that it is time Trident was scrapped and Scotland made a nuclear-free zone.

Not that this matters much. Labour is embarrassed but not surprised. The days are long gone when it openly embraced unilateral disarmament. Labour's Scottish conference still loyally votes to get rid of Trident but the party in London simply ignores it. Yet there is widespread opposition to Trident in Scotland, a political force which is being milked by the SNP and others. Many Labour activists are openly hostile to nuclear weapons of all kinds and would vote happily to get rid of them. This is a timely reminder that even if Labour wins this election it cannot count on mustering a majority for keeping Trident. The Scottish Parliament won't, of course, have the power to send Trident packing but it could make life difficult for the Ministry of Defence. It is a thought that the SNP could fail to win power and still find a majority for scrapping Trident with the help of dissidents in other parties.

March 5th
Tony Blair is in Glasgow at Labour's Scottish conference and doing some photo-calls and meet-the-people question-and-answer sessions. This time he invites newspaper correspondents to join him for a sandwich lunch. This is unusual because in most of his previous visits he has made a point of avoiding us. Blair remains touchy about the

Scottish media, newspapers in particular. His normal routine in Scotland is to talk to broadcasters only because he can control them more easily than he can print journalists. We gather in the penthouse of the Thistle Hotel where the Prime Minister, all smiles and handshakes, joins us.

What follows is revealing. Blair slouches in a chair, knees against a table around which he tells us to take seats. With an expansive wave he invites questions and says he would like to be off the record. We quickly get the impression he was bored with this whole idea and we make it known we would prefer him on the record. He agrees with some reluctance. The conversation turns, inevitably, to his personal popularity in Scotland which is still a talking point with party hacks and journalists and seems to excite attention in the rest of the UK. It is again being exploited by the Nationalists as a means of projecting him as an unwelcome interloper up from London to boss the Scots about. Unsurprisingly Blair takes exception to being portrayed as a latter-day Thatcher. He betrays his irritation that anyone should question his right as the British Prime Minister to take part in an election which is increasingly seen as a domestic Scottish affair.

In fact he has little cause – so far, anyway – to worry unduly about his personal poll ratings despite the growing misconception that he is exceptionally unpopular in Scotland. His middle-England image and the descriptions of him in various private Labour polls as "smarmy" are not reflected in any damning evidence of strong hostility towards him. He is not suffering as Margaret Thatcher did in her day – at least not so far. Thatcher broke the record for the lowest approval rating in history when *The Herald*'s System Three found that only 1% of the Scottish people thought she was doing a good job for Scotland. Blair's ratings are still not bad for a Prime Minister heading for mid term. But he is obviously peeved at a *Scotsman* ICM poll today suggesting that 61% of Scots think he should stay away from the election. Those pundits who predicted Blair would eventually become a victim in Scotland of so-called Thatcher Syndrome – ever decreasing popularity – have not been proved correct, but there is still time. On the evidence so far he is no less popular than predecessors including Harold Wilson, Jim Callaghan and even John Major. Thatcher was deeply disliked because she was incurably bossy and always thought she knew better (eg the poll tax) and she presided over the ruination of Scotland's traditional heavy industry which had been a source of national pride. The fact that she was seen as posh English was very much a secondary factor, according to polling evidence – but the myth that she was hated because of her Englishness survives.

Thatcher's trouble was that she kept coming back to Scotland to win acceptance but the more often she turned up the more catastrophic her ratings became. No doubt Tony Blair is aware of this. He shows every sign of listening carefully to advice from Donald Dewar and his Scottish strategists. Whenever he comes to Scotland he gives the impression that he is afraid of putting his foot in it and feeding a gaffe-hungry Scottish media.

When we raise this complicated and dangerous subject with Blair he observes bluntly that when he is in Scotland he is never asked questions (by the media, as opposed to voters) which he finds difficult to answer. In effect, he is telling us we always ask the wrong questions. Issues and policies are not discussed or analysed by the press, he complains, because we are preoccupied with his personality and giving the SNP too easy a ride. His Englishness is the kind of thing he dismisses as media-driven froth.

He then launch into a series of complaints about our interest in his middle-England persona and his attempts to turn Scottish Old Labour into a mirror image of New Labour in the South (at which he has had some success, it must be admitted). He leaves early to do a television interview and we return to the conference hall for his speech which turns out to be a stronger, more passionate version of what we had just heard. He defends his right to be in Scotland as leader of a British party and makes a plea to Old and New Labour, socialist and social democrat, to work together to defeat the SNP. It is the kind of appeal which he would not feel the need to make in England. On the platform he is undeniably impressive as an orator. We sit with our copies of his prepared speech as he launches into half an hour of passionate Nat-bashing invective. The second half of his text is abandoned completely in favour of an extempore burst of finger-stabbing rhetoric which plays very well with the comrades, or colleagues as they are mostly addressed nowadays. I cannot help but admire his style yet when I browse through my notes of his speech for the purposes of a story I am struck by the lack of substance. That's the trouble with his Third Way. It carries no discernible dogma, unless you count extreme moderation. His frequent argument that he is following a particular policy because it is "right" means nothing but many people are undeniably impressed by it.

Labour is still unable to shake off the Nats. System Three today has the SNP only one point behind Labour in first vote intentions and four behind in second voting. The whole advisability of Labour's constant Nat-bashing is now being questioned throughout Scotland. I wonder if Blair's increasing hostility to the SNP is being interpreted in some circles as his impatience with Scotland as a whole. After all he is constantly harping on about SNP supporters promoting separatism, building barriers, introducing passports and – more dangerously – he appears to be championing British patriotism as somehow a superior sentiment to Scottish patriotism. This is a questionable way to defend the Treaty of Union. Many Scots take the view that true separatism is simply impossible in the modern world of the European Union, the European single market, the European single currency, not to mention such global bodies as Nato, the UN and so on. The stuff about passports and border posts is transparently absurd and no-one in Scotland genuinely believes it for a moment. Even the BBC joked this morning about the Labour voter who walked into a video store and asked for a copy of Separatism Day.

Blair is, therefore, playing with fire and he knows it. He is either brave and correct or worryingly out of touch. Most of all he seems to take the view the Scottish general election is just another poll but most of us came to the view long ago that it is in fact an independence referendum – perhaps the first of several over the coming years. When such huge constitutional issues are debated and the future of the United Kingdom itself is in doubt, all those questions about how many computers school kids should have or how much students should pay in fees and other "normal" political issues become somehow redundant, yet these are what Blair wants discussed. He says they are the real issues and they are doubtless real enough to some people but he is also hiding from the reality of a threatened Scottish secession from the United Kingdom.

Donald Dewar shows annoyance when someone asks him why Labour does not further devolve its party structure in Scotland. He accuses people who ask such questions of following a Nationalist agenda. "And we're not Nationalists," he grumbles. This perfectly illustrates Labour's difficulty in dealing with the SNP. The party is a British structure struggling to make itself more Scottish, but knowing that if it does so it is perceived as appeasing Nationalism.

March 6th
Bob Thomson, the outgoing Scottish Labour Party treasurer, makes his farewell speech in which he has a swipe at the leadership (as he has done many times over the years). Being a veteran Home Ruler he uses his final report as treasurer to complain that "Labour is the least devolved of the British parties" and to call for a complete decentralisation of the party structure. He is warmly applauded – but only from the conference floor. Fellow executive members are less receptive.

March 9th
Harry and I chat about the editorial stance of *The Herald* in the elections. In my time with the paper, almost 30 years now, we have never supported a political party. We think we should not align ourselves with any party in the Scottish Parliament elections but there

is a sound case for taking a stance on Scottish independence. My inclination is to support it. How ridiculous and anti-democratic it is that not one newspaper of any significance in Scotland supports independence while some polls show that up to 50% or 60% of the electorate say they want it. The entire indigenous Scottish press is opposed to the idea of an independent Scotland and always has been. Even the *Scotsman* which has a history of supporting devolution gives the impression these days of supporting it only grudgingly. The *Scotsman* evidently cannot summon the courage to oppose it openly and has opted instead – probably under the influence of its editor-in-chief, Andrew Neil, an arch Tory, and his proprietors, the Barclay brothers – to support it in principle while cavilling at much of the detail of the constitutional settlement.

As for the London-based press selling in Scotland, it is almost all strongly Unionist and hostile to the SNP. True, the *Sun* fleetingly supported the Nationalists. That was in the days before it switched to New Labour after Blair struck a rapport with Rupert Murdoch. Much good it did the SNP which promptly saw its representation in Westminster halved at the next General Election. These days the Scottish edition of the *Daily Mirror* gives half-hearted support for independence but does not back the SNP.

I think the time has come for the views of so many Scots to be reflected more fairly and I would like *The Herald* to lead the way. This would certainly come as a shock to many of our readers, particularly the older generation which remembers our paper as more right wing than the Conservative Party. I can recall *The Glasgow Herald*, as we then called ourselves, publishing leaders which were soft on apartheid and which gave succour to the rebels in Ian Smith's Rhodesia. All that changed in the early 1970s with the campaign to save merchant shipbuilding on the Upper Clyde, a fight which did much to bring about our estrangement from the Tories – an estrangement which still exists today. But as of May, 1997, there are no Scottish Tory MPs. The country has changed politically almost beyond recognition and I think we have a duty to get involved in the new radicalised Scottish politics instead of merely looked askance at rapid change, as our timid rivals do.

This does not mean to say I think we should endorse the SNP. Far from it. Indeed, there is a case for allowing ourselves to be harder on the Nationalists than we have been. This is the most controversial decision any Editor – and he would have to be a brave one - could take in Scotland these days. If you exclude the dalliance between the *Sun* and the SNP there has been no editorial sympathy for independence since the era of the old *Bulletin* in the 1950s. Its fate is not exactly an inspiration for us today. James Reid was the editor of the *Bulletin*. He was fired and his newspaper was closed down. The management of the day said this had nothing to do with his editorial policy – well, they would – but there are still journalists around who remember things differently.

Commercial interests will bear on any decision to support independence. Some advertisers might pull out just when advertising revenues are set to fall anyway because of the state of the economy, but we might well gain a few more readers than we lose. Surely it must be worth a try. I don't envy Harry his decision. It will be interesting to see how our management reacts. Scottish Media Group results are out today showing pre-tax profits increased by 12% to £46 million. This makes us vulnerable to a takeover, apparently, and it could be that we might yet want some protection from the Labour government. If Donald Dewar and his colleagues in the Scottish Office got wind that we were about to endorse independence I cannot imagine them having much sympathy for us.

March 11th

The Herald has a good old-fashioned scoop tonight. Robbie Dinwoodie has been chipping away at a story doing the rounds with the SNP. His efforts mean we can report exclusively that the Nationalists want to invoke the Tartan Tax if they win power. This is a huge policy gamble. No-one expected it, especially after Labour's Budget cut of one penny off the basic rate of income tax. The taxation authority of the Holyrood Parliament will allow an administration to vary the British level of income tax in Scotland up or down by 3p in the Pound. The Nats want to use this power to cancel the 1p Budget cut in Scotland and to spend the money saved – which they say will be about £700m over four years of the Parliament – on education, health and housing. This will mean no tax rise, merely the foregoing of the Chancellor's minor cut, they will argue. In effect the Nationalists are about to present a dagger at the heart of New Labour and its Conservative-style tax-cutting preoccupation, inviting all those disillusioned with Blairism and yearning for a return to some old Labour values in Scotland to vote SNP.

Robbie and I spend the day lying in our teeth to our colleagues, all of whom suspect we have a good SNP story ahead of tomorrow's opening of the Nationalists' conference. At a convivial dinner with colleagues in Aberdeen Robbie is enjoying himself and I can tell he is finding it difficult to contain his secret. Around 11.30 he leans over the table and whispers with an evil smile: "The bombs are about to go off." Sure enough, our rivals' mobile phones start ringing around the table as their news desks react to our first edition back in Glasgow. We were not exactly popular with our colleagues but there will be no lasting hard feelings. We have good reason to feel very pleased with ourselves.

2

A Penny for Scotland

March 11th - April 5th

March 12th

Our story causes quite a stir at the conference where most of the 700 delegates only begin to learn of their own party's audacious tax policy by reading Robbie's story. They know this has put a firecracker under Labour whose spin-doctors are already working on plans to argue that Scotland will be hopelessly disadvantaged by a higher rate of income tax than the rest of the UK. Some of the press corps think the gamble could backfire drastically but they do concede that Labour suddenly has a problem. The Tartan Tax is, after all, a Labour invention. Labour leaders in Scotland have long argued the need to give the Scottish Parliament power to levy it. Donald Dewar and Chancellor Gordon Brown can hardly complain at the existence of that power now although they can and no doubt will question the SNP's wisdom in deciding to invoke it.

Alex Salmond has been busy with John Swinney, the Nationalists' Treasury spokesman and other senior figures, planning how to sell the idea to the membership and the voters. Their idea is to cut the feet from under Labour with a challenge to all patriotic Scots to pay a "Penny for Scotland" for better health and education and housing. It could work. Journalists at the conference are split and some are doubtful that the ploy will succeed, given that tax-cutting seems to be compulsory among popular governments these days. Some of my colleagues believe the SNP gamble is simply suicidal. I find it difficult to judge. A few weeks ago I wrote a column saying the SNP should forget using the Tartan Tax because it would be more trouble that it was worth. Then, 1p in the Pound translated to an estimated £150m but because of Budget changes it will now produce about £230m – making it rather more attractive to any administration. More importantly, this money can be raised over a period of years without increasing the basic rate in Scotland and instead merely keeping it at the pre-Budget level. Gordon Brown appears to have handed the SNP a new weapon and the Nationalists have decided to take Labour on. This is a real political issue now, giving new impetus to the campaign.

I hear whispers from various sources that the idea was resisted by some senior party figures. Even John Swinney himself had his doubts, I learn, and wanted to be persuaded that the policy would be bombproof. Concern was expressed in private by all wings of the party, left and right. But there appears genuinely to be no split. Margo MacDonald is outspoken in her criticisms, being quoted by one journalist as saying the other parties will soon be dancing round the SNP's funeral pyre. But she seems in a small minority.

Alex Salmond summons us to a news conference where he unveils SNP strategy for pushing this policy. The "Penny for Scotland" theme will be hammered home and the Budget cut will be scorned as a pre-election bribe by Labour. But first Salmond must get the policy through the conference.

March 13th
The big debate is fairly predictable. Only a clutch of diehards votes against the tax proposal and Margo MacDonald is not among them. Salmond carries the day easily but the big winner is John Swinney. He has been seen as a diffident performer and, although popular, he has never been recognised as a political heavyweight. But his speech is strong and unusually passionate. He receives a genuinely spontaneous standing ovation which almost brings him to tears. It is a poignant moment for those who know what he has been suffering. Swinney has been under enormous pressure, not least from the red-top tabloids which have wallowed in lurid accounts of his wife's infidelity. I think in that moment of on-stage emotion he felt reassured that he was among real friends and supporters, all eager to fight with him in the battles ahead.

The other papers have been trying to get even with *The Herald* after Robbie's scoop. *The Daily Mail* and *Daily Record* have, as expected, rubbished the Penny-for-Scotland idea. But the real heat on the SNP will come now from Labour.

Steve Goodwin, the Scottish correspondent of *The Independent,* checks out of the media centre in Aberdeen to head for his home in Newcastle. He says he's going back to his English tax haven.

March 14th

We are summoned to the Scottish Office for an "explanation" from the Chancellor, the Secretary of State for Scotland, and the Scottish industry minister on the effects of the Budget in Scotland. This is remarkable for a Sunday afternoon when ministers are normally relaxing and anxious to avoid the media. It says something for the SNP's ability to stir things up that suddenly we have three ministers popping up to do some Nat-bashing on their day off.

The Chancellor recites a long list of businessmen who are against the SNP's proposals including a number of figures associated with Rangers FC, a Scottish institution still seen nowadays as the Unionists at play. Those named are the usual suspects. The story would be more fun if the CBI and its members were coming down in favour of investing in public services but we would not dare suggest that to the Chancellor.

Gordon Brown is evidently wrong-footed by the SNP ploy. On radio he has just denounced the plan as irresponsible, claiming that the Nationalists would use the money to build customs barriers with England and embassies abroad and, for good measure, to invent a new currency. This is as absurd a riposte as could be imagined because the Nats have given repeated and categorical assurances about where the money will be spent. Even if they wanted to, the Nats would be unable to do as Brown says because they would be working inside a devolved state as distinct from an independent one. Some gullible people might swallow what Brown and others are saying, I suppose, if they keep saying it often enough despite it being blatantly untrue. Labour will have to come up with something more compelling than this tosh.

But Brown is unrepentent about his spluttering protests, still claiming the penny tax would destroy employment and ruin the economy because Scotland would no longer be on a level playing field with England. Strange how this argument was never used when Labour dreamed up the Tartan Tax and John Smith argued for a £2 per week increase in income tax to fund public services, suggesting people would prefer that to a tax cut. The SNP will have fun with that quote. I wish I had a pound for every time the Chancellor said he had a "duty" to point out the dangers of SNP policy. He is already coming under attack from other parties for using government funding for electioneering. At his side today in Glasgow he has Roger Williams and Anne Shevas, the two most senior information officers in the Scottish Office, along with Murray Elder from Donald Dewar's private office at what is just another Nat-bashing news conference. Labour really should not be allowed to get away with this. Tories, SNP and LibDems all claim this is an abuse of the civil service but the answer comes back that the Budget is government business and so civil servants are required to be there. The hypocrisy is breathtaking. If the Tories had behaved like this, Labour would have been furious.

I never thought I would witness a Labour Chancellor standing shoulder-to-shoulder in this manner with the tax-obsessed and reviled Scottish Tories and with Scottish big business. The Establishment is closing ranks against the SNP and quite soon I suspect the entire weight of the British State to fall on Alex Salmond and John Swinney. It only needs the Queen Mother to call for British unity in the face of Scottish Nationalism as she did in the 1979 Referendum and the anti-SNP alliance will be complete.

I ask Gordon Brown if he feels comfortable with such bedfellows and he says he is comfortable standing up for what is good for Scotland – and then he reminds me pointedly that *The Herald* has a reputation for being the business community's paper in the West of Scotland, as though we, too, had a duty to fall into line.

I admire the SNP for having the nerve to take Labour on. Whether the ploy will succeed is another matter. The serious Sunday papers have given the Nats fair treatment today but the tabloids are putting the boot in. I suspect that with six weeks or so left the SNP have plenty of time to get across their message but whether it will be well received is difficult to guess. At least we have a real political fight to enjoy.

March 22nd
To Edinburgh for the last sitting of the inappropriately-named Scottish Grand Committee. There was never much grand about it. This is, or was, a committee composed of MPs from Scotland only. For most of its life it never left Westminster but as Nationalism grew in Scotland it was encouraged to remove itself occasionally to Edinburgh and elsewhere in order, the Tory government of the day said, to let the people see how it worked. There is no evidence that they were impressed. The Scottish Grand, as it was known, was a talking shop with no powers whatsoever, which is the way the Unionists in Scotland wanted to keep it. Now even its supporters accept it is redundant.

I counted 20 or so MPs out of 72 who might have been there for the final sitting. They exchanged the usual ritual insults until Helen Liddell in her role as Deputy Secretary of State for Scotland – who is not standing for Holyrood - made a closing speech in which she said it was an honour to be the last minister to make a wind-up address to the committee. When she remarked that MPs would meet again in the Scottish Parliament, one of the SNP shouted across at her: "Aye, but you'll no be there."

Few will mourn the death of the Scottish Grand Committee. As Chancellor Seafield said at the adjournment of the Scottish Parliament in 1707 it is the "end of ane auld sang." In the case of the Scottish Grand the end has come not a moment too soon.

But at least this last meeting produces a story for a change. Having been told for the past few days in every Labour press release and government statement that their "Penny for Scotland" plan will be a disaster for small businesses, the Nats decided to have fun with a comment from last year by Henry McLeish, the Scottish Office devolution minister. To the SNP's delight he argued then, somewhat rashly, that the Tartan Tax would do small businesses no harm at all – and he was talking of perhaps 3p in the pound. The effect is hilarious. Labour's argument is turned on its head. No doubt soon we will have Labour dredging up some quote from the Nats showing they believe the Tartan Tax to be iniquitous.

I enjoy a newsworthy interview with Jim Wallace, leader of the Scottish Liberal Democrats, the man who is likely to be kingmaker in the Scottish Parliament. He and I find we had something in common. His introduction to politics was the Dumfries by-election of 1963 which also happened to be mine. I was then a young reporter on the Dumfries Standard. Niall MacPherson, the local Tory MP, had been given a peerage, and the Tories calculated that there was no risk in calling a by-election to replace him. A ridiculously pompous man called David Colville Anderson, QC, Solicitor General for Scotland, was foisted on the Dumfries Conservatives who had mostly wanted Hector Monro, a local laird and rugby playing farmer, as their candidate. My job was to follow the Liberal candidate, one Charles Abernethy, around Dumfriesshire for three weeks. For company I took Andree Bryce, an attractive girl from the front office of the Standard, (who has since survived more than 30 years of marriage to me). Our romantic time together talking during the drive between the Liberal candidate's meetings was ruined by the arrival on the scene of a young blade from the Borders with a vintage Rover which kept breaking down. This meant I had to give him lifts between villages. Since the Standard van was a two-seater he sat on Andree's knee as I became his unpaid chauffeur. This fellow, whom I always remember for playing gooseberry during my courtship of my wife, was to become famous later in life as David Steel, the Liberal leader, now Lord Steel.

Jim Wallace later fought Dumfries himself with no luck. Hector (now Lord) Monro duly became the long-serving Tory MP after Anderson disgraced himself in a sexual misadventure and had to resign abruptly. It was all hushed up but Anderson returned to public life years later and promptly got into the same sort of trouble, resigning again.

Wallace is one of only two Scottish LibDem MPs fighting for a seat in Holyrood. He will lead his party there and hopes to form a coalition with the largest party which will probably be Labour. The story I want from him is whether he foresees a pact with the SNP which would outrage Labour and make far bigger news.

To get him going I suggest there is no point in voting LibDem because everyone knows it is effectively a vote for Labour. To my surprise he comes up with the goods when he explains how it is possible to do a deal with the SNP. This is a departure from previous statements because he seems to be suggesting the SNP's insistence on a referendum on independence being a pre-condition of any coalition can be overcome.

Paddy Ashdown two weeks ago said categorically that the Scottish LibDems would never form a pact with "any party which seeks the break-up of the United Kingdom." This means, obviously, the SNP. But Ashdown is ahead of himself, it seems. He may be the federal leader but his writ does not run north of the border.

Wallace makes it quite clear that Ashdown is guilty of what he calls – with a smile – "over-enthusiastic interpretation" of LibDem procedures. Any decision on coalition will be taken by LibDem MSPs in Holyrood whose only duty will be to reflect as accurately as possible the sympathies of the party in Scotland, he says. Wallace is not worried by Ashdown's agenda in the south where he and Menzies Campbell and others like David Steel are desperate for proportional representation and jobs for LibDems in the Blair Cabinet. Having been excluded from the loop, Wallace feels free to negotiate with any or all sides in Edinburgh. When I mention this to a very high SNP figure I am met with raised eyebrows and an indication that the

SNP's unbreakable condition of a referendum might not be all that unbreakable after all – if it was to prove the only obstacle to the SNP coalescing with the LibDems. There is force to this reasoning. If the Nats win a majority – unlikely as of today – they could force through a referendum anyway. If they were a minority they would not be in a position to force through anything. The best they can hope for, it seems, is sufficient seats to muster a majority with help from mavericks like Dennis Canavan who – if elected, which is possible – would probably support independence. The Nats are forever predicting, probably correctly, that in the coming Scottish Parliament the MSPs who favour independence won't all be confined to the SNP.

March 23rd

Jim Wallace's comments in *The Herald* have caused a stir. There is something so annoyingly LibDem about the party's emerging strategy for Holyrood – all wait-and-see and compromise and middle-of-the road. I find it quite irritating. I decide to write a critical piece asking in so many words if there is any point to the LibDems or any compelling reason for their existence. Jim Wallace probably won't thank me. Yet someone has to say it; here we have a party which says it wants to be part of a coalition but won't say with whom, and that it wants to use the Tartan Tax to fund education, if necessary, but won't say if it believes it will be necessary. I cannot be alone in believing this approach to be unsustainable.

March 24th

Donald Dewar is in trouble for trying to discover the contents of a Scottish Affairs Select Committee report. The timing is beautiful. Almost to the minute that Nato announced it was now bombing the Serbs, sending every newsdesk in Britain into a frenzy, Labour has let it be known that one of its MPs, the obscure David Stewart from Inverness, has offered to resign from the committee. In normal times this tale would be a possible splash for the newspapers but Labour knows it can't compete with the start of war against Yugoslavia.

The Tories have been scenting blood since they forced Ernie Ross (Dundee West) to resign from the Foreign Affairs Select Committee after confessing to systematically leaking its views on the arms-to-Africa affair to the Foreign Secretary, Robin Cook. We have to be careful with Ross because he has taken legal action against *The Herald* in the courts for defamation arising from comments by Ian Davidson, MP for Glasgow Pollok who, along with Dennis Canavan (Falkirk West), was a victim of Labour's much-criticised selection procedures for Holyrood.

Ross's resignation in disgrace was not mourned. This latest case appears to be less serious, at least for David Stewart. He supplied information to Donald Dewar only after it had appeared on our front page. We told how MPs on the Labour-dominated committee had decided devolution could lead to Scottish independence – not at all the sort of thing government ministers expect or want to hear, especially at an electorally sensitive time like this.

It seems Donald was so agitated by our leak of the conclusions – which we regarded as rather a splendid scoop – that he contacted Stewart and demanded to know what was going on. This rather blatant approach by Dewar is helpful to Stewart who is likely to have his resignation offer accepted, but it shows Donald – good old Honest Donald – in a poor light. Ministers are not expected to go around asking for leaks – and most certainly not expected to get caught. Even Robin Cook did not do that.

For the moment the war in the Balkans is dominating the headlines but I suspect the Tories and SNP will return to Donald's troubles soon, perhaps demanding that he explains himself to the House privileges committee, which would be an embarrassing distraction in the run-up to the elections. Come to think of it, a few days ago Donald was protesting to some reporters that the Ernie Ross scandal was overblown and that it was as nothing compared with the way the Tories had behaved in office when they wanted the lowdown on what select committees might be up to. Now we see why he was so worried.

March 25th

In the High Court Mohammad Sarwar has been found not guilty of all charges by a majority verdict and is celebrating. Labour must now decide what to do with him. Some people in high places in the party will want to know why he lied about the famous loan – which the Crown said was a bribe – to one of his rival candidates, Badar Islam, who has emerged from this trial with what was left of his reputation in tatters. I have a long-standing arrangement with Sarwar, with whom I have always got on well, that he will speak to *The Herald* exclusively if he is acquitted.

March 26th

A hostile leader in *The Herald* this morning calls for Sarwar to step down despite his acquittal and has met, understandably, with a furious response. BBC news programmes have been questioning the need for it, given that the man now has no stain on his character. Sarwar is, understandably, greatly dismayed. I hear that *The Herald* has been denounced at the Mosque in Gorbals where Sarwar joined the faithful this morning. My interview with him is cancelled and then reinstated after he calms down.

At his home in Pollokshields his wife, Perveen, who was always by his side on the television shots of him arriving at and leaving court, lays into me about the coverage of his acquittal. She is nothing like the stereotypical Moslem wife, the docile junior partner who follows her husband everywhere at a respectful distance. Perveen lectures me about the faults of the media and Sarwar himself complains that only journalists ask questions suggesting there was no smoke without fire. The people, he says, accept he is innocent.

His telephone never stops and the doorbell rings continuously with people delivering flowers and other gifts and offering their good wishes. Eventually Sarwar calms down and begins to talk. He is plainly a very relieved man and thankful that his life has returned to some semblance of normality. While we are talking the news comes through from Delta House that his suspension from the Labour Party has been lifted. He begins to talk of seeking office again and getting down to concentrating, with no more distractions, on working for his constituents. His other ambition is to sue the *News of the World* which alleged he had been caught red-handed paying a bribe. Now that the jury has accepted his word that the bagful of £20 notes was simply a loan, Sarwar's chances of a lucrative settlement appear to have risen spectacularly. He roars with laughter and claps hands at the prospect and we part on good terms again. I must say that Sarwar is a difficult man to dislike, with his winning smile and gentle manner. I have not the heart to suggest to him that Labour might be ruthless when the time comes for reselection as a prospective candidate in Govan. Innocent he may be, but he has committed the unpardonable sin of producing bad headlines for New Labour. His only hope for the future is that the headlines would be even more hostile if Labour ditched him. I wonder how the Islamic community might react to an innocent man who just happens to be Britain's first Moslem MP being de-selected.

March 28th

Sean Connery is coming back to live in Scotland. The papers are full of his plans to buy a home in the Borders and live there for perhaps three months a year. Labour hates the idea because Connery, widely recognised as the most famous Scot in the world, is an unreconstructed Nat, even to the extent of having *Scotland for Ever* tattooed on his arm. Brian Wilson is making sarcastic comments about Connery's status as a tax exile while Connery continues to protest that he is nothing of the sort and that he pays taxes in Britain on his British earnings.

His decision will irritate and worry Labour ministers who were happy to exploit his huge popularity at the Referendum in 1997 when Donald Dewar and Gordon Brown and others queued to be photographed with the great star as he lent his support to the Yes-Yes campaign. But Donald and, it is said, Sam Galbraith, quietly cancelled the knighthood which had been pencilled in for him by the

"It's a Commander Bond, Mr Dewar ...
... says it's personal."

departing Tories. Talk about leaving a booby trap. When the news leaked, Labour's clumsy response was to smear Connery with old stories about a silly remark he made long years before about women needing an occasional slap. Labour briefed journalists that Connery was, in effect, a woman-beater. It was a nasty ploy which backfired after a ministerial source in London was exposed, and so Labour is being much more careful this time.

Whether Connery's reappearance on the hustings will make much difference this time is doubtful. He has booked Edinburgh Castle for a film premiere two weeks before polling day and so the Nats have high hopes that he will also make a high-profile appearance in their support. Some of the tabloids today are taking a tilt at him and his mysterious tax status, pointing out that he will not be liable for the SNP's one-penny tax, despite his vast wealth.

Harry Reid is amused at being listed in the *Sunday Times* as the 30th most powerful man in Scotland. The ST says: "Reid has the freedom to endorse whichever party he likes. Labour is increasingly jittery about his open-minded coverage of the SNP." By "open-minded" they must mean fair. There we have it. Scotland's leaders fret that a newspaper is fair. That rather says it all about the state of Scottish free speech, not to mention Scottish politics, today.

March 29th

Alex Salmond has just taken on the British Establishment again tonight with a denunciation of the Allied bombing in the Balkans, calling it an act of "unpardonable folly." He is the first significant UK politician to speak out and in doing so he must believe he is speaking for many, perhaps a majority, of the population who believe Nato has got its tactics wrong. Salmond has accused Nato's political leaders, ie Blair and Clinton, of speeding up the genocide in Kosovo instead of stopping it.

Not surprisingly there is a great flutter in the Labour doocot. Robin Cook goes completely over the top saying Salmond is standing shoulder to shoulder with Slobodan Milosevic and will be the toast of Belgrade. Similar sentiments are expressed by Defence Secretary George Robertson. Labour's tone is one of near hysteria. Salmond has again shown his talent for touching a raw nerve, just as he did in the bombing of Iraq when he spoke up against it, too. This time he has chosen a television party political broadcast to make his point. The SNP is usually not permitted equal time with the Prime Minister, leader of the Opposition and the Liberal Democrats because it is regarded in London as a mere "regional" party. But because there is an election coming in Scotland, the powers that be have decided Salmond is entitled to respond along with the other party leaders to the prime minister's broadcast to the nation on the Balkans crisis which is worsening by the day.

By breaking the British political consensus with his outspoken comments Salmond has cunningly got himself national UK exposure. In so many words he is saying that Nato troops are military lions led by political donkeys. He has also sparked a furious debate by giving voice to those – and there are undoubtedly many – who have deep misgivings about the tactical wisdom of Nato's actions. For Labour simply to dismiss this as near treason is ridiculous – but I wonder if it will be widely seen in that light. There must be many who think Salmond has a valid point but that this might not be the time to make it. The excessive Labour response is also testimony to the party's feverish preoccupation with controlling headlines. No-one knows better than Salmond how to get under Labour's skin. He knows, too, that he is probably speaking for many Old Labour voters in Scotland who are veterans of the peace marches of yesteryear and who still have a lingering fondness for Michael Foot-style peacemongering. Whatever happens, this will be another major issue in the campaign, along with taxation.

The Nats are nervous and calling *The Herald* tonight asking how we are treating the story. Harry promises we will be fair and balanced in our news coverage and that we will write a sympathetic leader. This will add force to the view being increasingly expressed, not least by Labour, that *The Herald* is going pro-SNP. I suspect there will be hell to pay but it should be fun.

March 30th

To the Scottish Office for a dull press conference with Lord "Gus" Macdonald, the Scottish Industry minister and our former boss at the Scottish Media Group where he was chairman until New Labour persuaded him to join the government. Gus is always civil to me but I know he is another of those who fret about us being "open-minded" towards the Nats. The last time we talked he was banging on about the damage which the Tartan Tax would do to Scotland. When I reminded him it was Labour's idea, he shrugged and changed the subject. As a journalist himself he knows he can push his politics only so far before he hits the brick wall of objectivity.

Today he is introducing businessmen who helped to write the 'Pathfinders to the Parliament' report, a series of recommendations and suggestions from a vast committee made up of the Scottish commercial and industrial establishment. Among their recommendations is the abolition of student tuition fees, or some of them, a policy supported now by the three Opposition parties. Gus is unfazed when I ask him how Labour responds to this, given that it is always claiming to be the party which best serves the Scottish business community. He skates out of trouble by reminding me that business policy will be a matter for the Scottish Parliament. This has become something of a mantra now whenever ministers are asked awkward policy questions. Gus is working well these days after a sticky start to his new career. It is said he was genuinely taken aback at the cynicism with which his ministerial appointment was received in Scotland. He was accused of being just another beneficiary of Labour cronyism. Yet his was undeniably a good appointment. Gus is plainly warming to the job. He likes nothing more than business jargon and he has a talent for quoting from a seemingly inexhaustible mental bank of statistics on the most obscure industrial topics.

For a while Gus was in danger of becoming something of a joke figure in the real world outside politics where he became known as the Minister for Job Losses. He has only just over a month to go before his short reign as a Scottish Office minister comes to an end and he must be hoping he can escape the run of recent industrial closures. He is not standing for the Scottish Parliament and I wonder what he will do next. Gus is wealthy and successful, not a natural politician but a good minister and a workaholic. Despite his barely concealed concern about *The Herald's* political tone and his none too subtle hints that we might be better disposed to the government, I wish him well.

Alex Salmond's comments have provoked an entertaining stushie. The Tories, bless them, come on the telephone asking my advice about how they should respond to Salmond's remarks. That's a first. Are they so bereft of confidence in Scotland these days that they have taken to asking people like me with no known sympathy for them how to go about their business? In my new role as Conservative Party adviser I suggest they should be aware that Salmond is speaking for a large section of the community in expressing doubts about the conduct of Nato's campaign against Slobodan Milosevic. It does not take long for me to learn that my advice is offered in vain. The Tories' first reaction shows they just cannot resist having a whack at Salmond – and in that they are in company of all three other major parties.

Labour ministers have been queuing all day to hurl abuse but the consensus seems to be that Robin Cook overstated his case embarrassingly when he said Salmond is the "toast of Belgrade" as he stands side by side with Milosevic. This is a manifestly absurd claim and today the SNP duly takes revenge with some rhetoric of its own to the effect that Cook is deranged about Nato's failure so far to bomb its way to a solution and that he is unfit to be Foreign Secretary.

But Salmond is privately concerned about how his comments will be received. He, too, asks me how they are going down. I am beginning to think I might have a career as a policy adviser. I suggest he should be firmer about supporting the troops while attacking the politicians – condemning the donkeys leading the lions. He did make a point in his broadcast of expressing support for the troops but the other parties ignored that, naturally, preferring to paint him as some sort of traitor. He takes my point and gives me a good interview saying he intends to continue in this vein, banking on the fact there is still time to get his views across before the elections.

Significantly, the television news tonight is full of stories about how Nato is causing the Serbs to speed up the genocide and ethnic cleansing of Kosovo, provoking a vast humanitarian crisis. Salmond might indeed be a political opportunist – aren't they all? – but he's an accomplished one. To my surprise the papers today are by no means opposed to Salmond. Even Allan Massie in the *Daily Mail* gives grudging recognition that Salmond has a strong case to argue and that he might be right. What worries me most is that I agree with Allan Massie.

Whenever the SNP claims the headlines, Labour calls a press conference. Helen Liddell wants us to listen to some routine Nat-bashing but her spokespeople are told in no uncertain terms by the press pack that there is no point. This is becoming a tedious habit with Labour. The last time Labour tried this trick of coaxing us away from the real story – which was Salmond today – it got not a line in any of the papers. *The Daily Record*, which is pro-Labour, leads the way today in explaining it has no intention of turning up to hear Mrs Liddell. I promise to look out for a press release but explain that I cannot attend a press conference (which is true – there is just no time) and now we have an impasse with the forceful New Labour media machine. Sometimes it's good to know New Labour needs us more than we need it, but the day will come – it always does – when the party takes its revenge on reporters who offend it. I suspect whoever turns up today for Mrs Liddell will be suitably rewarded with a little exclusive soon and I will get a rocket for my trouble.

April 1st
Grim news for the SNP. The latest System Three opinion poll for *The Herald* shows Labour suddenly moving clear with a 13-point lead in first vote support and eight points clear in second. This is exactly what the Nats prayed would not happen. But the odd thing is that when System Three asked people to choose between the SNP's "Penny for Scotland" idea and Gordon Brown's penny tax cut, more than half (52%) sided with the SNP. The lesson which can reasonably be drawn is that this is another example of the phenomenon which helped defeat Labour in 1992. People say they are willing to pay more taxes if doing so helps public services but when the same people go into the polling booth they don't vote to do so. John Smith was blamed for losing Labour the 1992 election when voters signalled that they were willing to pay higher taxes than the Tories were offering, but backtracked when it mattered. But it is worth remembering that although Labour did indeed fail miserably in England the same did not apply in Scotland where the party made gains despite a later surge by the SNP. Even so, there is a huge worry here for the Nats who know it is no good winning arguments if you don't win the votes.

This has all the signs of a landmark poll because it suggests for the first time since last July that the deadlock between Labour and the SNP has at last been broken. The one crumb of comfort for the SNP is that Labour has not increased its support in the crucial second vote although it remains strong at 40%. This sort of support would translate to about 60 seats for Labour in Holyrood, still not enough for an overall majority, and the Nats would be the Opposition. While this is bad news for the SNP, it is by no means the end. No-one seriously expected a Nationalist majority, except, perhaps, some of the more starry-eyed Nationalists. This poll merely suggests that the Nats will emerge as a smaller Opposition than they might have liked – but even becoming the official Opposition is progress for the SNP.

In private, though, their senior people are pretty gloomy. As of today their huge lead in the polls is consigned to memory and all the exciting progress they enjoyed last year is completely reversed. System Three offers some interesting reasons including Gordon Brown's well-received Labour Budget and a suspicion that Labour is gaining popularity temporarily because of the Balkans war. All governments tend to win support when the nation is in conflict – a point suddenly being made feverishly by the SNP. But what happens if Blair has a bad war? As of today the genocide in Kosovo appears to be continuing and there is now a catastrophic refugee problem which did not exist until Nato began bombing. This poll came too late for Salmond's broadcast to be a factor but previous polls have suggested his remarks were not popular. There seems a remarkable willingness in the London media to ignore them – perhaps in case they strike a chord and provoke questioning outside Scotland about the direction of the war? For the moment most of the London papers are still into jingoism with bloodthirsty headlines like "Clobber Slobbo" and "Bomb Bomb Bomb." It is rather unedifying. In Scotland the press is behaving differently, and rather unexpectedly. Although the *Daily Record* has reverted to slavish loyalty to Labour and is publishing increasingly vicious attacks on Salmond, the *Scotsman*, which abhors Nationalism, has given generous space to those who argue he is right. In *The Herald* we have argued today that he was brave to speak out although we had reservations about the tone of his comments. One of Labour's spin-doctors asked me today how I thought Salmond's remarks were playing. I said he could probably have been more careful with the wording of his broadcast – which, I am told, he wrote himself in a hurry – but that the message was seen as plausible and might attract sympathy over time. The reaction was icy. But the fact that Labour is phoning around asking the question seems significant. The Nats and Tories are doing the same, anxious to test opinion. This argument, it seems, will run right through to polling day and beyond because a humanitarian disaster on this scale cannot be resolved in a few days.

The Liberal Democrats have invited the media to join their campaign bus at a cost of £1300 per person. Willie Rennie, their spokesman, says apologetically that they are merely trying to recover some of their expenses. At *The Herald* we have no objection to this, despite the principle of paying for access. No access, no stories. If the other parties had done the same we would have had to stump up for them, too. It is political extortion but we seem to have little choice. Labour is not charging for Donald Dewar's bus (it probably has a benevolent millionaire picking up the tab) and the Tories have decided not to have a bus at all, while the Nats want £500 a head, which seems more reasonable. Charging the media for access has become part of political life nowadays and there seems little we can do about it. Information is a commodity to be bought and sold like soap powder and what right have we to complain? After all we make our livings from selling news. We don't give it away.

I take a call from Radio Clyde – which is notorious for its stingy payments – asking me to go on the air with my comments on paying for access. I argue that I am not too worried and that as journalists we shall merely put the cost on expenses. The interviewer sounds shocked and asks if the Scottish media should not band together and present a united resistance. (She admits being put up to this by her boss.) I reply that would be daft because journalism is a dog-eat-dog business and it would take only one news organisation to break ranks and get all the election stories of the day to itself. I know where Radio Clyde is coming from. It is too mean to stump up the money itself. Tough. It can make its own arrangements. The interviewer suggests that a few weeks on the French Riviera would cost less than being trapped on a bus for a month with Jim Wallace and a bunch of Liberal Democrats and would be a lot more fun. Maybe she has a point.

April 5th

After another weekend of bad polls for the SNP we are set for the formal start of campaigning tomorrow. Most of the pundits are agreed that as of today Labour will probably emerge comfortably as the biggest party in Holyrood with about 60 seats, still short of an overall majority but not that far from outright control. It is difficult to imagine a better start for Labour. Support seems to be draining from the Nationalists as the Balkans war continues to dominate the news agenda. With uncanny timing the Libyans have decided at last to hand over the two Lockerbie bombing suspects to the Scottish authorities gathered in the Netherlands. This might not do Labour much good but it surely won't do any harm. We have lived for a decade with stories of successive British governments failing to extradite the two Libyan suspects but now Nelson Mandela's intervention on Britain's behalf with Col Gadaffi appears to have succeeded. A deal has evidently been done on the Lockerbie case in return for the eventual lifting of sanctions against Libya. Meanwhile, the row over Alex Salmond's speech continues to attract mainly critical coverage.

A year or so ago it was all so different. The SNP was 14 points ahead of Labour at one stage in one of our System Three polls although I don't know of anyone who really believed it. George Reid of the SNP remarked then that the Nats might at last have achieved critical mass – but he said it with a disbelieving smile. So much has changed so quickly in Scottish politics. Labour was under constant attack this time last year for being too Thatcherite in Scotland and the papers were full of unremitting Labour sleaze and scandal. As of now Tommy Graham is expelled and silent, at least for the moment. The rebellious Pat Lally is working quietly as Lord Provost of Glasgow, having removed himself from the front pages although he is now setting about suing Labour which might embarrass the party briefly but probably not until after May 6. Dennis Canavan, having been thrown out of the Labour Party automatically for handing in his nomination papers in Falkirk West, where he will be standing as an Independent, is no longer making many waves. It's back to business as usual for Mohammad Sarwar and we have not had a decent local government scandal involving Labour for weeks. Gradually, Labour is resolving its difficulties just at the right time.

Clearly the SNP is about to come under more intense pressure than ever before. In this election the future of the United Kingdom is perceived to be in danger which means that the full might of the British State will be turned against Alex Salmond and his party. It will be bloody and probably dirty, but it should also be fun, especially if the Nats find a way of stopping the bleeding. Labour always said it would regain popularity as the people heard the message of Blairism. It might well be right. Any lingering notion that the Scottish Parliament elections will be a walkover for an Opposition party facing a government two years into office and suffering mid-term blues is now gone. In England Labour still enjoys popularity ratings of more than 50%. If that happens in Scotland, then Labour could yet surprise everyone – itself included – by winning a majority in Holyrood. This was never foreseen under the new electoral system. Only the Tories have ever won a majority of the popular vote in Scotland (taking 50.5% in 1955). Some of the number crunchers in the various party HQs have been putting post-war General Election results through their computers to discover how the results might translate in Holyrood. It seems only the Tories in 1955 and, possibly, Labour in 1966, would have won majorities in Holyrood, according to these calculations which, necessarily, are based for this purpose on the assumption that electors will cast their two Scottish Parliament votes for the same party or individual. It seems to me that the big danger for the Nationalists is the Tories making a significant comeback and regaining some of the ground lost to the SNP, but of that there is no sign.

3

Shooting the Messenger

April 6th - April 20th

April 6th

To Edinburgh to see off Donald Dewar on his round-Scotland electioneering bus tour. This marks the official launch of Labour's campaign. Donald intends travelling 2000 miles on his campaign bus, making more than 100 stops, in the four weeks remaining to polling. The suspicion among the cynics is that he is being bumped out of the way while the tougher Gordon Brown takes over the real work of running Labour's campaign. Donald turns up for a launch ceremony, choreographed mainly for television, at Parliament House, High Street, where the Scottish Parliament ceased to be in 1707 when it "adjourned" and Scotland lost her independence. It's raining and windy but just as Donald arrives the rain stops. The aspiring First Minister thinks this is a fine augury for Labour, and off he goes on an uncharacteristically harsh Nat-bashing rant about how the SNP is hiding its true colours and pretending to be a devolutionist party. Somebody must have written the script for him because this is not the natural Donald. As he often does on such occasions he departs from the text and inserts some characteristic Dewarisms. He accuses the SNP of ditching its obsession with independence by "magicking it away in a swirl of printer's ink." I think he means the SNP is being coy about separatism because it has produced its 10-point pledge card for Holyrood with independence for Scotland coming tenth on the list.

Donald starts a chain reaction. All over Scotland Labour politicians are taking up the theme, claiming the SNP is being dishonest and disingenuous by trying to play down the ugly and ruinous divorce it is planning from Britain and presenting itself instead as a devolutionist party. In Glasgow Henry McLeish and Douglas Alexander join in the chorus and we are told by Labour that Gordon Brown himself will be campaigning along the same lines in Glasgow tomorrow.

As we wait in the rain a television crew arrives with Charlie Whelan, the former spin-doctor to Gordon Brown and the man credited with the downfall of Peter Mandelson and Geoffrey Robinson. Charlie is working for *Scotland on Sunday* and *The Guardian* and has his own fly-on-the-wall television documentary team following in his footsteps. I recall with him how we met for the first time in Brussels when I worked there as European Editor of *The Herald*. He accompanied Brown on the Chancellor's first meeting of Ecofin, the EU's council of finance ministers. On that occasion Charlie gave a dreadful impression of New Labour at work when he scurried round the conference room shoving his hands over the lenses of television cameras while Brown briefed reporters. It was a silly incident which only added to Charlie's notoriety. But today he is unrepentent, boasting he enjoyed his time as a bovver boy. He might be deservedly notorious but he is a difficult man to dislike, despite, or because of, his studied bad manners.

BBC Radio 4 is covering Donald's departure and invites Charlie and me to debate the SNP's tax plans. Charlie refuses because, he says, he's "bloody freezing" and won't be interviewed while standing in the rain. But then he seems to remind himself that he's a journalist now and no longer in a position to call the shots. He launches into a critique of SNP tax policy, explaining that Nationalist tax rises will damage the economy. I point out that the SNP is not raising taxes at all, merely cancelling a proposed reduction – not at all the same thing – and that people in Scotland will not be paying any more under an SNP-run Edinburgh Parliament than they are now. Charlie's reaction is simply to ignore the facts and plough on about SNP tax rises. One thing about Charlie is his talent for never letting truth get in the way of a good libel.

And then it's off along the M8 to Bathgate which Labour has chosen as Donald's first port of call and where he formally opens the local party campaign rooms. This is the Westminster constituency of Tam Dalyell, Labour's most anti-devolution MP and the one Labour

MP in Scotland who refused to sign the Claim of Right a decade ago. Not surprisingly, Tam is not around on his home patch to greet Donald, or if he is, he is keeping out of sight.

Word soon arrives that Labour is concerned about the SNP's campaign launch earlier in the day. Labour's campaign bus is scheduled to take us from Bathgate to Glasgow Govan where Mohammad Sarwar is about to stage his public comeback by welcoming Donald. We are invited to skip Govan and disembark instead at Delta House, Labour's new Scottish HQ, to hear from Henry McLeish and Douglas Alexander who want to warn us yet again that the Nats are separatists and not devolutionists, despite their promise earlier in the day to make the Scottish Parliament work. After listening to them simply replaying Donald, the patience of Kenny McIntyre of the BBC finally snaps and he accuses them both of insulting the intelligence of Scottish voters who know perfectly well that the Nats stand for independence. Even Tom Brown, the voice of New Labour in the *Daily Record*, suggests that Labour's protests about the SNP pledge cards are irritatingly synthetic.

Back in the office I hear that Brian Cox, the Scottish actor, has been told by Labour that his services are no longer required for a party political broadcast. It seems Cox told the *Sunday Herald* that he was quite at ease with the idea of Scotland breaking the Union with England. This, of course, is Apache talk as far as Labour is concerned. Cox says Labour has taken a silly fit of pique. Labour considers him to be guilty of what might be called an unpardonable folly.

The Scottish Electoral Commission reports that the political parties have all disclosed the identities of those supporters providing more than £5000 in donations. Labour says it is not embarrassed to be seen to receive at least that amount from Jimmy Boyle, the notorious convicted murderer who has long since become reformed and who is now an established sculptor and voluntary campaigner in the fight against drug abuse. Sean Connery has given more than twice that amount to the SNP (these figures are only for the past three months) but the Tories have received £200,000 from Irvine Laidlaw which accounts for most of their donations in that period. I suppose this new transparency is a little piece of British political history which owes its existence to Lord Neill's report on standards in public life. Until now the political parties have been indecently shy about identifying some of their benefactors.

Ever on the lookout for a light line for the Diary in *The Herald*, I ask Murray Elder, who is a special adviser to Donald Dewar and famously dour, about the registration plate on Donald's bus. It is NIL 2542.

"What about the number?" I inquired.
"What about it?" replied Murray.
"There must be a joke there,"
"Why?"
"Well, it says NIL,"
"There's no joke," Murray replies. "You must be desperate today."

Ah, well, this is one campaign where we will not be laughing along with Labour.

Murray Elder's presence is normal at such events, as is that of David Whitton who earns a reported £80,000 a year as special adviser to Donald. The two are civil servants, never away from the boss's shoulder, but they are not allowed to take part in party political activity. David tells me he is now working for the Labour Party and no longer for the Scottish Office. No doubt Murray Elder, who is a former Labour general secretary in Scotland, is doing the same as of today. The big difference is, of course, that their salaries are no longer being paid from the public purse. The idea that civil servants suddenly step down during elections and become detached on a point of principle is a joke. The only difference here is that the taxpayer is no longer paying for them – and that will probably be temporary. I have no doubt that if Labour forms the Scottish government Murray Elder and David Whitton will be back in the service of Donald as if nothing had changed.

April 7th

We witness another new trend in electioneering. Labour is taking the second of its three bites at the publicity cherry in this election. Having despatched its campaign bus yesterday, Labour is formally launching its election pledge list today. Sometime next week it will unveil its manifesto. Each occasion is another photo opportunity and another chance to get on the telly. Donald Dewar has called a news conference for the formal unveiling of policies announced long ago, to wit Labour's hospital building programme, plans for improved schools, a new Drugs Enforcement Agency to be paid for with £4.5m of new money, 200 more police officers, new industrial apprenticeships, and so on.

But the hacks are mostly interested in the announcement today that JP Morgan, the American merchant bank, is locating in Glasgow. This decision was planned by Labour as a huge publicity coup but it has horribly backfired. A naughty journalist asks the boss of the bank if he would still have invested in Scotland had the country been independent.

The poor chap is as diplomatic as possible, shrugging off the question and saying that he is only interested in the highly educated local workforce. He adds as an afterthought that his bank decided on Glasgow because it suited its long-term corporate investment strategy. In other words: yes. Donald was come over faint, protesting indignantly that inward investors do not want to become involved in local politics.

All this is hugely entertaining because Donald is playing host today to Gordon Brown who is in Glasgow to issue apocalyptic warnings about the economic ruination of Scotland should the SNP win power in Holyrood. The Chancellor sweeps into Glasgow, making his entrance to the campaign in which he is widely regarded as the "real" leader, to deliver what turns out to be a crude but sustained assault on the SNP – unrestrained Natbashing. Donald hates it when Gordon Brown's power base in Scotland is mentioned because it suggests that as Scottish leader he is not up to the job of taking on the Nats. Donald introduces Gordon as an old friend and fellow campaigner. This does nothing to dispel the widespread suspicion that Donald is not a true believer in Blairism and New Labour and that Gordon is the true Labour power broker in Scotland.

But in typical New Labour fashion Gordon delivers a long and prepared text to a carefully invited audience (some of whom studiously refuse to applaud him, I notice). Donald, who is chairing the event, declines to accept questions afterwards. Gordon then shakes some hands and dodges reporters who are jostling to ask him why one of his most senior Treasury civil servant advisers was working inside Labour's campaign HQ in Glasgow last week. Opposition parties are ganging up to attack Labour for allegedly abusing the neutrality of the civil service, at taxpayers' expense, and they want to know if the official in question, Ed Milliband, will be getting his old job back at the Treasury when the election is over. It is a good question. Tony Blair has already signalled that the civil service will go into purdah on April 13 – when nominations close – but, of course, the election campaign will have been in full swing for a week by then. Even the guys from the pro-Labour *Daily Record* are keen to pursue the story. But Gordon brushes them aside, too. He spares no-one the cold shoulder. Charlie Whelan, his old adviser and pal, gives his former boss a bright smile of welcome. For his trouble he is ignored, cut dead. Even Charlie is persona non grata today, at least in public.

An unusual sight: David King, a friend of Old Labour from the *Record*, but who is also a plain-dealing reporter and knows a story when he sees it, is bundled out of the way by a young blonde woman from Brown's staff, as he approaches the Chancellor for a comment. It is now plain that Labour has something to hide. Brown disappears at speed as word arrives from London that Milliband resigned from the Treasury before he joined the Labour campaign. But the affair still stinks. The widespread expectation is that when the campaign is over Milliband will simply ease himself back into the Treasury to collect his public salary. None of this is playing happily with the civil servants of the Scottish Office information service who today are offering 14 press releases, most of which extol the virtues of their ministers' activities. I know from a couple of private conversations that they are embarrassed.

They have good reason, having just announced that Tony Blair will tomorrow make his second visit to Lanarkshire in a month and that the event will be held under the auspices of the Scottish Office. From Bellshill, the Prime Minister will fly to RAF Lossiemouth where he will meet military personnel and their families affected by the war in Yugoslavia. This, too, will be a government, as opposed to Labour, event. At some stage the Prime Minister will join the Labour campaign. Technically, none of this is sharp practice. But in constitutional terms it does seem wrong and exactly the type of abuse of government patronage of which the Opposition parties are complaining. There was a time when Labour expressed outrage at such behaviour by the Tories.

I take a call from the SNP asking how I consider the campaign to be going, as if they didn't know. It does not take Sherlock Holmes to detect a whiff of panic in the Nationalist ranks. Talk about whistling to keep their spirits up. The Nats keep banging on about the polls showing that not all is lost yet. Their trouble is that they see only the specialist questions like taxation and Kosovo which tend to show that their views have a constituency – which is true – but they ignore the obvious message that something dreadful has happened suddenly to their voter appeal. Robbie Dinwoodie judges that if there is a moment for the SNP to be in deep trouble it is now because they at least have time to claw back lost ground. That is correct but if Robbie is wrong then we are in for a truly boring election in which Labour, as usual in Scotland in recent times, sweeps all before it effortlessly. The Nats will do us all a favour if they continue to live a little dangerously. Otherwise this election is going to be a turn-off. It is difficult to be optimistic about a truly tense election, at least as of today.

The LibDems have produced their manifesto, showing they are open to raising 1p in the Pound through the Tartan Tax, just like the SNP, to safeguard education – but only if necessary. Ever anxious for a seat when there is a fence handy, they are behaving true to form. But they are eclipsed by their opponents today. Henry McLeish is suffering from a mauling by Jeremy Paxman on Newsnight after a BBC poll showing that Labour's own candidates are hopelessly split on issues like Trident and taxation. The poor old LibDems never seem quite to crack the secret of being taken seriously. Even Donald Dewar, their old ally in the Scottish Constitutional Convention, is talking today of going it alone as a minority Labour government in Scotland if need be.

Another sign of Labour control freakery in action. We are told that Alasdair Darling and Henry McLeish will be holding a joint press conference tomorrow but Labour refuses to say why, or even what the subject will be. This is blackmail, not to mention a departure in politics. We appear to be dealing with a party whose policies are a secret. But I cannot risk ignoring them in case they produce an important story. This means I must cancel my trip to Lanarkshire to cover the Prime Minister. McLeish and Darling had better be worth it.

April 8th
Back at Labour's campaign HQ I ask David King of the *Daily Record* what McLeish and Darling have to say. He tells me gently that it is all in the *Record* this morning. Labour has given the *Record* an exclusive – but it is one we can live without. It amounts to a claim that if Scotland became independent, the cost of setting up the bureaucracy to distribute social security would be more than £500m.

Darling says 70% of Scotland's families are in receipt of some kind of benefit which totals £9000m a year. This includes old age pensions and child benefit – quite an impressive sum, which tends to suggest the country is indeed dependent to a large degree on British public spending – until you realise that this is in line with the UK average.

A rather tedious press conference ensues where Darling shows irritation with suggestions that he is scaremongering because the technical equipment, computers, etc, required for social security transactions and payments exists already. An independent Scotland would surely inherit it as our share of the UK common service. Darling looks horrified and says this is all wrong. You see, he explains, the computers for these crucial services are all in English cities. This rather stretches credulity but he is insistent. I ask how other small European countries can manage to pay out far higher social security payments than Scotland if it is all so difficult. He disputes they are better off – though plainly they are. Having just returned from five years on the Continent, I need only the evidence of my own eyes. Luxembourg is the smallest independent state in the European Union and rich compared with Britain. Others are much the same, yet our ministers insist that Scotland, a country which exports whisky and electronics and is surrounded by oil, could not even meet the Maastricht criteria for the single currency. This flies in the face of academic evidence but, being politicians, they suffer from selective hearing.

We escape to the *Herald* office only to be summoned back immediately to Labour HQ where Henry McLeish and Douglas Alexander now want to respond to the SNP manifesto being launched today in Edinburgh. The Nats have had a rough time from the press corps and are privately down in the dumps, all because of the sudden drop in their poll ratings. Some reporters think they know in their hearts they are already staring at defeat.

And then suddenly another academic study of devolution is published, this time by the terribly respectable David Hume Institute in Edinburgh. It concludes, in so many words, that the SNP is right and that the costs of moving to independence are not prohibitive after all. Three wise men have concluded there is no good reason why an independent Scotland should not thrive economically. For the second day running, therefore, all of Labour's grisly predictions are upended by objective research. This has cheered up the Nats but whether it will have much impact on the voters remains to be seen.

Labour strategy seems clear enough. It is to meet each and every statement made by the SNP with an avalanche of ridicule and accusations of dishonesty. I just wonder if this overkill will not eventually backfire. Is the electorate impressed or even paying much attention? Difficult to say at this stage.

Tommy Graham tells me mournfully that he will probably not stand as an Independent candidate, Canavan-style, in Paisley North where he had been intending to challenge Wendy Alexander, the ultra-New Labour candidate, who until recently was one of Donald Dewar's closest advisers. Tommy still burns with resentment at his expulsion from the Labour Party after being found guilty of bringing it into disrepute. He says his doctor had diagnosed high blood pressure and ordered him to rest. He is also short of money for a campaign but he has endorsed the candidacy of Allan McGraw, a former footballer and ex-manager of Greenock Morton, who is a local hero in Renfrewshire. I tell Tommy I want to do the story tonight but he persuades me to sit on it until the weekend. The reason is that McGraw's agent will be Harry Revie who is suspended from the Labour Party for his (alleged) part in a local financial scandal in Paisley. Revie tells me that Labour offered to reinstate him if he promised not to seek re-election to the local council, but he is annoyed that this would prevent him working to clear his name. He protests his innocence and wants a proper inquiry so that he can acquit himself publicly. If he is seen working as an agent for an independent he will be expelled from the Labour Party automatically and he seems to accept his fate. But first he wants to return to the council office to clear his desk before the party bosses do it for him. Renfrewshire politics – little wonder Paisley is known as "a town called malice".

Word comes from Edinburgh that our colleagues are rebelling against the LibDems' charge of £1300 for a seat on their battle bus which today, we hear, had only one passenger. It seems I am wrong and that our rivals are indeed banding together and refusing to stump up. This sounds like a developing farce. I suggest our first reporter aboard should be a feature writer – but first I suppose we must stump up £1300 for the privilege. This story will run and run, even if the bus doesn't.

April 9th

All continues to go wrong for the Nats. The talk among reporters at Labour's morning press conference is along the lines of "what's wrong with Alex?" There are rumours of a rift between Salmond and the SNP chief executive, Mike Russell. Perhaps this is true, but I suspect these reports are exaggerated. The SNP is simply showing its first sign of cracking under huge pressure from the full Labour/government machine.

Gordon Brown is in town again, this time to explain how Labour is working for business. Business is most certainly working for Labour. In this morning's *Scotsman* there is a double-page advertisement, which must have cost many thousands, signed by a long list of businessmen arguing against the SNP. It is blatant anti-SNP propaganda but not paid for by Labour. This means the cost will not come out of Labour's £1.5m spending limit – and the trade unions, who are bigger backers than the business community, haven't even begun spending seriously on Labour's behalf.

The press corps puts up some persistent questioning of the Chancellor about taxation and he begins to show some irritation. The more he puts on that insouciant smile, the more you know he is becoming rattled. Reporters want to know how it is that the Tartan Tax is a fine and essential power for the Holyrood Parliament because, of course, it was Labour's brainchild – but a disastrous idea if it is wielded by the SNP. Brown himself refers to the tax-varying power as the "Tartan Tax." Strange how this phrase, which was coined as a pejorative term by Michael Forsyth, is now part of everyday language. The Nats and Labour use it without even a hint of embarrassment.

Brown easily avoids falling into the trap of saying that Labour will one day use the tax, just like the SNP. The best the hacks can coax from him is a vague suggestion that perhaps there might be circumstances a couple of decades hence when it might be invoked.

When the conference is over I ask Brown if he is enjoying his frequent trips to my old haunts in Brussels. He tells me he dislikes attending Ecofin, the EU council of finance ministers. But he seems preoccupied. Suddenly, he invites me to move out of earshot of the other reporters and tells me he is anxious that Labour should have a better relationship with *The Herald*. He reminds me, correctly, for the second time in this campaign, that ours is the business community's newspaper in Scotland. The unspoken message is plain: if only we at *The Herald* would mend our ways, the *Scotsman* would not be the only paper pulling in advertising which over the period of the campaign will be worth hundreds of thousands of pounds. I tell the Chancellor I am happy to hear that relations might be better improved and ask him what Labour objected to in *The Herald*. "You're not supportive," he complains. "You don't give us credit for the good things we are doing." Is his objection simply that we are fair to the SNP, I inquire? He does not take me up on that. Oddly, I had the impression he was not greatly concerned about us being fair to the Nats and the other parties; he seemed more upset that we were not on message with Labour. I promised to report to Harry. Back at the office Harry's reaction is one of annoyance and frustration, not least because we have just run four leaders in the previous few days in support of several New Labour polices.

This is now becoming very worrying because Labour is no longer trying even to be subtle. It is the old story: being objective or balanced is no longer enough with this government. You must be for them or you are classified as against them. Even the Tories in office, with whom we had many disagreements, never deliberately chose to fund our rivals as means of exerting editorial pressure. Harry tells me the management is expressing curiosity, even concern, wondering why we are losing a huge amount of income but, so far at least, our bosses have been supportive and seem to appreciate the principles involved.

Home reasonably early to watch the US Masters from Augusta and then an early night to unwind. No such luck. Just after midnight the telephone wakes me. It is Alex Salmond and he is furious. He wants to know if I am following up a story in the *Daily Record* first edition which claims he and Mike Russell are barely on speaking terms. This is the first I have heard of this particular suggestion although it does not surprise me, given what the rest of the press pack were saying earlier about suspected tensions inside the SNP. I tell him I am not interested in the story because I don't believe it although I advise him that there is certainly talk of the SNP already showing an air of tiredness. My impression – which I explain to him – is that he and Russell don't seem to be communicating in their accustomed workaday sense. In other words one SNP hand does not always seem to know what the other is doing. There is some evidence. Alex has promised me a couple of stories which have appeared first in newspapers elsewhere – simply because Mike was not aware of what Alex was up to. There is nothing exceptionally sinister about this. As far as I can discern it can be put down simply to the SNP – famously a two-man band – coming under increasing pressure and their organisation growing ragged. It does not come as much of a shock that the leading Nationalist figures are tiring and that the going is becoming ever tougher.

We discuss SNP tactics and he swears he is convinced he is winning with the Penny for Scotland policy and that his critical comments on Kosovo have not damaged his standing. This is not what the opinion polls have been saying, he admits, but he insists he is more impressed by reaction on the streets where his remarks are playing positively. If the sort of blatant misrepresentation and fabrication in the *Record* continues, he tells me, he will shut down the daily press conference to newspapers and invite television only. He tells me he has the seen the *Scotsman* advertisements and is well aware of what is going on with New Labour putting pressure on *The Herald*. That spells trouble for us, should it leak out, but it is probably too late already to prevent this becoming an awkward distraction.

I am frank with Alex about the Nationalists' difficulties, as I see them: I believe the SNP needs to sharpen up its presentation, particularly in pushing its Penny for Scotland tax. Why, for example, does the SNP not protest when Labour says it is raising tax? It is not. It is merely not cutting it – a crucial difference. I advise him to argue more forcefully that no-one in Scotland would pay more in tax under the SNP at Holyrood than they do today.

At the end of this first week of campaigning, Labour's press office telephones, wanting to know how the party election team has performed. I tell them that the way things are going Labour need to do very little because the pressure is all on the Nats. Labour knows this, obviously, but it is curious that even after the kind of easy week it has enjoyed, its spin-doctors still want reassurance – even from someone like me. Given that I am obviously regarded now as seriously off-message, perhaps I should be flattered.

April 10th

A telephone from Douglas Fraser at *The Observer* is alarming. He has heard how *The Herald* is being targeted by New Labour because of our editorial line and he wants some background. I tell him off the record of some but not all of our troubles.

He does not know about Brown's approach or Salmond's interest or pressure from Donald Dewar and his spin-doctor, David Whitton, who visited the office recently armed with sheaves of clippings to complain about our coverage. (That meeting was arranged after a leader in *The Herald* suggested Labour's endless scare stories about separatism were proving counter-productive. When Harry refused to name the writer of the offending leader, he was told by a high Labour official: "Well, whoever he is, he's got a thistle stuck up his arse." Harry was a little nervous about what to expect from Donald at that meeting but in the event they did not get down to specific examples of our sinning. Instead they enjoyed a civilised and enjoyable lunch together where nothing of note was agreed.)

Some light relief. Tommy Graham, tells me that his friend and local folk hero in Greenock, Allan McGraw, will indeed stand as an independent in West Renfrewshire. McGraw is one of the great characters of Scottish football. He can barely walk nowadays because he spent years foolishly taking cortisone injections to kill pain in his knees so that he could keep playing. He spent 35 years with Morton as player, captain, coach and manager where he was known as "Gunboat" and "Heid the Ba' McGraw." He has endorsements from Jim Baxter, formerly of Rangers and Scotland, and Bertie Auld, the Celtic Lisbon Lion. What a bunch. I suspect there will be a lot of entertainment down McGraw's way but not necessarily much success. Everyone should wish him luck. He is a popular enough figure to cause some enjoyable mischief even if he knows nothing about politics and cannot win.

April 11th
On its front page *The Observer* has broken the story about *The Herald* being boycotted by Labour because we are off-message. Well, the truth is out now and we shall see what happens. Douglas Fraser's report suggests we are about to watch even more money being poured into Labour-supporting papers including the *Daily Record* and *The Scotsman* because the party itself – as opposed to sympathetic businessmen – has not yet begun its newspaper advertising campaign. Philip Chalmers, Labour's head of advertising, is quoted saying the boycott of *The Herald* is deliberate because – interesting definition – we are not "worthy." Donald Dewar is quoted saying that we have become "an out and out nationalist newspaper." This beggars belief.

I cannot conceive of Donald thinking like that, never mind saying it. But there it is in black and white. When I have the chance I must ask him if he will confirm this is truly his view. *The Observer* says the relationship between Labour and *The Herald* began to deteriorate last year because of our coverage of the System Three opinion polls which gave the SNP a clear lead. Labour hated this at the time but that was hardly our fault. Talk about shooting messengers.

April 12th
To Labour's manifesto launch. In a smart new suit and safe New Labour tie Donald looks tense as he introduces a ridiculously huge document which looks like a colouring-in book. The manifesto is a rehash of old policies, all carefully worded. The point is quickly established by the journalists present that there is nothing in this wish list which could not be ordered by the Secretary of State for Scotland without any need for a Scottish Parliament. Donald brushes this suggestion aside saying a Scottish Parliament could, for example, have avoided the "embittering" experience of the poll tax. This is not the whole truth; a determined Scottish Secretary could also have resisted an idea like the poll tax, had he been so minded.

Labour's manifesto is not exactly a handy pocket-sized reference. It is 16" by 12" (I measured it) but it will be Labour's campaign bible until May 6. It also costs £5 and no doubt the party will make a few bob selling it. Donald completes his presentation and a group of party candidates and assorted jobsworths strategically positioned in the room dutifully applaud – at a press conference! There is something slightly North Korean about this.

I sense an unpleasant atmosphere about *The Herald* in the Labour ranks after the story in *The Observer*. Some of my colleagues express disgust with Labour's behaviour and encourage us to stick to our guns. They include Angus MacLeod of the *Daily Express* who is known to be a Labour sympathiser and Andy Nicoll of the *Sun*. I begin to feel a bit down and resentful about the whole affair. Throughout Donald's press conference I dutifully keep my hand raised to ask a question but somehow fail to catch his eye and eventually I give up. Now I am getting paranoid. Labour's decision to wheel in a phalanx of groupies to applaud Donald before and after he talks about the manifesto is stomach-churning. Even the Tories at their worst never tried that stunt.

I buttonhole David Whitton, Donald's chief spin-doctor, when the questioning is over and ask him if the remarks attributed to the Secretary of State about *The Herald* being "out and out Nationalist" are accurate. He tells me Donald never said such a thing. Similarly, he denies that Chalmers described *The Herald* as "unworthy." Why is it I find this hard to believe? I am reminded of a conversation with Dean Nelson of *The Observer* at the SNP conference in Aberdeen where he slammed the telephone down complaining bitterly about Donald putting about an allegation that he made up quotes along the lines of "one senior party insider admitted..." Some of the younger political correspondents do indeed make up quotes but I don't count Dean Nelson or Douglas Fraser among them. Later I am assured by one of Labour's press officers that there is no truth in *The Observer* story. This is odd because until I mentioned it to him he had no idea what I was talking about, having been out of Scotland when it appeared. So how could he be so certain that it was untrue?

Labour's launch passes without any tough questioning. I suspect the press pack is waiting for tomorrow's announcement from the Norwegian company Kvaerner about its plans for its Scottish operations. They are widely expected to include the closure or at least the sale of the Kvaerner shipyard in Govan – the SNP's top Labour target seat – and other outposts of the company empire in Scotland including the other side of the River Clyde in Clydebank. But just as Labour is congratulating itself on a trouble-free launch the Scottish TUC comes out with the agenda for its annual congress next week – and a fine collection of SNP policies it proves to be, what with condemnation of the Private Finance Initiative and demands for the Scottish Parliament to use the Tartan Tax, just like the

Nationalists propose, for better funding of public services. The Nats are cockahoop, delighted at last to have some of the heat taken off their miserable week. Labour is nonplussed and sullen, hoping the row will quickly be overtaken by events.

Labour puts out a party election broadcast on television to coincide with the launch of its manifesto. It is extremely negative and clearly meant to scare people off voting SNP. At its conclusion it invites viewers to join the Scottish Labour Party immediately, and it lists a number to call. This, it turns out, is a number for Labour in Millbank in London – a fact which the SNP gleefully points out within minutes. Things can be said to be looking up slightly for the Nats as of today but they are kidding themselves if they believe this marks the end of their problems.

Harry says we should not publicise our problems with New Labour's pressure. Robbie Dinwoodie agrees. I trust Robbie's judgment on matters like this. He has been around a long time on the Scottish political scene and despite his famous willingness to do battle with politicians he is a good thinker in a crisis. Alf Young, our deputy editor, says we must just carry on because we have no choice. Alf is furious at New Labour despite (or perhaps because of) his background as a Labour Party employee many years ago and he points out that one of the leading businessmen putting his name to the anti-SNP advertisements in the *Scotsman* is anxiously seeking government funding for a vast opencast mining programme across Scotland. It seems some of the businessmen in question are even less subtle than the Labour party.

April 13th
To break the monotony of my daily trips to Labour's press conferences I agree with Robbie that he should cover Labour in Glasgow today and I go to Edinburgh to keep in touch with what is happening inside the SNP. What a difference between the two parties' styles. The Nats

are in cheery form despite the awful publicity they have been suffering. I am told a strategy decision has been taken to be warm and welcoming to the media as a whole, including the *Daily Record* which has despatched the popular Dave King in place of Chris Deerin whose crime was to write the offending article about Salmond and Russell being barely on speaking terms. There is a friendly if slightly wary atmosphere among the Nats despite their resentment of the press – unlike Labour's conferences which are stiff and stage-managed.

Back in Glasgow Kvaerner has confirmed it is selling up. If it cannot find a buyer – tough. The yard in Govan will close along with the engineering works in Clydebank. The Nats are on their best behaviour, careful not to be seen trying to capitalise on the misfortune of the Scottish workforce but still blaming the crisis partly on Labour's economic policies of interest rates at double the Continental average and a Pound which is too strong for Scottish manufacturing – all because of the needs of the economy in the south-east of England. Treasury spokesman John Swinney and Nicola Sturgeon who is fighting Govan – top of the SNP's central belt target seats – endorse the government's efforts to find a buyer for Kvaerner.

Mike Russell takes me off for a beer and chat about SNP strategy. He seems genuinely mystified at the dreadful press the Nationalists have been suffering. He admits he was the author of the Salmond speech on Kosovo and that Alex changed bits of it. The final version was a joint effort. Mike insists the opinion polls do not reflect widespread anger at Salmond's comments and are, instead, merely the result of the government doing a good job in presenting its Budget as a giveaway. Mike reasons there is also at work the natural tendency to back the government at a time when the country is in military conflict. He agrees with me that another factor could be the complete absence in the papers – for the first time since the May, 1997 General Election – of any stories about Scottish Labour sleaze and scandal. Sarwar is forgotten, Tommy Graham downed by ill health and not standing for Holyrood, Pat Lally is behaving himself beautifully, and there have been no Labour local government scandal for weeks. All seems to be going Labour's way. It is significant, too, says Mike, that the SNP's poll rating has not slipped greatly; rather Labour's has increased. To my alarm Mike says he has a group of independence-supporting businessmen who plan to advertise – Labour style – in *The Herald* as a riposte to those attacking the SNP in the *Scotsman* and the *Daily Record*. "I realise this might cause you problems," he advises me. Thanks, pal. That is all we need: being the lucky recipient of politically directed advertising does not exactly do our dwindling credibility much good with Labour which will immediately point out that it is doing nothing different from the Nats. This is something we shall have to discuss.

Mike takes me back to SNP headquarters to show me the party election broadcast he has made personally for screening tonight. It is a simple affair but quite effective. Dougie Maclean, the Nationalist folk singer, is shown performing his hit song, Caledonia, while more and more Scots throw away their Labour Party lapel badges and one junks a picture of Tony Blair in a dustbin and joins a Pied Piper-style procession to independence. The imagery is a touch simplistic but the message quite positive – in sharp contrast to Labour's PEB from last night which was much more compelling but also ugly. It was made mostly in sinister black and white and was purely negative. Russell insists it was the worst example so far of American-style negative campaigning being introduced to Scotland. Labour's theme was a framed map of Britain being repeatedly and violently smashed as an allegory for the United Kingdom being destroyed by a messy divorce between Scotland and Britain. Having watched it myself and considered it excessively negative, not to say dishonest, I am relieved to see that my judgment is shared widely by colleagues, even those who are Labour. An old broadcasting colleague (who is well disposed to Labour) whispers to me there is talk again among the movers and shakers in the television industry of trying to have party political broadcasts banned, especially between elections, because they are seen by politicians simply as a licence to lie and by the television viewer as boring and a good reason to put the kettle on. This makes a good story. Mike Russell offers some cogent quotes and Labour responds by saying it was merely telling the truth in its broadcast about the real costs of a separate Scotland.

On the train back to Glasgow my mobile rings. It is Lorraine Davidson, Labour's spokeswoman, who says she has Donald Dewar on the line and he wants to speak to me. My first thought is that Robbie must have being doing his Braveheart routine again at the Labour news conference where we have ordered him to be diplomatic. But it transpires that Donald was not there, having taken the precaution of skipping his party's meeting with the media this morning lest he might be pursued about Kvaerner. Donald is speaking to me from a bus travelling across Aberdeenshire while I am between Glasgow and Edinburgh. The line is fractured three times. But I gather from fragments of conversation that he hopes I am being "serviced" by Labour on the Kvaerner problem and his reaction to it. Why is Donald suddenly coming to us and being so nice? Is Labour beginning to wonder if it might have gone too far in pressing its case with *The Herald* and is it worried that we might turn nasty?

Back at the office Harry seems to be unusually at ease with events. He won't tell me why. Perhaps he is just being fatalistic, which is his style. Arnold Kemp always told me Harry had a bizarre sense of humour. He is now talking about publicising Labour's pressure on us after all. I begin to wonder where all of this is going to end. Lorraine Davidson promises me Donald has said nothing about *The Herald* being "out and out Nationalist" and that he certainly does not believe it to be true. She also denies that Philip Chalmers described us as "unworthy" and suggests one of our management has been briefing irresponsibly. The plot thickens but I still find it difficult to believe that *The Observer* simply invented these quotes. They don't have that sort of ring to them.

April 14th

A dull campaign day is enlivened by several unexpected stories, none of which serves the best interests of New Labour. Mark Irvine of Unison, the public sector workers' union, has resigned from the Labour Party and issued a furious letter denouncing all New Labour's works, particularly on the private finance initiative. He is fed up supporting a party whose policies work against the interest of his members, he says. Other Unison leaders are said to share his views. This is an unwelcome embarrassment for the Labour campaign which has been progressing more or less untroubled from Day One.

Next, a remarkably eloquent and passionate letter in our correspondence column today attacks New Labour for betraying the ideals of the more consensual style of politics in Scotland promised by Donald Dewar. He has taken to suggesting that Labour will win an overall majority in Holyrood – which was not expected when Donald was doing his deal with Jim Wallace in the Constitutional Convention. Wallace is deeply displeased, complaining that Labour has abandoned its promise to change the discredited confrontational conduct of politics in Scotland and is reverting to the old Strathclyde Soviet style of rule. What did Wallace expect? Did he really believe for one minute that Labour and the SNP would bury their differences or that Labour would remain true to its talk of coalition if it got close to overall control?

The letter is from Helen Mackenzie whose husband, Michael, we learn, is an actor and Labour activist and leading figure in Equity, who made several party politicals for Labour during the 1970s and 1980s. I track him down to a theatre in Pitlochry and he tells me he thinks Monday's Labour party political was a "disgrace" and that the party should be ashamed of it.

This developing fuss delights the poor Nats, still miserable after their weekend of dreadful headlines. At last they have something to chew on, what with Kvaerner, the broadcast and the resignation of Mark Irvine.

As if all that was not enough the Nats have another couple of self-serving stories on which to capitalise. They have decided – shamelessly – to leak a copy of a Fraser of Allander Institute report suggesting that English public spending is about to rise by two-and-a-half times the rate of rise in Scotland in the years to 2001. This flatly contradicts Labour's repeated claim that Scotland will continue to receive special treatment from the Treasury. The Nats love it, because it suggests that Labour is discriminating against Scotland – exactly the type of grudge they love to nurse.

It seems the Institute was most helpful to everyone interested, taking care to send out copies of the report, which they know will be a political hot potato, in advance of publication later this week. But someone – we suspect a newspaper – has promptly leaked it to the Nats, apparently unaware that they, along with the other political parties, had received it already from the Institute. Naturally, the Nats want to use the report to force the debate. The institute will be none too pleased to know that the Nats cannot wait to start making hay and that they intend to break the embargo.

Our deputy editor, Alf Young, reputedly the only journalist in Scotland who understands the Barnett Formula, by which Scotland's share of public spending is supposed to be decided, will be doing the story. The Formula was invented by Labour's Joel Barnett when he was at the Treasury many years ago. Writing reliable stories about it is dreaded by most political journalists in Scotland whose numeracy stops at expense sheets. But Alf glories in this statistical stuff. I leave him busy pounding it out. The gist is that the Barnett Formula is supposed to ensure that Scotland's spending converges proportionally with England's over the years. But this seems to be not so much a convergence as a crush.

Meanwhile in Strasbourg Alex Falconer, the very Old Labour Euro-MP for Mid Scotland and Fife, has just come out on Radio Scotland with the startling comment that Alex Salmond "has been proved right" on Kosovo and the Nato bombing campaign. George Robertson responds through gritted teeth that Falconer represents only a tiny minority of Labour members' views – but I am not so sure. Falconer himself telephones me with an explanation of his views. I suspect he is simply having some fun, although there is no doubt he is sincere, being an old and incorrigible peacemonger. Alex is unashamedly Old Labour, having been a shop steward at Rosyth before his election to the European Parliament. He is the man who organised the famous anti-Blairite campaign to retain Clause Four of Labour's constitution and who was denounced by the Prime Minister for "infantile" behaviour. His crime was to persuade a majority of the Labour group in the European Parliament to sign a letter to *The Guardian* supporting retention. He has since been in trouble several times with the New Labour thought police but he cares not a whit. Alex has decided not to fight the European elections in June and he is simply having fun twisting New Labour's tail to the great annoyance of the party managers. Good for him. At least he holds sincere beliefs and is not afraid to speak up. Labour will be a duller party without him and others like him who are prepared to ignore the party managers and whips in the interests of free expression.

I hear that BBC Scotland is sniffing around Labour's efforts to exert pressure on *The Herald*. Harry seems unworried and tells me *The Times* is also showing an interest in the story. Here's hoping we get some publicity because I suspect that would be the last thing New Labour wants. Labour figures have taken to signalling that they ignored *The Herald*, not because of our political coverage, but because 70% of our readers are already New Labour, according to market research, and there would be no point, therefore, in spending lots of money to preach to the converted. That sounds corny. Can the *Scotsman* readership really be so different from ours? As for the *Record,* its readership must be even more overwhelmingly New Labour.

People are beginning to question why this is rather a flat election so far. The answer, I suspect, lies in Labour's determination to avoid trouble or controversy – hence, for example, the absence of Donald Dewar whenever there are awkward questions. If things carry on like this we will be facing a Paisley by-election writ large. Paisley in 1997 was where the Labour candidate, Douglas Alexander, who is now running Labour's Holyrood campaign and is a close ally of Gordon Brown, was known as the invisible man. Labour spin-doctors very seldom allowed him to meet the press and his only public appearances were photocalls announced at short notice so that photographers and reporters could not easily catch up with him. But such a boring by-election strategy worked a treat and I suspect the same tactic is about to work again on a national scale.

April 15th
I chair a Glasgow Chamber of Commerce breakfast at an agriculturally early hour. SNP, Tory and LibDem candidates are present on time in the Moat House Hotel but there is no sign of the Labour candidate, Brian Fitzpatrick. We decide there is no choice but to start without him and hope he turns up before it is too late. I spy my old colleague and friend Harry Conroy, who is Mohammad Sarwar's press adviser, in the audience. Harry is not so much Old Labour, more Ancient Labour. From the chair I suggest jokingly he might stand in for the missing Fitzpatrick. It would be hilarious: Harry is so hopelessly off message that the New Labour campaign gurus would be apoplectic – but it would be their own fault for letting us down. No such luck. Half way through the opening set of speeches Brian Fitzpatrick arrives breathlessly and takes his seat on the platform. Each candidate is given 10 minutes. Brian helps himself to 20 and regardless of all my deliberate coughing, fiddling with watch and tapping of table he just won't shut up. The other candidates, who have played the game, are beginning to look daggers.

We move to a question-and-answer session during which Fitzpatrick feverishly scribbles down points he wants to make. He explains that the reason for his late arrival is that he had to call into Delta House, Labour's HQ, for a briefing. In other words he had to undergo a brainwash before being let loose in front of live voters. Very New Labour. Just for fun we have a vote at the end of the speeches. Annabel Goldie, the Tory, emerges as the winner. In the real election she will have no chance in West Renfrewshire but should probably make it to Holyrood through the list.

On to Labour's morning press conference and suddenly we begin to see that at last Labour is not getting everything its own way. Douglas Alexander and his sister, Wendy, struggle to contend with the fallout from the Fraser of Allander report and Mark Irvine's resignation. They are even assailed by the New Labour-friendly *Daily Express* on the question of PFI and the party's deepening crisis with the STUC whose affiliates are mostly opposed in principle to private funding of the NHS. It seems some of the bad blood between Labour and the unions will be spilled at next week's annual congress in Glasgow. Neither of the Alexander siblings will indicate support for New Labour's administration in the city council where the leader, Frank McAveety, the party's candidate in Glasgow Shettleston, is about to sack the city's librarians. These people are very poorly paid and have been on strike for weeks. On Tony Blair's most recent visit to Glasgow they shouted abuse at him, to the amusement of passers-by who had not seen this type of thing for a long time in the city, probably not since Thatcher. The librarians, who seem to carry much public sympathy, are members of Unison, Mark Irvine's union, which has just given New Labour £200,000 and is the party's biggest financial backer in Scotland. Little wonder many of its members are growing weary of New Labour if this is the way it repays its gratitude. One of them complains in the paper today that the unions are nowadays treated by Labour merely as a milche cow and no longer as partners in a movement.

Angus MacKay, Labour's candidate in Edinburgh South - where Edinburgh Royal Infirmary is situated – claims he has been to the hospital and has talked to doctors and nurses who are, he claims, "delighted" with the fact that they enjoy wonderful facilities with which to practise their skills. Later in the day we discover another side to that story. The BMA denounces PFI funding of the hospital as "potentially an unmitigated disaster" and senior Unison figures join in the condemnation of New Labour for championing what they see as privatisation.

Tom Waterson, who is Unison branch secretary responsible for 1500 members, says he can no longer justify supporting Labour because it has moved well to the right of the Tories. On top of the Mark Irvine story this is more trouble for the Labour Party. There is much in this vein from others in Unison. Waterson says many Unison members and workers are voicing the same resentments. It will be instructive to see if Labour can contain this spreading revolt.

The news from Kosovo is awful. A Nato bomber has killed about 70 innocent refugees, having mistaken their tractors for armoured personnel carriers. This on top of the killing of a dozen or so civilians who were travelling on a train across a bridge when Nato bombed that, too. At Strasbourg the European Parliament has just voted in favour of Nato's campaign but nine Labour MEPs rebelled against the party line and two abstained. The nine include the usual Scottish suspects like Alex Falconer and Alex Smith. What makes this embarrassing for Labour in Scotland is that they have committed the disgraceful sin of voting with the SNP. Falconer is unrepentant, saying he agrees on peace policy with Ian Hudghton of the SNP. If Falconer were not already intending to retire he would not last a minute in the Labour reselection process. Smith, who has never done anyone any harm, has no future left with Labour in Europe anway. He has been purged already as an unwanted left-winger and is merely putting up a show of defiance before he becomes another of Labour's disappeared ones.

All in all this looks to have been Labour's worst day of the campaign so far, not helped by a poll in the *Daily Record* suggesting the SNP is now beginning to claw back lost ground. No doubt Labour's onslaught will soon become all the harder – but will it work? If the war carries on like this, Blair's strong support could begin to dwindle.

April 16th
By a farcical series of events we have a ridiculous error in *The Herald* today. Tom Waterson is reported as resigning from the Labour Party, following the example set by Mark Irvine. Only he didn't. He was never in the Labour Party. When I left the office last night my story quoted him saying he could "no longer justify supporting Labour." This was accurate. But a call from the newsdesk at midnight warned me that the *Sun* was carrying a report that Waterson has "quit Labour." It never occurred to me to ask Waterson about his party membership, or lack of it. The *Sun* story is written by Andy Nicoll who is a dependable pro. The news desk wants to know if we should write in a line to the effect that Waterson has quit, and I agree.

Over breakfast I continue to be troubled by the thought of lifting a story from the *Sun*. I call Andy to find out if his report is safe. My heart sinks when he tells me that some idiotic sub changed his story by writing in a resignation which never happened. We in turn have now written it into my story. So even when we get the story right we get it wrong. At the Labour campaign rooms the rest of the press corps fall about laughing. Andy thinks Waterson won't be too offended because he is unlikely to protest about being reported – even inaccurately – attacking Labour.

I meet Dean Nelson of *The Observer* for the first time since his story about *The Herald* being pressured by Labour. He assures me hand on heart that Donald did indeed say we were "out-and-out" Nationalists. Donald did not say it to Dean but he said it nonetheless, and Dean insists he can prove it. "I can show you the chair he was sitting on when he said it," he tells me. This row is not going away. In *The Times* today Magnus Linklater talks of "blatant" attempts by Labour to control press coverage and says that *The Herald* is the main victim now that Labour is withholding from us advertising worth £100,000. Linklater makes the point that the *Record* has fallen back into line with Labour and that the SNP is now complaining bitterly about Scotland's biggest tabloid being no more than a Labour election leaflet. Meanwhile, the *Scotsman* is becoming increasingly strident in its anti-SNP tone. According to Linklater: "Labour has not won many friends during the campaign. Its organisation is secretive, suspicious and hostile to the smallest sign of criticism." Too true.

Donald invites Craig Brown, the popular Scottish international football team coach, to come along to the morning election conference and endorse Labour's plan for a football academy. From the word go it is obvious that Brown is uncomfortable on a Labour platform. He is widely seen as an SNP sympathiser. Why Labour invited him at all is mystifying. Did no-one tell the spin-doctors this might be unwise? The exchanges are good knockabout stuff. Brown makes the reasonable point that he is not giving a political endorsement, merely a footballing one. But he is forced to admit that he did tell Alex Salmond during the World Cup last year that "I have voted the right way since Hamilton in 1967" – the day Winnie Ewing of the SNP won her famous by-election. Not only did he tell Alex Salmond that, he made the mistake of putting it in writing as a PS to a letter responding to a good luck message from Alex just before the Scotland-Brazil game. When Alex promptly read it out to an SNP rally it was met with "whoops of delight" according to our report at the time.

Poor Craig Brown keeps digging a hole for himself – with unstinting encouragement from the media – as New Labour's assembled fixers begin to twitch. He denies having endorsed Margo MacDonald in Edinburgh South but someone has brought along her election manifesto which makes it clear he is an admirer. Donald Dewar squirms and occasionally tries to come to Craig Brown's assistance. The hacks love it. Eventually, Donald decides that enough is enough and announces we are all invited to Hampden for a photocall with Jim Baxter and Billy McNeill and sundry other football icons.

Craig pleads to be excused because he has another engagement. It is all good clean fun – but Labour will hate the coverage.

This has not been a good week for Labour which continues to be haunted by its self-inflicted difficulties with PFI. Who would have thought a few weeks ago that the Scottish general election would be a khaki affair and that the main bone of contention would be something as recondite as the private finance initiative which Labour has now renamed the private public partnership (PPP)? What we need to bring this contest alive is some good old revivalist SNP crusading. The Nats are always at their best when they cause trouble and make a noise but they still seem strangely subdued. As Ian McWhirter notes in his column we need "more passion, less PFI." Labour's big potential pitfall now is the STUC which gathers in Glasgow next week when Unison and some other public services unions will be queuing up to complain about the principle of PFI.

Tonight we are running a story accusing Labour of misleading voters with its manifesto committing the party to work in the Scottish Parliament for the provision of eight "new" hospitals and 100 "new" school developments. We have established that so far four of the hospitals are being paid for privately and that work has already begun on some of them. We confirm that all 29 school developments in Glasgow – which are included in the 100 – are also PFI-funded. In other words Glasgow City Council has done all the administrative work on the schools with no recourse to the Labour Party and without any need for a Scottish Parliament. They could have been built by any local council or by the Secretary of State for Scotland sitting at his desk signing authorisation forms in Dover House in Whitehall.

I ask Labour for a list of the hospitals and schools but after 48 hours during which we telephone repeatedly for the information, a press officer calls to apologise for not providing it. No time, he said. We could persuade one of the Opposition parties to attack Labour on this issue but it is probably better to do it ourselves and take the credit or the criticism.

April 19th

Alex Salmond has nerve. He strides into the STUC today, pursued by umpteen camera crews and a posse of journalists, just a few minutes before Donald Dewar is due to make a speech and he very effectively disrupts Donald's arrival. In fact Donald finds it necessary to sneak in by a back door, causing huge offence to a group of Kvaerner demonstrators outside who are waiting to lobby him. Alex makes a point of giving endless television and radio interviews, taking up as much of Donald's time as possible. Lorraine Davidson, Labour's spin-nurse, makes her entry with an expression which would sink a battleship. Salmond is still chatting up the brothers in the cafeteria when Donald starts his speech inside. The Nationalist game plan is to cause maximum embarrassment to Labour over PFI – and Alex seems to succeed. He becomes involved in a heated exchange with one senior officer from Unison, John Lambie, a Labour loyalist, who insists indignantly that while PFI is wrong and should be resisted, no other party has come up with a feasible alternative. But the moment belongs to Alex who puts on his most self-satisfied smile and strides off in great fettle for some more street campaigning.

Nato calls in Brussels for an oil embargo against Yugoslavia which is good news for the Nats who lose no time pointing out that this is exactly what Alex Salmond has been suggesting since his speech against the bombing. It seems the Americans are impatient with the French and some other governments who believe the UN should be consulted first. Alex argues that Milosevic can be contained through a total trade embargo, oil included, and that Nato and the Americans have just conceded his point. Whether this will have much impact on Scottish electoral opinion is doubtful but it suggests this debate is only just beginning.

To an evening reception by Unison where the talk is all about the split between Labour and the STUC over PFI. Jimmy Reid is there and tells me the Unison delegates are furious with Labour for spreading the word that they have been silenced by the Labour spin machine. A couple of Unison members confirm that there is going to be an almighty row. For the first time I meet Jimmy Knapp, the railwaymen's leader, who is exactly like his television image. He is a true party loyalist despite his Old Labour image. Robbie Dinwoodie, being an unreconstructed leftie, asks him if there is any policy of New Labour which he would not support, and after a moment's thought Knapp says No. Well, at least you know where you are with a man like Jimmy Knapp which is why, despite all the disparaging comments in the press about his Ayrshire accent and old-fashioned political views, he remains a respected and trusted figure.

Jim Devine of Unison, who is Robin Cook's main fixer in Scotland, suggests Labour is picking up more than half of the vote in Livingston and in Ochil which are SNP prime target seats. If this is true, then the SNP appears to be in for a fearful defeat across Scotland. Devine is an old campaigner and knows his stuff. His theory is that Labour's internal difficulties are mainly resolved and that the row over candidate selections and Blair being too Right wing, etc, are complaints articulated now only by disillusioned activists. As evidence he cites the continuing popularity of New Labour in the polls. He has a point. For all that the chattering classes resent New Labour, the people remain well disposed to it across the UK, including Scotland.

April 20th
Yet more bad news for the Nats. In an NOP poll for the *Daily Express* they have fallen all of 21 points behind Labour in a matter of weeks, which means Labour is now within touching distance of an overall majority in Holyrood – something which, I suspect, was not foreseen by Donald Dewar even in his most optimistic moments. Mike Russell of the SNP invites me to Edinburgh for another chat and assures me hand on heart that this finding is entirely at odds with what the Nationalists are hearing on the streets. Experience tells me to be wary

of such protestations, regardless of which party is making them, in times like these. Mike previews for me the second of the SNP's party election broadcasts which is due to be screened tomorrow night. This one is directed, written and narrated by David Hayman and consists only of rather repetitive slow motion shots in black and white of children at play in a street while various policies are recited in Hayman's voiceover. Mike seems very pleased with it but slightly cross when I say it is not, in my opinion, as good as his own programme screened last week.

He advises me that despite the *Express* poll and other evidence of the skids being under the SNP he and Alex will not be changing tactics. The Nats will continue to campaign on the theme of Scotland's penny – a strategy in which they do seem to have genuine faith – and will try to make a virtue out of being seen to be positive, unlike Labour whose Nat-bashing continues relentlessly. The Nats believe they have not been damaged by Alex Salmond's "unpardonable folly" speech and insist they will not be softening their line on Kosovo. Their big problem, Mike reasons, is the Balkans war. It seems to be doing for Tony Blair what the Falklands war did for Margaret Thatcher and there is not much the SNP can do about that.

Sean Connery is supposed to be coming to Edinburgh for a preview of his latest movie and will take the opportunity, Mike hopes, to make a short speech at a Nationalist rally next week. By that time, if the trend in the polls continues, the Nats will need more than 007 to dig them out of this trouble. Oddly, the *Express* is predicting that despite the sudden collapse of support in voting intentions, the Nats might even gain a seat because of a quirk in the new Additional Member System of voting for Holyrood. So, if future polls continue to go against the SNP there might still be hope that the inbuilt corrective mechanism of AMS could come to the aid of the Nationalists. But NOP shows Labour now with 49% of first votes. Another slight jump and they could be looking at overall control – and no whingeing from losers about unfair voting systems.

Before leaving Edinburgh I call System Three to ask Chris Eynon, our polling guru, to confirm that our so-called superpoll result will be ready for Thursday's paper. This will be the biggest and most important poll of the election – using a sample more than three times the routine monthly survey – and the rest of the media knows it is imminent. To my surprise Chris produces the result there and then, having speeded up the translation of fieldwork to results. We now have to keep the findings a secret, something which is never easy when the rival parties and their spies are on tenterhooks waiting for the findings to be leaked.

The superpoll is a catastrophe for the Nats. The SNP is now trailing Labour by 20 points in first vote intentions and almost as much in the second vote – a phenomenal collapse which indicates the Nationalist effort has been scuppered by something. But what? Kosovo? The Scotland's Penny campaign? The Balkans war generally or Salmond's comments in particular? We shall have to research this in some detail before we commit ourselves to print.

In the light of this finding I pull my story about the SNP's decision not to change tactics. After this they simply must do something to stop the bleeding. This looks like the moment of truth for the Nationalists. Are they yet again going to fall at the last fence? Will the Scottish electors again go for the safe option despite all the indications of the past few months? It is astonishing that the SNP and Labour have been deadlocked or at least within a couple of points of each other since July last year, and that within the space of a month or so the SNP vote should suddenly collapse. This is not a case of Labour gaining. It is a clear case of the SNP haemorrhaging support, and no-one for the moment quite knows why.

My theory is that any backlash against Salmond after his criticism of Nato is probably marginal. I am relieved to see this view is supported by the poll which suggests 70% of people say it will make no difference to how they vote. But it could be the effect of the war generally. My country right or wrong and all that. The poor old Nats simply don't know what is about to hit them tomorrow when we break the news. This is one poll result which is guaranteed blanket coverage. From here on the Nats will need a miracle, fast, and the campaign itself will need the kiss of life if it is not to expire now as a contest.

4

Swings and More Swings

21st April - 5th May

April 21st

Robbie and I skip the morning press conferences to get stuck into reporting the poll, but the telephone never stops. Other reporters and the parties – SNP and Tories in particular – keep calling to ask for the results. They must wait for a while. We want to keep them quiet so that we can organise some good coverage for *The Herald* and System Three. Eventually Mike Russell more or less demands to be told and I give him an idea of what he is in for. This is enough for the Nats to go into some sort of semi-secret session to reassess their strategy. They are hypersensitive about what they are up to, but we hear that Salmond wants a radical reassessment of the campaign.

What can they do? It is now too late for them simply to announce they are abandoning their main policies and trying another tack. This is panic time. The Penny for Scotland campaign will continue, they tell us privately, and they do seem genuinely to believe it is working on the doorsteps. Perhaps it still needs to be explained more clearly to voters, most of whom seem unmoved. Kosovo seems to be the bigger difficulty, according to System Three, where the broad effect on voting intentions is neutral with only a small minority saying they are less likely to vote SNP. This all sounds find, of course, except that the SNP is disappearing through the floor. Twenty points behind in the space of a fortnight after being deadlocked with Labour for six months demands an explanation. Something has gone horribly wrong.

Mike Russell sounds bitter about the media, especially the tabloids. A million copies a day are sold by the *Daily Record* and the *Daily Mail* in Scotland, all more or less telling people not to vote for the SNP, he complains. I gather from him that the Nationalists' change of direction – touchingly, they refuse to call this a relaunch – means a return to old-fashioned barnstorming. They will continue to be civil to the media, Mike assures me, but they will take their case directly to voters all over the country, by-passing the hostile press. In other words there will be less in the way of set-piece news conferences which the tabloids use merely as an excuse to pour on the condemnation. From now on if the papers want a story they must take to the road with the campaign teams and simply report what SNP leaders are saying.

It all sounds rather desperate but the Nats know they have little or no choice. They want to sound more positive, Mike Russell says, and that means putting themselves forward as the Scottish champions of good against the greed of New Labour in privatising hospitals, preaching tax cuts, and so on. Tony Blair will be depicted (again) as the new Thatcher. Sean Connery, inevitably, will be invited to address a rally.

In other words, most of what the SNP has left to offer has been tried before. This is all so familiar. Labour has Glasgow plastered in posters and I cannot recall seeing one from the SNP, or anyone else for that matter. Money is no object to Labour and however much the media dislikes its news management techniques, they are working to perfection. All Labour must do now is nothing in particular, and the battle will be won. How boring. Labour's machine has killed off the election in jig time and the excitement is now gone, if it ever really existed. The only question remaining is whether Labour can break the 50% barrier and win the popular majority, something few people believed was possible.

It is a bizarre thought but who would have suggested a few weeks ago that the Scottish general election would be wiped almost completely from the front pages for a month and that its direction would be determined largely by events in a place called Kosovo of which most people in Scotland have never even heard?

Just when I am finishing the main poll story into my office walks Charlie Whelan followed by a film crew with floodlights and microphones. Before I know it I am on camera with the bold boy asking all sorts of questions about the campaign and its progress. Harry has already warned me he thinks we are being set up by the Labour Party. Charlie is rumoured still to be working for Gordon Brown behind the scenes and there are stories in the papers that Peter Mandelson has been wheeled out of obscurity to lend Labour a hand – not that it seems to need it right now.

Filming continues in the editor's office with the grinning Charlie trying to wind us up with accusations that we are the voice of Scottish nationalism. He lolls around in a chair making provocative comments and trying to lure one of us into saying something rash. Quite good fun, I must admit.

When he sees he is not getting anywhere Charlie gets more serious. The conversation turns to the SNP and its travails. We let him into the secret of our poll figures on the strict understanding he will keep them to himself until the first edition is up and they become public knowledge. His views are interesting. Charlie considers the most senior Nationalists were mad to allow Alex Salmond to make such a statement as he did on Kosovo without first researching the likely effect. No focus groups, no brainstorming sessions – Charlie invokes all the terribly New Labour stuff that people mock.

Yet it is difficult to argue with him. Charlie explains that if he had been spin-doctor for the SNP he would have ensured the Penny for Scotland campaign was stillborn. Labour learned its lesson on tax in 1992, he reminded us. Maybe he is right. The SNP did take the decision in a matter of hours after hearing Gordon Brown's Budget speech, although John Swinney told me at the time that the party had also hired System Three to do some research on that very question. We shall have to wait and see what happens on the tax issue in the coming two weeks but I would not be surprised if Charlie is proved right on that, too. After all, its effect might be neutral, as some Nats insist it will be, but whatever it is, it is certainly not proving a stunning vote-winner.

I have the feeling that today is the Nationalists' moment of truth. If they cannot now reverse the trend they are finished, and Labour will be by far the biggest party in Holyrood with about 63 seats, just short of an overall majority.

The most awful prospect which must haunt Alex Salmond tonight is that perhaps the worst is not yet over. As of this day his leadership ability is unlikely ever to go unquestioned again.

April 22nd

Naturally, the Nats are shattered but putting on a brave show in public. Our splash headline this morning is *SNP in Freefall* and the front page of *The Herald* is being shown regularly on television news programmes and quoted extensively on radio and in all of the other papers. At the SNP morning conference the atmosphere is icy. Alex Salmond is asked repeatedly about his relationship with the media after his very public complaints about being turned over by the press, particularly the tabloids, and he stonewalls, saying with his most benign smile that he takes us as he finds us. He offers a beautifully mixed metaphor when he said his golfing dad always told him to play the ball as it lies and not shoot the messenger.

His response to the awfulness of the poll is to quote John Paul Jones: "I have not yet begun to fight." The thought occurs that Jones is regarded in the United States as a great American hero who had a talent for taking on the full might of the British State in battle, and winning. But in his native Scotland he is remembered as a pirate who would have been none the worse of a good hanging. The allegory seems rather neat in the circumstances, given that Alex is the SNP leader who has given Labour most trouble and the only one ever to take the Nationalists into a major election on 33% of the vote. Now the buccaneering Salmond could be walking the plank soon if things don't improve rapidly.

Throughout the press corps there is dismay that this poll has finally killed off what was an already dull campaign. If the Nats really are dead and buried already, after promising so much in recent months, then they might as well chuck it now – but they have no choice but to plod on and hope for a miracle. As of today it seems the only question worth asking is the size of Labour's representation in Holyrood. With 63 seats, as suggested by System Three, Labour would be two short of an overall majority. Can it manage the rest? No-one knows yet whether this poll marks the nadir of SNP misfortune or whether – Salmond's nightmare – things might get even worse still before they (perhaps) get better.

The one cheering possibility in all of this, which delights the media, is that Dennis Canavan is given a fighting chance by System Three of making it to Holyrood via the Central regional list and – beautiful prospect – he could, with a bit of luck, end up holding the balance of power. That would be too wonderful for words.

I have never seen the Nats so low, not even after some of their most bitterly-disappointing defeats over the years. This must have been just about the worst day in their history.

Mike Russell tells me he was in a television studio last night when he was approached by Gilmour Parvin of the Scottish Tory Reform Group. Parvin introduced himself and told Mike: "I hope you die soon." Mike, rather taken aback, naturally, muttered something about hoping that Parvin reformed himself soon. Where do the Tories get them?

To lunch with Gordon Brown who is making another of his interminable speeches to one of those specially invited audiences of business suits, so beloved of New Labour. This time the questions have been vetted in advance, we are told, and several of them come from local schoolchildren. Those of us at the press table are forbidden to ask anything and the Chancellor does not wish to see us later. Talk about New Labour media control. It is becoming shameless.

As usual at these events there is a question from Ian McMillan, chief executive of the Scottish CBI. Ian is becoming famous for always asking the same question. Will Mr Brown promise that if Labour wins control of Holyrood it will not return the power to set the uniform business rate to local councils? Naturally, Ian always receives the same answer. The Chancellor gives a long and convoluted response which is a fine example of sustained evasion. Ian sits down with a frown. No doubt he will be at the next Gordon Brown speech and will be asking the same question and getting the same answer. How long can he keep it up? Perhaps Gordon should save him the trouble by sending his reply in writing so that Ian can stop travelling all over Scotland repeating himself.

The four main Scottish party leaders make up the panel on BBC Question Time. When I arrive home there is a message to call Alex Salmond who wants me to watch the tape to see his response to questions about Kosovo in which he makes the point I suggested to him last week about expressing his deep concern for the safety of British and Nato service personnel. He emphasises that his criticisms are directed at the political direction of Nato and its strategy, not at the essential need to stop Milosevic. I watch him refusing to withdraw his comments about the war being an unpardonable folly and arguing that he has been proved right by events, particularly now that the Americans are calling with increasing urgency for a complete oil blockade. His remarks play well with the audience which, as usual in these televised debates, appears to include a preponderance of noisy Nats. The SNP spin machine is adept at loading audiences despite all the best efforts of the BBC to achieve balance. The audience police will be there to make sure each party has an equal number but they cannot control the noise produced by the SNP section. As ever Alex wins easily on the clapometer.

April 23rd

St George's Day, although the thought never crossed my mind until Harry phones to say I am wanted on Newsnight with Jeremy Paxman to discuss England's relationship with the rest of the UK. To mark the occasion, Scotland's "unfair" extra share of public spending and the West Lothian question are up for discussion and I am to be joined by Trevor Phillips, a black journalist who wants to be become Mayor London in May, 2000, and Teresa Gorman, the famously right-wing

Conservative MP and notorious Scottophobe.

Feeling deeply nervous I take the Shuttle to London – leaving poor Robbie to do all the work at home – where I am introduced at the Television Centre to Mrs Gorman who turns out to be an engaging and rather likable character, if obviously a touch eccentric. I had been prepared to dislike her immediately but she is all giggles and smiles before we enter the studio. She tries to test me by accusing the Scots of hating the English and of being subsidy junkies who deny the people of England their rightful share of the UK economic cake. She is an English nationalist, no question. She recalls with a smile that she once wrote a provocative article for *The Herald* on the subject of Scots stealing England's money – an article which, as I recall, was intended to kick up a storm of protest from chip-on-the-shoulder Scots but which was regarded by most people as a blatant wind-up.

The debate is to go out live – a rather daunting thought – and I am not made any more at ease at the thought of Paxman's famously ferocious interviewing style being directed at me. The three of us are told to perch on stools for a 16-minute discussion and as the programme begins we see for the first time on a studio monitor a videotaped report claiming public spending in Dumfries and Galloway is much higher than across the border in Cumbria.

Paxman then comes immediately to me demanding that I should justify this kind of scandalous mistreatment of the English. I mutter something about spending levels in Scotland being higher for very justifiable reasons and attempt to explain that subsidies also flow south in the form of whisky duty and oil revenues, all of which go in their billions to the Treasury in London and mostly stay there.

Paxman responds with his falling-about-in-amazement routine. It quickly becomes evident that this debate is meant to be a bit of knockabout which is why they have Teresa on the show. True to form she launches into an assault on the Scots who, she protests, are running the government and England and keeping control of Britain's money while misappropriating large amounts of it to send north. The Scots use to be needy, she says, now they are greedy.

She also complains that England is increasingly being bossed about by Scots. My response is: "Tough. Now you know how it feels." I explain that for almost 300 years the Scots had become accustomed to English MPs running the UK, never more so than during the Thatcher era when the Tories and their allies in the Lords went about piledriving the poll tax into Scotland despite the overwhelming opposition of Scottish MPs. Teresa merely sees this as another reason for Scotland wanting to be independent – she has a point – and then she launches into another tirade about the EU refusing to recognise the UK as a state while attempting to dismember it into regions as part of a dastardly divide-and-rule plot by Brussels.

Teresa is forceful enough as a performer. Her trouble is that she never lets any respect for facts trouble her. So this debate was not one for students of the British constitution. It was more like a late-night pub argument, but good fun for all that.

Teresa had told me before going on air how she had just come back from holiday in Portugal. The thought had occurred to me earlier that if I had the chance on air I might explain how fortunate she is to live in the rich south-east of England where all she need do when going abroad is pop along to her subsidised (by me) London tube and take it to her nearest international airport. But if she had been a hill farmer in Galloway or a crofter in South Uist she would have had huge expense and inconvenience just trying to reach the type of public service Londoners take for granted. Come to think of it, I could have told Teresa of places in Scotland where people pay road tax when they have no roads. If that is not a subsidy, what is?

Sadly, my chances are time-barred by Jeremy Paxman. He closes the discussion by asking me if I have any advice for the people of England. My immediate thought is to say that the Welsh, Scots and even the troubled Irish are all working out their constitutional futures in the changing world for themselves, while the English fiddle. My advice to the English would be: "Get a life."

But I lose my nerve, thinking that might be seen as too flippant. Instead I suggest that England should have its own grand committee, and that it should be made more useful than the one the Scots have just ditched. I predict that Scottish MPs empowered to vote on purely English matters will probably choose to go shopping during Commons divisions. As we leave the studio I confess to Paxman that I find the experience of appearing on live, networked television enjoyable but terrifying. He puts on that famous expression of astonishment. He does not appear to have a nerve in his body. He's a cool one, a true broadcasting professional. Like every other journalist at this time he is wondering if the shine that New Labour still enjoys almost two years into office – when it should be in mid-term blues and unpopular – will finally be lost if, or when, the Balkans war goes wrong. I certainly would not wish to be a British minister on the receiving end of his questions when that day comes.

April 25th
My old friend from my Brussels days, Grant Baird, who has just retired as chief executive of Scottish Financial Enterprise, indicates he is willing to step into the campaign with a public denunciation of Labour's scaremongering about the cost of independence – and to give me an exclusive interview. Being one of the best known economists in Scotland, Grant carries intellectual clout and seems willing to make a public stand despite the panning he will probably suffer at the hands of Labour's propaganda machine. His views are interesting not least because they are rather right wing on economic policy – which in normal circumstances would go down well with New Labour. His wife, Glynne, who made it to the SNP's Holyrood list of approved candidates but failed to find a nomination, is distraught at the collapse of the SNP's campaign and furious with the media, but delighted that Grant is prepared to make a protest.

The gist of Grant's argument is that a report under huge headlines in today's *Scotland on Sunday* is typically alarmist. It claims that an independent Scotland would have a £10 billion deficit. This is becoming something of an auction. Any advance on £10 billion? Do we hear £11 billion from New Labour? No doubt we will soon.

This latest report comes from the Centre for Economics and Business Research which is run by Douglas McWilliams whom Grant remembers as the Thatcherite chief economist of the Confederation of British Industry. McWilliams's conclusion is that a devolved Scotland run by Labour would be unsuccessful economically, but that an independent Scotland would be prosperous, provided it was run by a pro-business, pro-enterprise government.

Not surprisingly *Scotland on Sunday* has played down the independence conclusions while making a great splash about the deficit McWilliams says would face Scotland. Grant describes the figures as "total nonsense" but when he realises I am about to quote him saying so he asks me to change this to "seriously flawed." Economists appear eager to argue with each other but never to lose sight of the need to be courteous.

The UK had a £22 billion deficit, according to Grant, when Ken Clarke left office at the end of the Tory administration. Nowadays the UK is moving into the black and it must follow, therefore, that Scotland's share (normally about 9%) will mean the Scottish deficit is much smaller than the £10 billion being shouted about by McWilliams and his colleagues – perhaps non-existent eventually. Grant is further annoyed at the government's persistent talking down of the Scottish economy in matters like our prospects of meeting the Maastricht criteria for the European single currency. He is an expert on this, being the man who set up, and made a success of, Scotland Europa, the Scottish lobbying presence in Brussels. In his view Scotland would not have the slightest difficulty joining the European single currency because our economy is already in better shape than some, if not most, of the eurozone nations. In this he is in complete agreement with Professor Andrew Hughes Hallett of Strathclyde University who has greatly annoyed Labour by disagreeing with its claims that Scotland is unfit for the euro. Grant agrees that if the Belgians, who can't run a whelk stall, and the Italians and others with enormous deficits can meet the criteria then Scotland would have little difficulty doing likewise. (Belgium's debt was 120% of GDP at one point, when the Maastricht criterion was 60% but the Belgians still made the grade.)

Andrew Wilson, the SNP's Treasury spokesman, calls to make the point that the survey was commissioned for *Scotland on Sunday*, presumably with the authority of Andrew Neil, the famously anti-Nationalist editor-in-chief of Scotsman Publications. His views mirror those of his proprietors, the Barclay twins (who are right-wing and anti-Maastricht). Wilson reminds me that Andrew Neil set up his own Scottish Policy Institute last year. I wonder why it was not given the chance to do a hatchet job on SNP economics. Perhaps Neil thinks there might be a conflict but at any rate his institute appears to have been stillborn.

Sean Connery continues to attract the wrath of New Labour whose spin-doctors are now getting anxious about his big speech in Edinburgh tomorrow. George Foulkes, the development minister, accuses Connery of being a hypocrite because he lives in style in the Bahamas while paying no tax in the UK. Yet, says Foulkes, Connery wants Scots to pay more tax, as suggested by the SNP. I wonder if Foulkes might be hearing from Connery's lawyers about that accusation. Connery has always denied being a tax dodger, claiming he pays UK tax on all of his UK earnings. This is becoming quite a nasty and personalised little vendetta against Connery by New Labour whose ministers were not so long ago queuing to be photographed with the great man as they sought his endorsement for the establishment of a Scottish Parliament. In a letter to voters Connery attacks the Tories who have also been making sarcastic comments about his tax status. He also has a go at New Labour which he says will not provide the better Scotland everyone is entitled to expect from Holyrood. Connery's main complaint is that Tony Blair runs New Labour and if New Labour is elected, he will run Holyrood, too, which is not how Home Rule is supposed to work. The SNP is to distribute a million copies of his letter.

Ian Austin, one of New Labour's in-your-face media minders, telephones to ask what I have written today. The cheek of it. He must have heard we are doing something which might not be in Labour's best interests and is curious to find out what. This is becoming a routine with Labour's election HQ. If they have the slightest suspicion of an unhelpful headline in the next day's papers they are on the telephone wanting to know the details so that they can issue a spoiler. Is what I have written to appear on the front page, he wants to know? Can I tell him what it is? Eventually I have to be frank and say I can't possibly tell him. That makes it worse, of course, which I find mildly satisfying. He'll find out soon enough.

Grant Baird tells me he has given an interview to BBC radio on condition it is not broadcast until tomorrow morning by which time *The Herald* will be on the streets. My slight concern is that New Labour might start trying a whispering campaign against Grant in revenge for his comments. That would be despicable and I hope I am wrong.

April 26th
Well, the great man is in town and we shall see what difference the Connery factor makes. This is quite a day in Edinburgh. The Nats are desperate for something or someone to cheer, and who better for them than Sean Connery? The gathering is surprisingly small, with less than 300 of the party faithful. It seems a remarkably modest turnout for the great Nationalist superstar, benefactor and champion. I suppose the idea is simply to get Connery on television supporting the cause. Party officials anxiously direct latecomers to the empty seats in a little theatre in the Edinburgh International Conference Centre – it would never do if he walked into an auditorium which was not full. How Labour and the Tories and LibDems would love that. The thought occurs that the Nats could have attracted thousands of hero-worshippers just by inviting them in from the street.

Connery's speech, if you could call it that, is a surprise. There is no razzmatazz, no invective, no barnstorming of the kind promised.

He attacks the press – which is predictable, given the nasty coverage he has suffered personally from the *Daily Record* – and he speaks for only five minutes. But it is powerful stuff. His speech is his own work and he makes a point of saying so, emphasising that the SNP and its spin-doctors have had nothing to do with it. That much quickly becomes obvious. Connery is not just upset by the tabloids, he is furious and his anger is plain. The speech turns out to be a five-minute homily in which he preaches simple patriotism, sentimental but heartfelt, which is so characteristically Scottish. Pride in the country, love of the land and its people – and a sense of hurt that Scotland is not, as he put it, an equal with every other nation in the world.

First he launches into a defence of his cinema work for Scotland, saying he has always put Scotland first and never sought personal gain. (He spends millions helping Scottish youngsters through his charitable work which is conducted privately and goes largely unrecognised.) It says something for Connery's passionate commitment to Scotland that despite his fame and the adulation he attracts he seeks no recognition for this charity work; indeed he shuns publicity in that respect.

Then, to cheers, he launches into an attack on the press, complaining that he is ashamed of the media's recent behaviour. He growls and grumbles in that amazing voice of his – and the Nats love him to death for it, for they are suffering as never before in any election I can remember. They really do believe they have been assaulted quite unfairly by the press and they are right to complain. For the moment they just want a fillip and Connery certainly provides it. Perhaps they are just being naïve about the tabloids. What did they expect when the full firepower of the British State started exploding around their heads? Now the media, mainly the London-based papers, are doing to Connery and Salmond what the *Sun* did to Neil Kinnock in 1992.

Connery mourns the abandonment of political consensus – most people outside the political parties do – and he attacks Labour for the conduct of what he calls its "control freaks" who, he says, use fear and intimidation to scare people off voting for real change in Scotland. No-one can argue with that. Even Labour is not in the business of denying it, so complacent and self-satisfied has it become now that a poll in today's Scotsman shows it 18 points ahead, thanks largely to its negative campaigning.

The big question as of today is whether Connery's magic is still potent. It does seem rather daft, after all, in a mature western democracy, that a film star can make a significant difference to voting patterns. The BBC carries a vox pop of Glaswegians who think, mostly, that Connery wonderful and sexy and a great Scottish icon – but is making no real difference to the campaign. It is entertaining to watch the Tories and Labour and LibDems walking on eggshells when they criticise the SNP for producing him. Donald Dewar says on television that the election is not about celebrity head counts – this from the man who tried to coax an endorsement from Craig Brown last week and is endlessly pursuing famous business tycoons for support - while Raymond Robertson of the Tories and Malcolm Bruce of the LibDems studiously make a point of saying what a wonderful and popular actor Connery is, before daring to rubbish his politics.

What I like about Connery today is that he does not flinch despite the battering he and the Nats have taken in the past few days. He does not have to do all this, after all, and he must know the headlines in the tabloids will be hostile yet again. But he is prepared to soldier on because he believes in what he is doing. And he has been doing it all his life. This is the same Connery who sent a message of good wishes to Winnie Ewing before the famous Hamilton by-election in 1967.

Being mugged by the tabloids must be especially tough on one who has become accustomed to nothing but constant hero-worship over many decades. Very few hugely successful men about to turn 70 would risk losing a lifetime's popularity for a political party. Connery's nationalism is based on uncomplicated patriotism and he cannot understand why people in Scotland seem so reluctant to demand independence. He's not the only one. If the SNP truly knew the answer to that oddity they would not be in the mess they are in today. But one ray of hope is offered by the *Scotsman* poll. It suggests that the SNP might have hit rock bottom, thus offering the faint prospect of the Nationalists staging some sort of comeback before May 6.

Connery slips away through a back door to annoy the waiting press. I am invited by Alex Salmond to join him and Winnie Ewing and various other party bigwigs in a hospitality room. For the first time since Black Thursday last week the Nats seem genuinely cheered up. Alex believes our System Three poll was so dreadful that it might have engendered a sort of backlash against complacent Labour. He might be right. ICM in the Scotsman and other polls are showing that his Kosovo speech is not playing badly although the pundits are still saying the timing was wrong and the language a touch careless. And as of today the war is not going Blair's way. Margo MacDonald says that after May 6 she will demand a thorough examination of the media's role in this election. Her determination is that the SNP will never suffer from such a hostile press in future, especially when even in bad times it continues to attract so much of the popular vote. A long and bitter debate looms on that issue.

Yet even on what was undeniably a good day for the Nats they still have no luck. Sean Connery and his intervention in this campaign should have given them huge headlines. And what happens? Jill Dando, the popular BBC television personality, has just been murdered brutally on her own doorstep in London. It is a shocking and sensational story, easily enough to consign Connery and the SNP's good day to the inside pages.

April 27th
Labour is haunted today by the ghost of Peter Mandelson. A new biography of Mandelson by Donald McIntyre of the *Independent* claims a deal to have a power-sharing pact in the Scottish Parliament was agreed informally by Blair, Cook, Dewar and various other New

Labour bigwigs, and Ashdown and the Liberal Democrats, three years ago at a meeting in London. Donald Dewar looks shifty when the subject is raised and swears blind it is not true. At least it gives the Nats some much-needed ammunition. Mike Russell claims this is in effect a plot for a coup d'etat and what he calls the "big boys" in London have been caught in the act of carving up the running of the Scottish Parliament already. If true, it certainly begs the question: what is the point of voting LibDem if you are voting in a Labour-dominated Parliament?

There is a ring of truth about this. I recall my conversation with Jim Wallace when he said he would not countenance a deal unless it involved LibDem Cabinet posts – in proportion to the party's number of MSPs – and his insistence that any pact would have to be formal. He does not want a return to what he calls "Steel-Callaghan Lib-Labbery" in which the two parties merely voted together on certain issues when it suited them. Most of the reporters involved in this take the view that a deal has been done quietly but only in principle and then only if Labour really needs the LibDems (and the working assumption is always that the new voting system will make that likely). Come to think of it, the story would be better if Labour was now saying the LibDems could get lost and that an overall majority – even a tiny one – meant an end to all talk of coalitions. This is treason as far as Jim Wallace and the LibDems are concerned. Wallace pops up on television to say that he was not at the alleged meeting and Ashdown does not have the authority to take decisions on behalf of the Scottish party. But the reality is that Ashdown had huge influence if not direct constitutional control then. And Blair's Third Way is all about keeping the Tories out of power for a generation, most probably by means of a Labour-LibDem pact sooner or later, and that the Scottish Parliament could be the testing ground.

My spies tell me the Nats are about to announce the launch of their own newspaper. This is an old idea being resurrected briefly and the decision to go ahead, I hear, was taken after our System Three poll was about to be published last week. Well, at least they were serious about going over the heads of the hated Scottish media direct to the people. Having your own newspaper is the best answer to having more than a dozen newspapers, all of which show varying degrees of hostility to the SNP. Apparently the Nats have no millionaire on hand this time to pick up the bills so the safe bet is that this will be a souped up election leaflet produced by sympathetic journalists. There will be no cover price and no advertising. No wonder it is scheduled to last only until polling day.

This reminds me of a story I wrote last year when there was talk of the Nats launching their own very real newspaper or, failing that, buying an existing title. It rankles with them that on a good day the SNP can command almost half of the Scottish vote and yet there is not a single newspaper in the land which is prepared to endorse independence, far less the party itself. Some senior Nats have long taken the view that starting a newspaper of their own is the only answer to their perennial problem of a hostile press. They take encouragement from Eamon De Valera in Ireland who was so disgusted with the Irish press than he launched his own newspaper which became the most popular of its kind in the country. Similarly in Poland the Solidarity movement launched a paper which did the same.

Word comes from Nicola Sturgeon that the wobble of last week is over and that the SNP is again back on track in Govan. Tommy Graham tells me that in his area the doorstep reaction does not bear out the polls. From Skye Jim Mather of the SNP insists he cannot reconcile the System Three finding with what he is hearing. And Kate Higgins from Galloway says she can't wait to get back there where the feeling for the SNP is good and that the seat is safe. Can it be that there might be something happening which we don't yet know about? The weekend polls should make very interesting reading. Perhaps the campaign is not yet over after all.

April 28th

To Clydebank to meet Canon Kenyon Wright (the Grand Kenyon as I like to call him) the veteran clergyman and Home Rule campaigner who has announced he will stand as in Independent in Scotland West. Kenyon is a lovely man, quite bereft of the talent to be a venal politician. I suspect he will be unsuccessful, which would be a great pity. He was a leading activist in the Scottish Constitutional Convention which begat the Claim of Right which begat the Scottish Parliament. His greatest moment came when he delivered a famous line in his speech 10 years ago at the signing of the Claim of Right. On that occasion he questioned what would happen when "that voice we have come to know so well" – meaning Margaret Thatcher's - said No to a Scottish Parliament, and he proclaimed: "But we say we are the people, and we say Yes."

Kenyon is having a press conference and has brought along two old pals, Jimmy Reid, the shipyard trade unionist-turned-journalist, and William McIlvanney, the author, to endorse him. A great couple of characters. I never fail to marvel at McIlvanney's effortless eloquence and Reid's warmth of character. They make a great double act. Both are compulsive talkers when they have a captive audience and poor old Kenyon struggles to get a word in. Campbell Christie, now retired as general secretary of the STUC, sends a message of good wishes (diplomatically saying he hopes for a Labour administration). Harry Conroy, who does some PR for Kenyon, telephones me just as we are settling down for a chat and shamelessly orders me to ask Kenyon whether he wants to run for Speaker (or Presiding Officer in the prosaic language of New Labour). Kenyon is, of course, anxious to be asked. He wants the chance to make a point of dismissing the very idea, doubtless with a modest smile, pointing out that you don't run for Speaker, you have to be asked. But everyone knows he would kill for the job. Sadly, he probably won't be elected and, besides, it is now being suggested by Labour (in London, naturally) that other aspiring MSPs are being groomed. That should put David Steel's nose out of joint. He has been after the job for long enough and until now has been favourite.

Jimmy Reid bemoans the "disgrace" that the parties could not figure out a way to give Kenyon a free run, and Willie McIlvanney pleads for idealism and less cynicism in the Scottish Parliament. For himself Kenyon eventually manages to squeeze in a word to the effect that he is promising to make no promises – a refreshing change for a parliamentary candidate – and that he will remain off-message for all parties. Would that there were more like him. I wish him luck.

Well, it seems the Nats were not talking complete nonsense about their prospects after all. Chris Eynon of System Three gives me the figures for our latest poll and they are sensational. This will be our final survey before the real thing and it is about to bring a dull election to life with a bang. Suddenly, the race is on again. Alex Salmond's new "Braveheart" campaign in which he ignores the newspapers and goes direct to voters appears to be working – or else something very odd is happening to Scottish public opinion. This latest poll shows the gap narrowing in a week from 20 points to eleven in the first vote and from 13 to three in the second. This will take some interpretation. I can't recall volatility on this scale ever before in Scotland although Harry Reid insists the same kind of thing has happened in England in General Elections towards the close of campaigning.

The number of Undecideds has fallen sharply and most of them appear be moving to the Nationalists. Just why this should be is difficult to discern. One of the theories Robbie and I discuss is the terrible press which the Nats suffered last week. The vilification of Connery as a tax dodger by those in the Labour Party who curried favour with him in the Referendum seems to have had an effect as well. Perhaps the Scots don't appreciate Labour's negative campaign and believe the Nats are being treated unfairly. Then there is the fear that a clear majority Labour vote would turn the Scottish Parliament into just another Labour soviet like Glasgow City Council and the old Strathclyde region where the leader, Charlie Gray, famously complained that his biggest problem was remembering the names of his massed ranks of fellow Labour councillors.

Perhaps it is Kosovo and the fact that the UN is now echoing Alex Salmond in calling for an oil blockade. Salmond was laughed out of court when he suggested that. A theory advanced by Alf Young, who has been poring over the statistics, is that the Budget petrol tax increase imposed by Gordon Brown is beginning to hurt Labour in the rural areas where all the parties have been exploiting its unpopularity. On the basis of this poll the SNP would gain Glasgow Govan – which is a quirky seat at the best of times – but its three other predicted gains are all in rural areas such as Caithness, Inverness-shire, and Ochil. Young people in particular appear to have been turned off by Labour's hardnose style and are switching to the SNP.

Anent the tabloids, I see in the *Record* a London-based journalist, Quentin Letts, suggesting in a piece about English nationalism: "All it would take is a few killings of English children in Scotland. All it could take is an English Salmond to come along and appeal to the Lionheart Factor." He writes this stuff in the context of Slobodan Milosevic moving into Kosovo and making cynical appeals to Serbian nationalist sentiment. It is as if he genuinely equates Scottish nationalism with genocide and ethnic cleansing. Can this guy be serious? What kind of newspaper publishes such bilge? This type of idiocy offends public opinion in Scotland where the bigger newspapers are traditionally less slavishly committed to political parties than their counterparts south of the Border. If I was Alex Salmond I would pay Mr Quentin Letts a lot of money to keep writing like this. He seems to be working wonders for the SNP.

But this is still only a poll and it leaves us with an obvious difficulty. How can it be so hugely different from last week's? Malcolm Dickson, a political academic at Strathclyde University, who does analysis articles for *The Herald*, is on the case. Malcolm says it is quite feasible that public opinion has indeed changed considerably. Sean Connery's intervention is not much of a factor, it seems, because the publicity surrounding his appearance for the SNP came on the last day of fieldwork, too late to have a major impact. If there was indeed damage to the SNP campaign caused by Salmond's "unpardonable folly" speech then it appears to have disappeared.

The same applies to the Penny for Scotland campaign which is now apparently working rather well. The Nats will be cockahoop when they hear all this. But the best bit is that we are publishing the poll in tonight's paper and that means the new Nat newspaper due out tomorrow will be scooped on a great Nat story on Day One. Well, they can't have everything.

April 30th
Our splash story is headed *It's Not Over Yet* and suddenly the campaign is alive again – even more than before. It provokes Andrew Neil in the *Scotsman* to pen a diatribe about *The Herald* and its support for the SNP, accusing me in effect of talking up the Nats. He writes off the poll as a rogue and seems to think we will be made to look daft. We'll see. Funny how the Union's greatest supporters can be panicked by just one poll. Maybe they are more uneasy than we realise.

Today the Nats publish their long-awaited economic strategy for independence. John Swinney, the SNP Treasury spokesman, has refused to let us have an advance look at it, despite earnest pleading from me. It follows, therefore, there must be something in this document of which the Nats are afraid. John has assured me privately that there is no deficit involved in the SNP's costing of independence. This is something they have always maintained and I am mindful of John's statement, made to me in the knowledge that I would be quoting him, that "there is no deficit – structural or otherwise."

It has to be said Alex Salmond and John then proceed to make an inglorious hash of their press conference at which they unveil the document. This is perhaps the biggest press conference of the campaign so far for the SNP and it is mishandled. Alex simply refuses to put a figure on the cost of – or benefit to – an independent Scotland from the year 2000. He is asked several times and tries to dodge the question, inviting other people to ask other questions (which they do not) and he tries to offload the questions on John. But eventually after much needless obfuscation he admits that an independent Scotland would be £1.5 billion in the red in its first year, but that it would quickly move into the black in subsequent years.

This is what the media have been waiting for and they waste no time in reporting the fact. Labour's machine slips into gear immediately and within three hours Gordon Brown summons the press to offer them 14 pages of detailed rebuttal and another three of his comments. You have to hand it to Labour. Gordon Brown might be careless with the truth about the SNP's figures and costings and he might indulge himself with bizarre assumptions – for example, he says an independent Scotland would need a separate mint, an idea which is widely seen as a joke – but he certainly knows how to respond under pressure. He does enough to ensure that the Nats do not have it all their own way.

The papers are full of Gordon Brown's house on the banks of the Forth being burgled. After his press conference I ask him if everything is back to normal at home. Gordon tells me it is his second housebreaking. On the first occasion the police advised him that his home had been completely ransacked and that papers were strewn all over the floor. "Nothing was taken," he tells me. "It's always like that."

On Radio 4 I am asked to debate the role of the Scottish media with Alan Cochrane of the *Daily Telegraph*. He is a likable right-wing ex-*Daily Express* bruiser with a bestial east-coast accent who holds no candles for the SNP. But we agree on one thing. The Scottish press might be hostile to the Nationalists but it needs them and wishes them well in one respect. When the SNP makes waves it makes Scottish politics come alive. Alan argues that Connery is just a vainglorious actor who takes for granted being idolised, and is unwilling to take the heat which can be generated by politics. He suggests that celebrities who proffer endorsements should be able to take criticism when the going gets hard. My point is that Connery is, of course, offering his services to the SNP in the sure and certain knowledge that he will be pilloried for it. And he now has confirmation.

I am kept out of bed by Radio 5 who want the same sort of conversation with the mischievous Joan Burnie. She defends the *Record* – she has to, it pays her wages – and we agree to disagree on the role of the media. Joan's is something of a lone voice on the *Record* these days. She was invited to the Connery bash but found that one of her colleagues had pinched her accreditation. A row ensued, but with La Burnie there is only ever one winner. Her colleague did not go to Sean's party, but she did.

The *Record* has a poll tomorrow which confirms the trend suggested by our System Three. When word of this spreads there is general hilarity among the hacks at the thought of the editorial team in the *Record* office trying desperately to figure out a way to turn an SNP propaganda coup to Labour's advantage. In fairness to the *Record* it manages to put the story on page 1. An act of conscience, perhaps.

May 2nd

The Sunday polls are conflicting but Mike Russell tells me that he still believes the SNP can become the biggest party in Holyrood. There does seem to be a roll going for the Nats, but polls in *Scotland on Sunday* and the *Sunday Herald* suggest the gap is not as close as in System Three's survey for us last week. Still, there seems agreement all round in the Sunday papers that Labour won't win an outright majority and the fight is now on to see if the SNP and LibDems together can outnumber Labour in Holyrood.

An old pal telephones to say he has heard that some of Bill Clinton's political consultants are working in Scotland. If this is true it could be a good story – and one which Labour must have seen good reason to hush up. How Scots might take to Clinton's people working for Labour – it must be Labour, no-one else would use them, given Blair's friendship with the US president – is a moot point. I suspect that being a contrary lot the Scots might be rather miffed at finding out that Labour was secretly trying to manipulate their political views in this way. I cannot raise anyone in Washington, where this political consultancy is based, for details about what these guys are up to in Glasgow. I learn from an article in the New York Times that the consultants involved are James Carville, Stanley Greenberg and Bob Shrum. Carville is said to be the man who told Clinton: "It's the economy, stupid." Greenberg was Clinton's pollster in 1992 and Shrum wrote Clinton's 1999 State of the Union speech. They are said to be working for Ehud Barak, the Labour candidate challenging Benjamin Netanyahu in the Israeli elections, and earning $400,000 for their trouble. I check a few Glasgow hotels but none of these names is registered which is not surprising. Some political consultants love publicity, others hate it. Tomorrow we must start some serious digging.

May 3rd
Some strange goings on. Owen Dudley Edwards, the Irish academic who lives in Edinburgh, claims a Labour canvasser has asked him to vote Tory with his second vote in order to stop the SNP. It makes a story in a couple of tabloids, not least because people have been slung out of the Labour Party for this kind of thing – and for much less. Labour denies the charge but is known to be worried. A story in the New Labour-friendly *Express*, whose Angus MacLeod has good Labour contacts, says the party is suddenly worried by its own private polling. Coming from the *Express* this is rather startling. While these stories do not prove that a swing back to the SNP is under way, they certainly encourage suspicion that there is indeed movement of the kind the SNP is proclaiming.

I spend my day calling the United States, trying to track down Stan
Greenberg whose office won't put me in touch with him or, at first,
even speak to me. There must be something in this tale, I conclude,
because Greenberg's people seem to have something to hide, but it is
difficult to stand up the story without some more hard facts. Bob
Shrum is said to be in Israel with Greenberg. A couple of academics
tell me Greenberg is rich and successful and if he is indeed working
for Labour on the Scottish elections then he won't be coming cheap.

Eventually a call comes from one of Greenberg's colleagues who
denies any involvement in the Scottish election campaign but admits
to doing UK polling for Labour with Philip Gould, the guru of focus
groups and opinion research, who takes great credit for his part in
Labour's General Election triumph. When I ask why an experienced
old hand like Greenberg would say categorically on tape that he has
elections in Scotland on May 6 but now says he has not, I am given
no reply.

Labour's David Whitton also telephones back with a blank denial
of involvement by Greenberg. His call comes within a minute of
Greenberg's. Seems a bit of a coincidence and I am naturally
suspicious that there has been some quick collusion, but there is not
much more I can do to stand up the story which has now to be along
the lines of "Labour last night denied ...." One day, perhaps the full
story will come out.

Alf Young learns that the Institute of Fiscal Studies has produced a
report which appears to vindicate the SNP's hopes for the Penny for
Scotland campaign. This is truly remarkable because the IFS is just
about the ultimate authority in these matters, widely respected and
regarded as strictly neutral. This is the sort of backing the SNP would
have dreamed of a few weeks ago and it begs the question: did Alex
Salmond make a strategic mistake leaving the debate about the SNP's
entire economic strategy until this late stage in the campaign? With
endorsements like this, the Nationalists would have made it so much
more difficult for Gordon Brown and Labour to discredit their

projections. The IFS concludes that the changes will be progressive for 90% of Scottish households. Only for the richest 10% does the impact begin to tail off because the tax-varying power applies only to the basic rate of tax and does not cover income that attracts the 40% higher rate.

The Nats seem to sense something is up today. They are on the telephone asking what we are writing about. This is getting ridiculous. Journalists are paid to tell stories, I know, but we are supposed to tell them to readers first, not to rival politicians who are trying to use us as narks for other parties. Labour is also on the telephone again, wondering what we might be publishing tonight. Telling them nothing and asking them to wait for the paper to come out just makes them more curious. Creeping paranoia is the order of the day in both Labour and SNP camps.

In today's *Guardian* I am being blamed personally and by name for losing *The Herald* £100,000 worth of advertising. An article by Douglas Fraser reprises the story of Labour's pressure on the Scottish press and the SNP's battles with the tabloids and the *Scotsman*. There's not much new in it but Fraser states uncompromisingly: "The SNP has had its most sympathetic coverage from *The Herald*, under the political editorship [sic] of Murray Ritchie. Other political writers are closer to Labour sources but Ritchie's tone so irked Labour it withdrew the £100,000 it could have been expected to spend in election advertising." Thanks, Douglas. I go in hope that our accountants and managers are not keen readers of the *Guardian*'s media section.

Harry is writing the first of our election leaders. He wants to clear the air about the relationship between *The Herald* and the political parties and has argued a trenchant case in defence of our decision to be even-handed in our coverage. To add some entertainment value he says he will let readers into the secret of his row with the senior

Labour figure who accused one of our leader writers of having "a thistle up his arse." Ah, well, the angry spinner was no doubt speaking informally and off the record, on lobby terms, etc, etc, as these people do, but he was being naughty just the same, doing nothing to dispel the worry about so-called Labour control freaks. He's lucky Harry does not identify him.

May 4th
A poll in the *Daily Express* shows Labour support dropping and the SNP narrowing the gap. More worry for Labour in the closing stages – and the *Scotsman*'s poll is still to come tomorrow. There is a growing feeling among the press corps that this affair could be closer than we have assumed.

The media have been asked by the Scottish Office to take a couple of hours out from the campaign for a familiarisation tour of the temporary Scottish Parliament in the General Assembly building. We duly turn up to find that it all looks very grand but someone has been playing fast and loose with access arrangements for the press. We had all agreed with the parties and the Scottish Office that the Parliament would be open and accessible for everyone, journalists especially. I never expected to win my argument that it should be as accessible as the European Parliaments in Brussels and Strasbourg where reporters can go almost anywhere except into the debating chamber, but this is ridiculous.

Someone in the Scottish Office has changed the agreement governing access to the temporary Parliament. MSPs will, it seems, be able to leave by side doors, giving reporters no chance to buttonhole them. We are barred from the Members' coffee room and various other areas including corridors off which doors lead into the chamber. We cannot even use the front entrance and must take a detour through the courtyard, past the famous statue of John Knox, and enter by the back door – rather a time-consuming journey especially for reporters fretting about deadlines.

Our Scottish Office minder quotes "security" and looks embarrassed because he knows this arrangement is nothing like what was agreed over months of discussions about Parliamentary rules and procedures for the media. He suggests with a blush that some reporters might be tempted to burst into the debating chamber and cause a scene if they were allowed into the Members' corridor with its doors leading to the chamber.

Robbie Dinwoodie points out that if someone was silly enough to behave like that he or she would do it only once before permanently forfeiting credentials, not to mention a career. There is, after all, nothing to stop someone doing this in the House of Commons, for example, but no-one can recall such an event taking place.

There are about 20 of us on this familiarisation trip and we give the access arrangements a unanimous thumbs down. This has nothing to do with politicians, we suspect, but with the Scottish Office civil servants whose mindset is that reporters and publicity and openness are all dangers and to be avoided. We shall have to re-educate them. There is going to be a row but we will win in the end. Whether the end comes in time for the first meeting on May 12 is another matter.

The Nats are seeking publicity for a Commons written reply they have coaxed from George Mudie, the English junior education minister. He has admitted that the number of students absolved of paying tuition fees next year will fall to 30%. This appears to have been wrung from the government just in good time for an eve-of-poll row. John Swinney asked the same question of Helen Liddell, the Scottish Office education minister, and was told she would reply "as soon as possible" – ie after the Scottish general election. But Mudie's answer has let the cat out of the bag because the government has always sought to defend its imposition of these unpopular fees by pointing out that 40% of students will not pay them because their families can't afford them. Now the figure is slipping and will continue to slip – and the SNP has it in writing.

Tommy Sheridan of the Scottish Socialist Party calls to complain that he is not getting much publicity in *The Herald*. The cheek of him. *The Herald* is about the only paper that has given him a fair deal. Today he is in typically rebellious mood, leading his supporters to the home – Tommy's says it's a palace – of Gordon Jackson who is fighting Govan for Labour. Gordon bought a big villa in the constituency but it is not in an area of Govan which might be regarded as typical. He lives in a posh, middle-class enclave and wants to avoid hassle or publicity at this stage in the game – which is, of course, exactly why Tommy and his followers have picked on him. There's nothing Govan folk like more than an important personage being pricked. We send a photographer to watch Tommy at work. Poor Gordon. He's a decent and worried man who took on the awkward challenge of keeping Govan for Labour in the face of party scandals, shipyard closures and rising unemployment. Now he is being vilified for being rich, which he undoubtedly is. My problem is that I admire Tommy's impertinence and I like Gordon as a man. You can lose too many friends in journalism, especially in elections.

Harry Reid wants Robbie to be with Alex Salmond on election night in Banff and Buchan. But there is a problem with logistics. Salmond's count will be in Macduff which means the journey back to Glasgow or Edinburgh around dawn will be tricky. Robbie discovers that Salmond has a helicopter and inquires if he might cadge a lift – only to discover that the said helicopter has been supplied by the *Scotsman* as part of a deal for serialising an upcoming biography of Salmond. Harry spits blood, as if it was Robbie's fault. There is no justice.

Scottish Television sends a crew to the Herald office for an interview with me about proportional representation to be screened on election night. Any sense of self-regard at being a television pundit is quickly punctured when the interviewer lets slip that it is for screening during the "boring" bit between the close of poll and the first result being declared. We all have our uses

May 5th

The last day of campaigning and I am to be vetted for my accreditation for the Scottish Parliament. I have a form to complete which asks my mother's maiden name (she died in her 80s a decade ago) and whether I have ever been involved in espionage, sabotage or terrorism. I am also required to declare if I have ever taken part in activities aimed at overthrowing the democratic rule of the country or been associated closely with people trying to do so. How tempting to say yes to that last bit. After all I did associate closely with several Scottish Tories for a while (purely professionally). Whoever dreamed up this form might not see the joke. Best play safe and answer no.

Looking back, this has been a roller coaster campaign for Labour and the SNP. Labour's machine has been ruthlessly effective and not always for the most edifying reasons. By common consent this has been a very negative election from Labour under the leadership of Gordon Brown and his inner circle. Reports are surfacing of discontent behind the scenes in the Scottish Labour Party at the way in which its own senior officials and spin-doctors have been sidelined as Brown and the Millbank people have taken over. Donald Dewar has put in occasional appearances at press conferences but most of the time he has been safely out of the way doing what he is best at – meeting the public and pumping the flesh. My abiding image of this campaign is of that notorious Labour party election broadcast showing smashed picture frames and violent divorce. Not pretty, but who can deny it has been effective? Scots, it seems, are easily scared.

For the Nats the fight never really started in earnest until our System Three poll midway through the campaign which we splashed under headline: *SNP in Freefall.* That galvanised Salmond who had looked uncharacteristically diffident at the start. No-one knows yet what was wrong with him. It is still a mystery. Perhaps his back was hurting again or perhaps he was unwell. Whatever it was, his disposition became much sunnier immediately our second poll was published and he has been firing on all cylinders ever since. On several television debates in the past few days he has easily outshone Donald Dewar.

The Scotsman's ICM poll today puts Labour comfortably ahead in both votes but not quite so comfortably as before, suggesting that the SNP is indeed making a comeback. Mike Russell thinks the Nats can yet spring a surprise although he frets that they might just have run out of time. One excitable Nat footsoldier in Dumfries tells me he thinks the SNP will take the constituency (this despite Labour sitting on a majority of almost 10,000). As Robbie says, politicians do have a wonderful capacity to believe their own publicity sometimes when they become afflicted by candidatitis towards the end of campaigns.

The Tories are pleased with themselves and with David McLetchie who was something of a forlorn figure five weeks ago. He has had a good campaign and after constant exposure on television and in the papers he is no longer the nonentity he was such a short time ago. McLetchie has also shown a sense of fun, which is more than the others have managed. In his "Torycopter" he has hopped around Scotland and seen much more of it than the other leaders in their battlebuses. He it was who produced one of the more entertaining gaffs of the campaign when he agreed that when the economics of independence are argued the winner's prize must to go to Alex Salmond. This was widely interpreted by some of the papers as an embarrassing error of judgment but most reasonable people would probably conclude he was just telling the truth. Those most outraged were the old hardline Unionists who hate the whole idea of the Tories apologising for not being more sympathetic to Scotland in the past. These people still cannot thole the idea of Home Rule or the Scottish Parliament.

McLetchie is no mug and he might even have been something of a revelation - but that is not to say he is yet popular. Given that he started this campaign without a single Scottish Tory seat in Westminster, it follows that the only way his fortunes can go is up.

No matter how many seats the Tories win in Holyrood, their final tally will be an advance on zero and so McLetchie should be safe for a while from a leadership challenge.

As for the Liberal Democrats, well, they went through the campaign stuck on their fence as usual, not saying if they would raise the Tartan Tax and not saying which party they would prefer to coalesce with in government. They have given the (accurate) impression of being coalition obsessives. Yet it is plain that their practice of seeking friends in rival parties is foreign to Scottish politics and to the electorate. Voters want to know if there is any point in supporting the LibDems when they are simply destined to become quasi-Labour MSPs. As of tonight there is some idle speculation among some of the press corps and the other parties that the LibDems are about to be the big losers in this election because Scottish voters do not yet have the coalition mentality. Electors seem to want consensus in principle but they tend to balk at the idea of voting for one party which will promptly throw in its lot with another. In normal times the Scottish LibDems, so strong in localised voting, would be expected to hold on to their existing seats but there is talk of them losing Argyll and perhaps a couple of other seats and coming fourth of the main parties.

Our eve-of-poll leader, written by Harry, offers no endorsement of any party – which is *Herald* tradition – and calls instead for a Parliament which makes a real difference to Scotland with a new style of politics. I can put my hand on heart and say that *The Herald* has genuinely made an effort to be fair to all parties which is more than our principal rivals even considered. I am surprised and a little saddened by the role of the Scottish press. It has always been predominantly conservative but seldom blatantly party political – compared with most of the London papers – but it emerges from this election as feverishly hostile to the second political party of the land. It seems unfair, even undemocratic, however much you might disagree with the SNP or independence.

I console myself with the thought that Labour will probably not win an outright majority. That would be too much. Even some Labour activists are privately saying they would not want such an outcome at the birth of the much anticipated new democracy. The whole point of adopting this electoral system was to prevent the establishment of another Scottish Labour soviet.

Labour thoroughly deserves to prosper in this election because its victory two years ago in the General Election paved the way for the successful Referendum and the Scotland Act and, now, the Scottish general election. You have to give Labour due credit for keeping its word on devolution and doing so promptly, even if the motivating force for all of this is the threat from Scottish nationalism. That threat is now greater than ever before. Let's face it, if this is the best Labour can manage at a time when it is running the most popular government in history, two years into its term of office, what will happen in a Scottish Parliament election when Labour is deeply unpopular, a circumstance which must come about one day? No party wins all of the elections all of the time, even in Scotland. The SNP's time will surely come. Perhaps an early spell in opposition will do it some good.

5

Moments of Truth

6th May - 7th June

May 6th

I decide to revive an old *Herald* custom: Election Day golf. A crowd
of us heads off to play Hilton Park and we receive a soaking for our
trouble but it is good fun and agreeably relaxing before the big night.
After voting and taking a nap in the afternoon it is time to begin
working through the night.

The BBC has an opinion poll – its press office denies it is an exit poll
but the broadcasters keep referring to it as such – which suggests
Labour will win no overall majority and that the Nationalists will
take up to 47 seats. Labour must be worried by that - and even more
worried as the first result is announced. Tom McCabe, the council
leader in South Lanarkshire, claims his place in history at 11.15 pm
as the first Member of the Scottish Parliament in the safe Labour
seat of Hamilton South. This is the constituency (much changed)
which Winnie Ewing won for the SNP more than 30 years ago to
announce the arrival of Scottish Nationalism as a serious force. On
that occasion Labour made a mess of its campaign and the Tories
managed to make a spectacular cock-up of theirs. The SNP has never
stopped talking about it since. But the swing tonight of 10% from
Labour to the SNP on a low turnout is enough to suggest this could
be a happy night for the Nationalists.

McCabe's majority is 7176, less than half that of George
Robertson, the Defence Secretary, at the General Election. As the
results start coming in, swings of this magnitude are repeated in
constituencies including East Kilbride, Falkirk East and Motherwell
and Wishaw. It soon becomes obvious that the SNP is performing
strongly but is still unable to make the breakthrough it needs in the
central belt where Labour is most powerful. It is the same old problem

for the Nats. None of their huge swings brings an SNP gain. Even in Hamilton North and Bellshill where the swing is 13% the Labour majority remains comfortably in control. We begin to see again the huge advantage of first-past-the-post voting to the Labour Party in Scotland where its mountainous majorities are impervious to the stiffest challenges. Crafty old Donald Dewar knew exactly what he was doing when he insisted that electoral reform should not remove first-past-the-post voting which gives Labour its inbuilt advantage in Scotland.

The routine of Labour victories in safe seats continues. And then comes Falkirk West. This is Scotland's answer to the downfall of Michael Portillo. Dennis Canavan, the man spurned by Labour's selection panel and denounced by Donald Dewar as "just not good enough" despite 25 years as an MP at Westminster, trounces Labour to retain his own seat. I am sure the whole of Scotland is chuckling except of course those gathered round the television set in Delta House. This is a phenomenal result for Dennis. We all expected him to win a Holyrood seat via the list system, but to take the result by a mile in constituency voting is truly sensational. I cannot recall anything like that happening in Scotland in modern times.

Dennis takes 55% of the vote, a stunning personal triumph. He is now assured of his place in history as a political folk hero. One story has it that Labour was so worried this week about Dennis doing well that the party bussed in a group of students to help in canvassing. When the kids reached the centre of Falkirk they promptly switched sides and went to work for Dennis. They were speaking for most of the voters in Falkirk West where there has been outrage ever since his rejection by what he sees as a cabal of party fixers.

Dennis makes a dignified speech in which he calls for reconciliation with Labour but he cannot resist twisting the knife in Donald Dewar's ribs. "I had no option but to let the voters decide if I was good enough," he says, to ecstatic cheering. That picture of Dennis with his arms raised in triumph and a smile a mile wide must be destined to become one of the abiding images of the campaign.

Reporters at the Falkirk West count suggest that even Dennis himself is surprised at the scale of his victory. As a born rebel he will be an adornment – and a troublemaker, I hope – in the Scottish Parliament and is now likely to enjoy some sport at Labour's expense in Westminster before he is forced out there, too. Tam Dalyell, a fellow free spirit, who has always criticised Labour's treatment of Dennis, releases a statement calling for him to be readmitted to the Labour Party. This is met with deafening silence.

Things are beginning to go wrong for the SNP. Nicola Sturgeon fails to take Glasgow Govan, to the undisguised delight of Gordon Jackson who is normally noted for his gloomy countenance and who is suddenly sporting a grin of Canavan proportions. For Gordon this is also a deserved triumph after being written off by so many people, including much of the media. Curiously, the SNP's tilt at Govan has produced a swing of only 1% and there is no immediate explanation. But a pattern is becoming clear. The Nationalists are making the deepest cuts in Labour's majorities in seats where Labour can affords to lose thousands of votes and still hang on with relative ease. In seats where the SNP needs its biggest swings it is not getting them.

Alex Neil, a veteran Nationalist, who seems to have spent a lifetime trying to wrest Kilmarnock and Loudoun from Labour, has failed again because his swing is only 4%, leaving Labour with a majority of 2760. He can take comfort in the fact that he will still go to the Scottish Parliament via the regional party list while the constituency itself is now reduced to the status of marginal.

Much the same happens in Ochil which was another of the SNP's top target seats. George Reid gives the Nats a swing of 3.5%, not enough to dislodge Labour. He intends now to step down from the SNP executive and take a tilt at becoming Presiding Officer or Speaker at Holyrood where he will have a seat via the list. If I was Alex Salmond I would tell George to forget the idea; he brings experience to the SNP and a gravitas which not too many of its MSP's will be able to match.

And then suddenly there is panic among the Nats. The BBC suggests that Roseanna Cunningham will lose Perth and that Alasdair Morgan will lose Galloway, both formerly Tory constituencies. A call to SNP HQ in Edinburgh produces the suggestion that everything in these two seats is fine and this is simply the Tories enjoying some mischief. But the Nats would say that, wouldn't they? To the party's immense relief Roseanna Cunningham duly wins but her majority is cut because of a slight swing back to the Tories. In Galloway Alasdair Morgan suffers a 2% swing to the Tories but hangs on with his majority reduced to 3201.

It is now evident that, perversely, the SNP is performing least well in it own strongholds. No-one seems able to explain this, at least not yet. In Moray Margaret Ewing becomes the first of the Ewing dynasty to go to Holyrood – in fact she is the first Nationalist MSP – but she, too, has had her troubles with a swing to Labour of almost 5%. At least there is a plausible explanation in her case. Moray is home to RAF Kinloss where service personnel (many of them English) are based. Some of them are currently off bombing Serbia and will not have enjoyed Alex Salmond's remarks about Nato's activities being an "unpardonable folly."

But the bold boy defies the trend. Alex Salmond coasts home in Banff and Buchan on a 2% swing from the Tories to SNP – only to find himself stranded after the count in Macduff. This is a matter of some inconvenience and frustration to him and great satisfaction to me. One of the *Scotsman*'s writers is working on a biography of Salmond and has persuaded his paper to fly the leader back to Edinburgh after the count as part of a publishing deal. Being our principal competitor, the *Scotsman*, naturally, offers seats to the Press Association reporter and some other journalists but refuses a request from Robbie Dinwoodie. I am delighted to hear from Robbie, who is cackling with glee, that the helicopter has been grounded by fog and that Salmond must make other arrangements for his return to the capital.

It seems the Tories are not going to win any constituency seats. Their best hope is seen as Eastwood which was the safest Conservative seat in Scotland until the General Election and where John Young, a veteran Glasgow councillor, is the Holyrood candidate. He is a rare species, a Scottish Tory with a Scottish accent and a track record as a bonnie fechter. He has a record of continuous success in elections going back more than 30 years. He even keeps on winning in the soviet which is Glasgow city council these days. But even John Young can't crack this one. He goes down by a couple of thousand votes despite managing a small swing back to Labour.

In Renfrewshire West Annabel Goldie, who is tipped as a future Tory leader in Scotland, comes third behind the SNP and Labour, her progress blocked by Patricia Godman, wife of Norman, Labour MP for Inverclyde, who is also being talked about as a candidate for Presiding Officer. Yet the Tories have put up a good enough show in Glasgow and the West of Scotland for both John Young and Annabel Goldie to go to Holyrood through the party list.

I am pleased to see my old drinking pal, Bailie Bill Aitken, another Glasgow Tory, is also heading for Holyrood. He had the most thankless task in Scotland - taking on Donald Dewar in Glasgow Anniesland where he came third behind the SNP as Donald annexed almost 60% of the vote despite another of those swings to the Nats, this time 3%.

The Tory who has performed worst in Glasgow is Michael Fry, the historian and journalist, notorious for his right-wing polemics in the broadsheets and his penchant for gracious living, especially when the drinks are on expenses. Michael has been entertaining *Herald* readers with accounts of his exploits and appears to have fallen victim to his own propaganda, suggesting that he might improve his party's performance and spring a surprise in that most hopeless of Tory causes, Glasgow Maryhill. Our editorial indulgence of Michael has caused some comment from readers and from other candidates who are miffed at his self-publicising writings. Harry has permitted this slight deviation from the rigidities of fair play on the reasonable basis that Michael's reports are tongue-in-cheek and that his cavalier confidence offers an entertaining hostage to fortune. After his protestations that he knows better than the Tory party machine how to campaign in lost-cause seats, Michael comes a miserable fifth with 5% of the vote, making him less popular than the Scottish Socialist Party. I look forward to his excuse.

No such troubles for Phil Gallie, the pugnacious Tory who lost his Ayr seat in the General Election slaughter. Phil has twice told me he thinks he has a real chance of taking back Ayr and it seems he might be proved right. Ayr is now about to announce the result of a second recount but, sadly for Phil, who is one of the more entertaining characters of Scottish politics, he fails by a frustrating 25 votes despite a swing of 7% from Labour to the Tories.

In Edinburgh Pentlands, once the Westminster seat of Sir Malcolm Rifkind, former Foreign Secretary, the Tories' hopes are dashed again when David McLetchie fails narrowly. It is the same story for Lord James Douglas-Hamilton in Edinburgh West although both should survive because of the party list.

In Glasgow Pollok, Tommy Sheridan of the Scottish Socialist Party takes 22% of the vote, suggesting that System Three and other opinion polls have been wrong about his chances of getting elected through the party list. Our suspicions are duly confirmed when he comes fifth among the seven list MSPs for Glasgow amid scenes at the Glasgow count of backslapping, clenched fists and the air being punched. With dissidents like Tommy Sheridan and Dennis Canavan among the MSPs, this Parliament is beginning to look interesting,

In the head count of MSPs Labour is leading by miles but list voting has still to come into play after most of the constituency results are announced. Remarkably, the Holyrood constituency map of Scotland is so far unchanged from Westminster if you discount Falkirk West which goes on the record as a Labour loss although the MSP is the same individual – Dennis Canavan.

And then comes the news that the LibDems have gained Aberdeen South from Labour. The personable Nicol Stephen, one of the LibDem stars in Scotland, who lost his Westminster seat in 1992, is back having knocked over a Labour majority of 3365 with a swing of 6%. This looks like being a better night than expected for the LibDems who seem to be holding their constituency seats easily and have still the top-up seats to look forward to.

Another change: Fergus Ewing, son of Winnie, husband of Margaret, gives the SNP something to cheer by taking Inverness, Nairn and Lochaber, but only narrowly. This is one of the tightest marginals in Britain and has been snatched from Labour with a swing to the Nats of less than 3%.

Dundee West appears about to provide a sensation. This is Ernie Ross's seat in Westminster and it must be that his widely publicised troubles about being a government nark in the Arms to Africa scandal, which prompted his resignation in disgrace from the Foreign Affairs Select Committee, have damaged the Holyrood candidate's chances. But the SNP just fails after a recount, and Kate MacLean holds on with a Labour majority of only 121 despite a whopping 16% swing to the Nationalist candidate, Calum Cashley.

Notable failures so far include Donnie Munro, Labour's choice in Ross, Skye and Inverness West. All credit to Munro, who has suffered some mickey-taking because of his stylised hair and eccentric clothes (he was the lead singer with the Gaelic rock group Runrig). Munro had been in line for a safe Glasgow seat but chose instead (or was persuaded by the Glasgow Labour mafia) to try his luck in the Highlands. One obvious theory is that the hated Skye bridge tolls did for him, especially after the SNP pledged to abolish them. My occasional golfing partner and eternal SNP optimist, Jim Mather, comes third in Skye in what is another success for the LibDems and their veteran Highland fighter, John Farquhar Munro.

Lorraine Mann is a prime mover in the Highlands and Islands Alliance whose candidates have campaigned partly on the original idea of making the work of an MSP a job-sharing affair. She is noted for her anti-nuclear campaigning and a sharp debating style which once famously silenced George Robertson in a major television argument. The results suggest the failure of the Alliance is abject, which is odd, given that other minority parties seem to be doing well.

Annabelle Ewing, Winnie's daughter, is the one member of the Ewing clan not to succeed. She has been fighting Stirling for the SNP and has encouraged a swing of 11% from Labour but, again, Labour holds on. Brian Monteith, who had expressed hopes of winning back this constituency for the Tories (it was held at Westminster by Sir Michael Forsyth until the General Election) comes third but he will still become an MSP because of the list.

There will be no Holyrood seat for Keith Geddes, the Labour president of the Scottish Convention of Local Authorities and, therefore, a high-profile councillor. He chose to stand for Holyrood in the knowledge that if he succeeded he would have to quit local government. For him the list offers no safety net. Labour is the party which stands to gain least from the new voting system, and Geddes, a talented politician, is a victim of that system. Having failed to gain a constituency nomination he put his name and his faith in the party list – and it failed him.

Let's hear it for Robbie the Pict – or "Mr Pict" as the Queen's private secretary addresses him when responding to his many letters to Her Majesty on Scotland's ills. Robbie, popular eccentric, fighter of lost causes and tireless champion of the Highland campaign against Skye bridge tolls, loses another battle but lives to fight another day in his own crazy style – soon, I hope.

Around 8 am I update the front page story for the umpteenth time and head home in a taxi, struggling to stay awake. I collapse into bed and as my head hits the pillow the telephone rings with someone wanting a live interview for Talk Radio in London. I mumble a few words and find that suddenly I can't sleep. There is no peace.

May 7th
The Lothians count is late, delayed overnight by some administrative incompetence, but it springs the final surprise of the campaign. Frances Horsburgh, my bleary-eyed *Herald* colleague at the Edinburgh count, calls to say Robin Harper has been elected via the lists and will go down in history as the first Green parliamentarian in the United Kingdom. Even the other candidates are pleased for him. There are tears and congratulations. The thought occurs that the SNP will be quite happy with this. With Robin Harper, Dennis Canavan and Tommy Sheridan in the Scottish Parliament – not to mention Labour's John McAllion from Dundee East – the number of MSPs who support an independent Scotland or are at least soft on the idea will be significantly more than the number of SNP MSPs.

The Lothians list has found room for Lord Steel of Aikwood who must be back in the race as a candidate for Presiding Officer. The SNP's Margo MacDonald, who did well but not well enough to win Edinburgh South, joins the left-wing Kenny McAskill in Holyrood, two results which will boost the Nationalist numbers but should also increase future internal party pressure on Alex Salmond. Margo is a critic of Salmond but, uncharacteristically, has forced herself to keep quiet about her well-known misgivings during the campaign.

The final result is really nothing like most of the polls predicted in terms of percentage support for the parties. Where some of the polls had Labour with half the vote and touching overall control the result shows Labour did not even reach 40% in first votes and it could win only 33% in second votes. On seats, the polls were less inaccurate. The final shakedown means a hung Scottish Parliament. Labour has 56 seats, the SNP 35, Tories 18 (all from the list), LibDems 17, SSP 1, Greens 1 and Dennis Canavan.

May 10th
After a long weekend of rest and recuperation Donald Dewar and Jim Wallace are in Edinburgh for talks on forming a coalition. They meet in secret in the new Parliament offices in High Street behind

closed doors fronted by security personnel and signs marked: No Media Access. So much for the new Scottish politics of openness and transparency. Robbie and I spend the morning moving into our new offices in Lawnmarket while the coalition talks continue in the administrative centre round the corner. Eventually the silence is broken by a call from David Whitton to say there will be a press briefing. At the same time the LibDems announced a news conference at their party HQ at Haymarket. In the event Whitton is accompanied at his briefing in a committee room by Michael Moore, the LibDem MP, who seems to have taken over the role of party spokesman. Willie Rennie and Tony Hutson, both of whom are official LibDem spokesmen, listen in at the back of the room, obviously demoted for the duration of the talks. Even Peter Curtis, spokesman for Jim Wallace, tells me he is being told nothing. This is unusual behaviour for the LibDems who would normally kill for a spot of publicity.

Whitton brushes aside a comment by Alastair Campbell, official spokesman for Tony Blair, that the Prime Minister is "involved" in the talks between Dewar and Wallace. An uncomfortable Whitton explains this by telling reporters that "when we say he is involved we don't mean he is involved as such" and goes on in this vein to persuade us that this should not be interpreted as London interfering in the process. I think he might be right, despite the cynicism.

Ashdown, who has been in close touch with Wallace, and Blair are often reported as being believers in co-operation. This is, after all, supposed to be at the heart of the Blair project. It would be surprising if Blair really was getting in Donald's way but it is also true to say that Blair would not relish stumping up the price of a Scottish government abandoning student tuition fees, especially when the Treasury under Gordon Brown has said it will not write cheques to cover the cost. Tuition fees are now the major obstacle to agreement and there are hints that the talks could last days. This is grim news. There is nothing worse than a newsdesk wanting a front-page story when there is nothing to write except descriptions of never-ending secrecy.

I decide to write a story suggesting there will be no quick deal, despite Donald Dewar's wishes, and I base this on the continuing dispute over tuition fees. Harry calls to say he has been tipped off that the LibDems are being bought off on tuition fees and there might be agreement soon. This worries me because it conflicts directly with what Robbie and I are hearing. I am relieved to take a call from 10 Downing Street. It seems the Prime Minister is anxious that we should take account of a statement by Scottish university principals. They point out that scrapping tuition fees might be a neat idea but want to know who will stump up. They also question the benefit to the poorest families. If the Prime Minister's office is troubling to telephone round drawing attention to the drawbacks of scrapping tuition fees it must mean they are still being discussed. Robbie and I rewrite the story, this time to make it harder.

In the Deacon Brodie bar across from the media centre we find some LibDems in a huddle over drinks. They include Donald Gorrie who has been returned to the Parliament via the list and he seems in fine fettle. He is wearing the kilt and says he has been to a funeral. For one who is normally rather unsmiling and not given to banter he is joking and chatting as if he had not a care in the world. Given that he is not a fan of Labour and is a fierce critic of tuition fees, I take this as a further sign that things are going his way and that our judgment on what is happening behind those locked doors might be right.

May 11th
A long day in Edinburgh. Neil Rafferty of the Press Association offers a glimpse of the future. Having just left the new Parliament building but having forgotten something, he tries to go back in. He is ordered by a bumptious young security guard not to deviate from the floor to which he is heading. "If you do," this guard threatens, "you will have your badge confiscated and your livelihood will be lost." Welcome to the new Scotland.

Lord Steel of Aikwood, known to my generation as the Boy David, wants to be Speaker or Presiding Officer as the government would prefer, in the new chamber. Nowadays he sees himself as an elder statesman, which I suppose is fair enough, and he fancies playing a prominent role in Edinburgh. Good luck to him. He has always supported Home Rule but he is undeniably getting on a bit in the view of some people who would prefer a younger candidate.

George Reid of the SNP has similar ambitions and lots of experience and we hear now that Patricia Godman's name is being mentioned by Labour. She is a new MSP but has the advantage of being a woman. Another candidate is rumoured to be the Glasgow Tory, Councillor John Young, who failed to win Eastwood but has arrived via the list. The three men are oldies but if, as rumoured, the Presiding Officer will be chosen by secret ballot any one of the four candidates should have a decent chance.

The Labour-LibDem coalition talks continue in secret. I bump into Donald Gorrie of the LibDems who is fuming at the very idea that they are still even talking about tuition fees. He protests that Labour's leaders in Scotland must grow up as democrats and change their attitudes. Gorrie is a remarkable man. He has just given £10,000 of his own money to the Scottish LibDems, saying his kids are grown up and off his hands. At least he is a politician who puts his money where his mouth is. He tells me on the record there should be more to a Scottish Parliament than a simple transfer of power from Tony Blair to Donald Dewar and that it should be "not just another Stalinist-style State." Donald Gorrie is of the old school who believes a Parliament and its policies should be guided by its Members and not by a whipped executive. He wants the Scottish Parliament to be "nothing like the waste of space which is Westminster." He is disgusted with Labour's spin on the talks about tuition fees, condemning it as "disgraceful" for suggesting the LibDems might be about to cave in. I asked him if his party yet might be preparing to reconsider its absolute commitment to the abolition of tuition fees and he replies angrily: "If it is, then certain people will be in big trouble."

After claims that Tony Blair is meddling in the Scottish elections – denied by Labour, music to the ears of the SNP – Labour's former assistant general secretary has said Scotland has no right to "go it alone." Matthew Taylor, who now runs the Institute for Public Policy Research, say rather crassly that devolution is about allowing Scots to make decisions about Scotland but that this has become confused with internal party decision-making."

He keeps digging the hole he is in when he says: "There is another view which I suspect is widely held among senior Labour politicians. It sees membership of a party as indicating acceptance of its core political identity." This provokes Alex Salmond to accuse Taylor of having "blown the last scrap of pretence off the coalition talks and exposed the naked truth that London Labour is running the show."

Frank McAveety, Glasgow City Council Labour group leader, is caught walking up the Mound by a television crew who want his views on the suitability of the Church of Scotland building for its meetings. Being in Edinburgh but from Glasgow, McAveety replies: "Very nice place but if it had been in Glasgow we'd have had it stonecleaned."

The SNP is muttering about its MSPs taking the oath of allegiance to the Queen. A couple of them complain over drinks in the Jolly Judge, which looks like becoming the Nats' watering hole, that they did not get themselves elected to the first Scottish Parliament since 1707 to swear fealty to Her Majesty. There is talk of taking the oath in Gaelic but the rules insist English has to be the first language. Some want to make a protest before taking the oath, just to underline the point they are swearing loyalty under duress. But they will all take it one way or another – or they won't become MSPs.

May 12th

This is the day they're calling Democracy Day. Edinburgh's High Street has come alive for the first sitting of a Scottish Parliament in 292 years and there is a buzz about the town. Even the Scots tend to forget that Edinburgh was one of the great European capitals in its day, certainly one of the most beautiful. But, while the Kirk and the legal fraternity remained loyal to Edinburgh, they were not enough to replace a legislature, government, and a diplomatic corps. For too long Edinburgh has been provincialised – if you exclude the annual Festival - but perhaps for not much longer as of today.

MSPs and their families and the media mob converge on the Assembly Hall building which we notice is flying the Union flag. No-one is quite sure whether this is normal. Professor Neil MacCormick, who will be contesting the Euro-elections for the SNP, tells me he thinks it usually flies the flag of Edinburgh University. As from today, of course, it is home to a Parliament within the British State. Someone seems to have ordered the raising of the Union flag just as a wee reminder, but at least whoever did so had the decency to run up the Saltire as well.

Paul Grice, the interim clerk, claims his place in history as the first man to speak in the Scottish Parliament for almost three centuries when he addresses the MSPs and says "welcome" before asking them to take their seats. He is obviously aware of the moment and he sounds nervous. The instant he speaks there is complete silence and a feeling of tension. It takes something to silence a roomful of normally garrulous politicians. Winnie Ewing has the dubious distinction of being identified as the Oldest Member (she's 69) and is first to swear fealty to "Her Majesty, Queen Elizabeth." Notice the absence of numerals after the name. Queen Elizabeth is, of course, the first of Scotland and the second only of England, and many Scots are touchy about the distinction which was ignored at the time of her Coronation.

Winnie takes the oath in English with no attempt to rewrite the script in front of her. Then she repeats it in Gaelic. This was her chance as a recidivist Nat to add something seditious without the assembled oath police knowing although, presumably, there must have been someone there with the Gaelic waiting to pounce on any covert departure from the strict wording. Torcuil Crichton of the *Sunday Herald*, whose first language is Gaelic, is beside me in the press gallery and pronounces that Winnie does indeed have a grasp of the language and has been faithful to the script a second time.

Perhaps surprisingly, very few MSPs are in the kilt. This is a sign of the times. Not so long ago anyone wearing the kilt was assumed to be a Nationalist. Nowadays the kilt is worn routinely at weddings or at international sports events. Curiously, the people who (mostly) no longer feel compelled to wear it are the Nationalists but I can spot none of them kilted. Keith Raffan, an ex-Tory MP and now a born-again LibDem, is sporting the tartan - Raffan looking raffish. Some of us wonder if there is such a beast as Clan Raffan. I notice that Edinburgh's creme-de-la-creme of descriptive writers are gathered to polish their epithets and some of them are not exactly old campaigners for Home Rule. I note with satisfaction that Allan Massie of the *Scotsman* and *Daily Mail* is wearing a black tie.

Winnie and the other Nationalist MSPs sport white roses - Hugh MacDiarmid's "little white rose of Scotland that smells sharp and sweet - and breaks the heart." She takes the chair and watches as Donald Dewar swears the oath of allegiance. Alex Salmond is next but before he does so he makes a little speech making clear that his "primary loyalty is to the people of Scotland." He points out that the people of Scotland are sovereign. "All of our Members of the Scottish Parliament take this view," he says and then he makes his peace with Her Majesty.

Dennis Canavan, who has spent the entire day grinning and handshaking, explains that he, too, has problems with the oath and makes clear in a short preamble that he is swearing allegiance to the sovereign and not the people only because he is legally compelled to do so. He is followed by the man already known in Edinburgh as Mister Happy, Robin Harper of the Greens. His smile outdazzles even Dennis's and he likewise expresses reservations about taking the oath. We begin to wonder if this is about to become a farce. If all the other 33 SNP Members follow Winnie or Alex Salmond we will be here for hours listening to them protesting before swearing allegiance but it seems that Alex, mercifully, has spoken for all of them.

And then a great moment of theatre. Up steps Tommy Sheridan in his role as a party leader (of the Scottish Socialist Party and its only MSP) who also makes his point about taking the oath under protest. "Before making an affirmation I would like to declare that as a democratically elected socialist my vision for Scotland is of it being a democratic socialist republic where supreme sovereignty lies with the people of Scotland and not with an unelected monarch and I therefore take this affirmation under protest," he says. As he begins to recite the oath he raises his right hand as a clenched fist, to the great amusement of the chamber. There are disapproving frowns from Donald and some of the Tories. At the conclusion of this daft ceremonial no less than one third of the Scottish Parliament's first roll call has balked at taking the loyal oath. Westminster this is not. Yet the punishment for failing to take it is far tougher in the Scottish Parliament than in Westminster. MPs in London are simply barred from entering the chamber until they swear allegiance but in Scotland they would face a by-election within weeks.

Labour's Susan Deacon takes the oath while her daughter, Claire, aged 21 months, calls "hello" and "mummy" from the gallery to the general delight of all assembled. Ms Deacon is so nervous and disconcerted that she forgets to sign the register and has to be recalled. This is supposed to be a modern Parliament keeping family hours and Ms Deacon's swearing-in is the first sign of that. Somehow I can't see that scene being played out in the House of Commons.

Nick Johnston of the Tories takes his oath in English and Catalan (his wife's language) for no obvious purpose. Two SNP Members are caught rule-breaking, one deliberately. Dorothy-Grace Elder, columnist and campaigner, is detected inserting a few words of her own into the oath. She, it is reported, muttered "the people of

Scotland" just ahead of the mention of Her Majesty before leaving the chamber. But she is collared. The Parliament's lawyers advise the SNP that she must take the oath again. Within minutes she is likewise "advised" by Mike Russell, her party chief executive, to behave properly, which she does. In the corridor later she admits to me with a shrug and a grin: "It was a fair cop." Gil Paterson also falls foul of the process and is asked if he has a "problem" with going through it all over again. He swears his allegiance a second time and later tells me he still hasn't a clue what he did wrong the first time. Gil is a Nationalist to his fingertips but he looks so innocent that I have to believe him.

I notice Canon Kenyon Wright looking down on this fun and games and the strange mixture of absurd ritual and tension from his seat in the gallery and I wonder what he is thinking after his failure to become elected to the Parliament which he did so much to create. He tells me he thinks the fuss over oaths is unnecessary and rather daft. All members of the Scottish Constitutional Convention – which means all Labour MPs at the time except Tam Dalyell - signed the Claim of Right, he reminds me, confirming their party's belief that the people of Scotland, and not any Parliament, are sovereign. "They all signed it except the Tories and the SNP – and so they can't deny the sovereignty of the people," says Kenyon. But no-one seems to have told the powers that be. Kenyon should know. He keeps the Claim of Right, signed first by John Smith and then himself, locked away in the Convention's office.

Winnie Ewing is never one to miss a chance. She makes a little speech at the close of this first session and an uncompromising Nationalist battle cry it turns out to be. She reminds MSPs that the old Scottish Parliament was "adjourned" all those years ago but not abolished. "I want to start with the words I have always wanted to say, or hear somebody else say – the Scottish Parliament, adjourned on the twenty-fifth day of March, 1707, is hereby reconvened."

The start of a new sang indeed, and the MSPs and everyone else applaud in what I suspect will prove to be a rare sign of mutual good will and unity. Later, someone whispers to me that Andy Nicoll of the *Sun* was the one who suggested this idea to Winnie. Good for him – and her.

Robbie and I adjourn also – to the Bow Bar, where the customers are watching the proceedings on a television news programme. When Tommy Sheridan is shown with fist clenched there is an outbreak of cheering.

May 13th

Back to Edinburgh – I now seem to be living permanently on the ghastly rattletrap which is the Glasgow-Edinburgh train – to see Tommy Sheridan and Hugh Kerr, the ex-Labour Euro-MP who was purged by the Blairites for being too left wing. He is standing for the Scottish Socialists in the European elections on June 10. After all this overdosing on politics it is a grim thought that the day is already upon us when nominations close for the Euro-elections. Tommy and Hugh are met to protest at the size of the deposit (£5000) demanded of the parties. They argue there should be no money involved and that any candidate with 250 supporters' names on a nomination sheet should be permitted to contest the elections without charge.

Tommy's clenched fist as he took the loyal oath is now a familiar image after all the publicity. We stand talking on the High Street as Tommy poses for pictures for *The Herald* and some passers-by wave to him, a few giving the clenched fist as they shout good wishes. He tries hard not to show how pleased he is with himself. I suspect we are seeing the birth of a folk hero. He has, after all, beaten the system, just like Dennis.

To Parliament for Donald Dewar's coronation as First Minister. Nothing seems to go quite to plan. Donald is elected easily enough because the Lib Dems choose to vote with Labour, an early sign that the talks about coalition, still dragging on, might not be in as deep trouble as some suspect. Indeed the word is that a deal is all but done. To Labour's embarrassment and the widespread delight of others, Dennis Canavan wreaks spectacular revenge for being rejected as a Labour candidate in the elections. He makes a speech in which he taunts Donald about asking the LibDems to buy a "pig in a poke" – looking directly at the First Minister-to-be as he speaks - reminding everyone how Donald described him as "not good enough" to be an MSP.

To Donald's consternation Dennis then strides across the floor of the debating chamber with hand outstretched saying he wants to shake hands because he bears no malice. It is splendid theatre but Sir David Steel in the chair is rather po-faced about it, warning Dennis that he will be punished in future if he crosses the floor in this manner again. For his part Donald is furious and although he puts on a brave smile he is obviously embarrassed, not least by the cheering and applause which greets Dennis's little trick.

Dennis is quick to point out that he is best suited to be First Minister because he is an Independent and the MSP with the largest majority. He launches into an attack on the "shabby deal cobbled up behind closed doors between the Labour Party and the Liberal Democrats." Scorning the mooted review of tuition fees, he complains: "We have just had a review - it was called an election. I am against this review and a so-called Lib-Lab pact because we don't know what is in it apart from a fudge," he says. This is the first moment of real political debate and it is good fun, but still rather stilted and genteel.

Naturally, the SNP Members are delighted with Dennis as he denounces Donald Dewar's "dead-of-night deals" and tells him to his face: "Above all, the First Minister of Scotland must be someone who will speak for Scotland, not someone who will act as Tony Blair's puppet."

When the vote to nominate Donald as First Minister is taken there is confusion. Winnie Ewing presses the wrong button and the whole affair has to be gone through again. Some unkind soul in the press gallery says she thinks she's at the bingo.

Eventually, the deed is done and Donald is First Minister of Scotland with 71 votes. Alex Salmond gets 35, exactly the

Nationalists' voting strength in the chamber, David McLetchie of the Tories has 17 votes and Dennis Canavan three – from himself plus Sheridan and Harper, his proposer and seconder. It is the first example of the arithmetic of coalition. Sir David, who is now non-partisan in the job of Presiding Officer, does not vote. Keith Raffan abstains and a Tory, Murray Tosh, is posted absent.

Ben Wallace of the Tories wins the dubious distinction of being the first MSP to be ticked off for raising a bogus point of order. He is cried down by LibDems when he accuses them of a "sell-out" on the tuition fees issue and is accused in turn by Sir David of allowing behaviour in the chamber to degenerate to the standards of "that place some of us are glad to leave."

Donald Dewar says his nomination is a great privilege and I suspect he is rather emotional behind that schoolmasterly expression. He has, all credit to him, spent years working for Home Rule although he never calls it that (too many Nationalist overtones). This is probably his greatest moment after the Referendum result of 1997 and even the Opposition MSPs seem genuinely pleased for him as a man, if not as a Labour luminary. Donald says the Parliament is no longer a political pamphlet, a campaign trail, or a waving flag. "It is real. It is here. We are a country with a past and that past has shaped us. But we must shape our future. That is our task."

Other leaders start the congratulations. Alex Salmond, now officially leader of the Opposition, promises Donald that the SNP will be formidable in their new role on issues such as tuition fees and the privatisation of public services. For the LibDems Jim Wallace wishes Donald every success. "I hope that together we will show that this is a Parliament that can make a difference for the people of Scotland." David McLetchie also wishes Donald well. It is all very friendly and even sincere. I wonder how long this can last before it is business and abuse as usual.

The LibDems are still closeted in never-ending discussion about Labour's offer of a coalition deal and the press are kept well away, gathered for hours on end in groups on the pavement outside Parliament HQ. Alison Hardie of the *Scotsman* and I decide to test the rules by sneaking off and taking an underpass below George IV Bridge from Parliament HQ. This leads to a building across the street where the LibDems are meeting to discuss Labour's conditions for joining a coalition. Until now this underpass has been forbidden territory for the media but as from today, we think, though we're not sure, we are now permitted to be there. Alison and I go exploring and when we surface at the other end we find ourselves outside a room from which we can discern the voice of Jim Wallace. He is trying to sell the so-called Partnership Agreement to his fellow MSPs. We turn off our mobile phones lest we are discovered and accused of eavesdropping. After a few minutes I lose my nerve. The price of being caught could be my accreditation and I would hate to give that imperious security guard the satisfaction of saying "told you so." We slink back to the media pack. There was a time when initiative like this would have been rewarded by an Editor with a pay rise and promotion. In the changing world of newspapers you are more liable to be fired if complaining party spin-doctors have their way.

A contact whispers to me that Jim Wallace has been offered the job of Deputy First Minister as part of the coalition package. I get confirmation from two other sources and, bingo, we have a good exclusive. Back in Glasgow I give a lift to Angus MacLeod of the *Express* from Queen Street station to the West End. By now it is first edition time and Angus asks what I have written, knowing it will be public knowledge within minutes when the paper hits the street. I reply that I have a good story about Wallace becoming Donald Dewar's number two. "No," says Angus confidently. "Henry McLeish would never stand for it." I suspect Angus might have a message to call his newsdesk when he gets home.

Back in Edinburgh Donald Gorrie gives Robbie a great quote. Labour, Gorrie says, "are the biggest bunch of liars you could ever meet." If this is how the LibDems regard their partners and friends in government, what do they think of their opponents?

May 14th

Some of us have doubts about the nomenclature used by the Parliament. First Minister seems rather like a title from pre-Berlin Wall East Germany. Presiding Officer sounds more suitable for a court martial. These terms are laid down by New Labour which is terrified of the Parliament getting ideas above its station. Titles like premier or Prime Minister or Speaker or President are deemed to smack of independence or Nationalism and are to be resisted at any price. This is hardly surprising from the party which talks about devolution because it can't bear to utter the words Home Rule.

Now the Tories and SNP with a little encouragement from Robbie and me have taken up the title issue about which we first wrote last year. Gerry O'Brien, spin-doctor to the Tories, is delighted to put McLetchie's name to calls for the title First Minister to be changed to Premier. We know that Tony Blair is reluctant to see another Prime Minister in Britain. (What would he have done in the days when Northern Ireland had its own Prime Minister?) McLetchie says the Presiding Officer should be known as Speaker. This is too much like Westminster for the Nats who want him (or her) known as President, which I think is better and more in keeping with a modern Parliament.

Much bickering continues among the LibDem MSPs about their proposed coalition deal with Labour and McLetchie wants to add to their troubles. He tells us that from now on the Tories will be boycotting television and radio debates on Scottish devolved affairs where both Labour and the LibDems were represented. "They are one party now," McLetchie says. "Why should they be entitled to double representation in the media?" Good point.

Alex Salmond tells me he wants the Scottish Parliament to debate the war in Yugoslavia despite the fact it has no responsibility for foreign affairs. News has just come through that Nato is suspected of slaughtering as many as 100 innocent civilians by dropping cluster bombs on them in Kosovo. Salmond claims majority Scottish opinion now has "serious misgivings" about the conduct of the war by Nato. Plainly, he is still irked by the hostile reaction to his "unpardonable folly" speech, especially now that events seem to be proving he might well have been correct.

Still unrepentant, he complains that this latest tragedy is just the latest consequence of Nato policy. He predicts that because of the way Nato is conducting the campaign there will continue to be serious and tragic mistakes. He sees them as inevitable and argues that Nato cannot conduct an air campaign without causing serious collateral damage. This, he believes, has become clear with the bombing of trains, buses, television stations and the Chinese embassy in Belgrade and now, it appears, villages in Kosovo.

All of this makes a good exclusive for *The Herald*. Whether he is right about Scottish opinion remains to be seen but mistakes by Nato on this scale can hardly be doing the government's case much good. How the SNP must wish the war had never happened – or at least had begun to go wrong for Tony Blair and George Robertson much earlier in the Scottish election campaign.

May 17th

Donald Dewar goes to see the Queen at Holyrood Palace. In a sign of the devolutionary times Her Majesty comes to Edinburgh instead of Donald going to London. The Queen and the new First Minister Designate, as he is announced, are televised chatting before Donald goes to Parliament House which was home to the independent Scottish legislature until 1707 and is now the headquarters of the legal establishment. There, Donald is sworn in by the Lord President of the Court of Session, Lord Rodger. Poor Donald has to do quite a long of swearing these days. He must swear allegiance to the Crown – not a problem for a good Unionist like our Donald – and then take an oath of office, and for good measure he must also take an oath as Keeper of the Scottish Seal which was until today known as the Great Seal of Scotland. We are told this artefact is the earliest seal of the Scottish kings and was first used by Duncan II in 1094. All documents from the kings were despatched bearing the Seal. History hangs heavy, even in the brand new Scotland.

David Whitton has been busy spinning for Donald who has had all the time in the world to choose his Cabinet but decides to delay his formal announcement until the evening news goes out on live television. In the best traditions of 10 Downing Street he summons his preferred few one by one to Bute House in Edinburgh, his official residence, where they wave to photographers on the steps as the door opens magically for them at their moment of arrival. The Scottish Office advises journalists to be there early and that we might have to hang around for three hours before the Cabinet is announced and paraded on the pavement. No questions will be taken, we are advised.

This is too much. They now want us to behave like extras in a television production. Donald's people appear to want journalists there just for the purpose of shouting questions across the street, thus lending some atmosphere to the occasion. We decide to boycott the whole scheme. Robbie pops along late just to pick up the official list of ministers when it is handed out and I watch the news on television in our new and rather commodious office in Lawnmarket.

No real surprises. Sam Galbraith is not given health despite his earlier jobs as a neuro-surgeon and Scottish Office health minister. Instead he is given schools. Jack McConnell becomes minister of finance, a sort of Scottish equivalent to the Chief Secretary to the Treasury, which means he will be in charge of checking just how the money from the block grant is spent. No doubt he will busy himself quickly with an accurate costing of tuition fees. The problem of fees themselves comes with the further education portfolio which goes to Henry McLeish, still reportedly smarting over his expected role as Donald's deputy going to Jim Wallace. Wallace in turn is confirmed as Donald's number two – news which brings me some relief at getting my prediction right – and is put in charge of home affairs which gives the lie to stories over the weekend that he will be a mere figurehead.

But the big surprise is the failure of Helen Liddell to become Secretary of State for Scotland. That job goes instead to John Reid, formerly transport minister, who is reputedly neither a Blairite nor a Brownie. It seems Helen's conversion to Blairism has not played well in Scotland and now the Prime Minister has sent her to transport where she will be another Blair loyalist keeping an eye on John Prescott. The deputy Prime Minister is said to be "livid" at her arrival. Helen Liddell's fate is also a sign that Blair is not turning Scots away from English ministries as was expected. Helen, a Scot, will now have control of transport in England but not much say north of the Border where most transport policy is devolved.

Some grumpy LibDem MSPs are still talking about voting down tuition fees even as Jim Wallace is posing with the Cabinet for the official group picture. As of today it seems the fees issue could still bring down the coalition. But cynicism is becoming widespread. Some journalists believe that with their promised independent inquiry into fees, Dewar and Wallace have bought sufficient time to overcome hostility to the Partnership Agreement in general and tuition fees in particular. There is some force to this view. I don't believe the coalition itself is the cause of anger so much as the fact that the LibDems simply abandoned their promise that fees would be non-negotiable. Now they have several months to calm the indignation of their supporters while working on a powerful case to put before the committee of inquiry. If it is not stuffed with Labour cronies and can find a way out of this impasse all will be clear for a coalition lasting the full four years. If not, then it is difficult to see both fees and the coalition surviving into the winter.

It is late when Robbie and I finishing filing. We head for the Lawnmarket exit where a new swipe-card security system is in operation – except that it isn't operating as it should. We are unable to make it through locked doors to the Parliament HQ exit and are trapped in the media centre. In desperation I use my mobile phone to call the security desk and explain our predicament. This is met with guffaws by the security staff who eventually turn up to release us. While waiting to be rescued I recall a conversation with an official who visited our office on Day One and asked us if we were familiar with the fire escape. "Are you saying this place is a fire hazard?" I inquired. "Not really," was the answer. "You could say it is an officially approved fire hazard." I think I know what he meant. Tomorrow I really will check the fire escape.

May 19th
To lunch with Robbie and some others of the media pack from the Parliament. We head for the Grassmarket, much gentrified since the last time I saw it, where the restaurants have their tables and parasols on the pavements in warm sunshine. We have a most enjoyable al fresco meal with excessive supplies of white wine, a pleasant reminder of my days in Brussels and Strasbourg reporting the European Parliament. Edinburgh is much prettier than most Continental cities although the sun is less dependable. In a curious way I see Scotland growing up. This is the way the press in real democracies likes to live, after all. It is all rather heartwarming. On the way back to the office Robbie is so inspired by this experience that he buys a huge Saltire for £7 on the pretext that our new office needs a curtain to reduce glare on his laptop screen. That's just what we need: a Saltire hanging from *The Herald* office in the Scottish Parliament. It would only serve to encourage Donald Dewar's worst suspicions.

Fiona Ross of Scottish Television who has superb Labour contacts is running a good exclusive to the effect that Alex Rowley has been fired as general secretary of the Scottish Labour Party. She reports that Rowley, a disciple of Gordon Brown, was summoned to Millbank in London overnight and told to "resign." There is hell to pay, we hear, inside the Scottish Labour Party where Rowley has been sidelined by John Rafferty, an old friend of Donald Dewar, since before the election. Rafferty is now tipped to become Donald's chief of staff. This sort of thing is meat and drink to the SNP which is busy banging on about London Labour control freaks creating havoc in Scotland. Sometimes Labour really is its own worst enemy. But the election is over and public reaction no longer matters. Rowley's fate has been awaited for long enough. The story I ran earlier this year that he had resigned in frustration but had been persuaded to change his mind seems to have been well founded despite all the denials at the time. He was known to be very unhappy with the direction of events.

I hear there have been questions raised about Rowley's personal life and criticisms of his professional abilities as an organiser and even snide comments about his strong Fife accent. Much of this seems quite unfair but it is typical of New Labour's whispering techniques. The truth is that Gordon Brown was probably too heavy handed in pushing Rowley into the job. At least that seems to be the view of some of Gordon's enemies in London. Even Donald is reported to be angry at the decision, especially at the way it was handled. The race will now be on to get Rowley to tell his story to one of the papers. Fat chance. He will go quietly on agreed terms. They all do.

Rowley's downfall follows the surprising choice of Alex Mosson as Lord Provost of Glasgow. This involves another classic example of New Labour character assassination. Mosson is very Old Labour and he is no angel, but on the morning of his election he is suddenly exposed by the *Daily Record* as having convictions for housebreaking and assault.

The background is that Mosson is a recovering alcoholic who has not had a drink for more than 20 years. His troubles with the courts were caused by his youthful drinking and he has led a blameless life since becoming teetotal. Even those who are his political rivals are disgusted at this type of smear tactic. His own children knew nothing about this aspect of his background until it appeared in the *Record*. But to general approval the contest for the Provostship was won by Mosson comfortably. It seems that others in the Labour group were also so angry at his private history being leaked that a considerable number of them voted for him out of sympathy. If his enemies who leaked this story had left well alone he might have lost anyway.

May 20th

The new Scottish Cabinet holds its inaugural meeting in the drawing room of Bute House, Edinburgh. When David Whitton briefs the Parliamentary correspondents soon afterwards he lets it be known that John Rafferty, who ran Labour's ruthless but successful election campaign from Delta House in Glasgow, had sat through the entire proceedings. We quickly assume Rafferty must be running Donald's private office as has been predicted for a couple of weeks. But Whitton seems reluctant to say so.

After some humming and hawing about this odd event – an unelected party bureaucrat attending the first Scottish Cabinet meeting and no reason given beyond the fact that the famously low-profile Rafferty is now a "special adviser to the First Minister" – the journalists spill out on the street. And, lo, who is spotted on the pavement but the said Mr Rafferty who is promptly mobbed. With a look of horror on his face he rushes off across the street, refusing to say a word beyond referring us to David Whitton.

Four hours later David sends out a message to the effect that John Rafferty has been appointed as chief of staff of the First Minister's office and is no longer merely on unpaid leave from his old post as head of the Lotteries Board in Scotland. The question now arises: why was his appointment kept quiet? It seems the explanation is innocent and that the paperwork had simply not kept pace with recent fast-moving events. This little episode does not inspire faith in the promised new transparent and open government of Scotland but at least it shows that Donald Dewar and his senior staff can be pushed by a grumbling press into being more communicative. A useful precedent seems to have been set.

Alex Rowley, now gone from Labour, tells me that he had plans to modernise the party in Scotland and suggests obliquely that this could have been the reason for his sudden departure. In an interview for *The Herald* he is careful not to go into details with me because he has indeed reached some type of agreement not to go public. He probably stands to lose money if he breaks his word. But the import of his comments is clear: he found himself with no future because his face no longer fitted and London seemed to want to keep control of the party in Scotland. This is hugely sensitive and exactly the kind of thing Labour hates being discussed in the media because, of course, the party is so vulnerable to Nationalist accusations of being in thrall to London. Labour cannot credibly campaign for political autonomy from London rule while slavishly following the party line as laid down by Millbank. The story being put about by Labour itself is that Rowley was simply not up to the job and should never have been given it at the insistence of his mentor, Gordon Brown. Most journalists suspect there is force to Rowley's argument – but also to the party's.

May 21st
Lord (Gus) Macdonald is guest of honour at the Bank of Scotland press awards in Edinburgh. He makes a witty speech but one which is essentially New Labour's defence of the press in the Scottish elections. It also serves as a reminder that Labour is now very firmly installed as the Establishment in Scotland – and no mistake. There's not much chance of a dissenting voice at events like this nowadays.

Gus argues that the *Record* was never as hard on Salmond as the *Sun* was on Kinnock in the 1992 General Election. So that must make everything all right, then. He lists some SNP politicians who have columns in various newspapers including Dorothy-Grace Elder (who was sacked by *Scotland on Sunday* because her column was partisan and who was only reinstated after an internal editorial department row). It's true that Jim Sillars, Margo MacDonald and Roseanna Cunningham have columns in the tabloids but this hardly constitutes balance when you consider that the Scottish press generally is bulging with columns from Tory and Labour champions such as Brian Meek,

Gerald Warner, Michael Fry, Ruth Wishart and many more. Gus also manages to ignore completely the comparison in the *Record* between Salmond and Milosevic and he dismisses the Connery smear as a joke.

It was amusing to watch New Labour ministers, including industry minister Brian Wilson, forcing themselves to applaud Fidelma Cook as she picked up her gong for exposing Donald Dewar's cancellation of Sean Connery's knighthood. It was Brian who was widely credited with arranging the black propaganda against Connery and the accusation that the star once supported the idea of smacking a misbehaving woman.

Someone has decided it is a good idea to give a "lifetime achievement" award to Brian Thomson ("Mr Brian" of D C Thomson of Dundee, publishers of several newspapers including the *Sunday Post*, and, of course, the *Beano* and *Dandy*) who is now a frail old man. There was a time when he was a hated figure among British journalists because of his family's anti-trade union history. But here we all applaud him politely, particularly the younger set who do not remember the bad old days when membership of the NUJ had to be kept a secret in the Thomson empire. Nowadays anti-union attitudes are almost the norm, especially with proprietors like Rupert Murdoch who pioneered union-bashing at Wapping in the 1980s. The irony of this occasion is not lost on Mr Brian who reminds us that he once worked for the *Red Letter Weekly* (not to mention the *Beano*). Brian Wilson, once one of Brian Thomson's most vociferous critics, joins in the applause, just like the rest of us, as Mr Brian totters back to his seat. So do I. We are all getting older.

May 24th
Labour's launch of its European election campaign goes smoothly, not least because Donald Dewar and the new Scottish Secretary, John Reid, address the massed ranks of the party's MPs, MSPs and Euro-MPs plus assorted apparatchiks while the media are kept at the back of the room and not permitted to ask questions. Very New Labour

but effective, as usual. John Reid makes an amusing speech in which he recalls Tony Blair's advice when appointing him as transport minister. Blair suggested transport was a tough portfolio and that no-one had ever been successful in it apart from Mussolini. "But I don't think Mussolini is a good role model for New Labour – yet," Reid says, deadpan.

Reporters are eventually invited to a side room with Donald and John Reid who, we are advised, will take questions. We want to know why Labour has no Scottish manifesto, an omission which seems a gift to the other parties all of whom are anxious to keep beating Donald with accusations that he is being operated by remote control from Millbank. Donald offers no plausible explanation apart from pointing out that Labour at a UK level has signed up for the European Parliament socialist group campaign document (which is vague and non-committal). There is no British manifesto either, he points out. Donald praises the excellent work of Labour Euro-MPs from Scotland and appears mildly irritated when I ask him why, in that case, Labour has effectively deselected so many of them – Alex Smith and Hugh McMahon being prime examples. The truth is, of course, that the Blairites are using the closed list system for this election as a means of purging the party of left-wingers and other off-message MEPs. Donald deftly flannels his way out of this one by talking of democratic selection procedures, etc.

I manage a few private minutes with Donald and take my first chance in weeks to ask him if he really did say, as *The Observer* claimed before the Holyrood election, that *The Herald* was "out and out Nationalist." He looks fretful and denies ever saying any such thing. I ask if he believes it, regardless of whether he said it or not, and he tells me that all politicians in the heat of election campaigns sometimes see "tinges" of Nationalism in some Scottish newspapers. I suspect that is as close to the truth as we will ever get.

Donald seems to be directing his anger at other newspapers these days and appears to have agreed a sort of peace with *The Herald*. He is back to being his old courteous self. Now his resentments are aimed at the Sundays because of their coverage of John Rafferty who has been portrayed as some sort of unelected and meddling Svengali. Donald says he has known Rafferty for 20 years and trusts him completely as a close personal friend. He is shocked that Rafferty should be portrayed as some sort of Blairite spy whose job is to keep the Scottish Labour Party accountable to London.

Donald is so annoyed that I believe him. For once, New Labour's presentational skills have been found wanting and suspicions about Rafferty and his role have been allowed to grow unchecked. Alf Young suggests the way for Rafferty to clear the air is to tell the whole story of his appointment and ambitions by giving *The Herald* an exclusive interview. Alf, who is also an old associate of Rafferty from their days long ago in the Labour Party, offers to conduct the interview himself. When I put this idea to David Whitton the answer is a categorical No. Whitton cites as one of his reasons the fact that Rafferty is now bound by the civil service code but the unspoken truth, I suspect, is that Rafferty is hypersensitive to publicity of any kind. He hates it, witness his ridiculous anxiety to run away when approached in the street last week.

Some amusement is caused by David Steel's rather pompous edicts to MSPs. In his role as Presiding Officer he wants procedures which would disbar MSPs from singing or drinking alcohol in the chamber of the Parliament. There must be no bad language or threatening of other Members. What a shame. Steel is emerging as a party pooper, par excellence.

May 28th

The week ends with a series of good going rows. Labour is considering making the Parliament withhold funding for Opposition MSPs, most of whom were elected via the party lists. Party strategists believe – correctly, no doubt - that their rivals would simply use the money to set up offices dedicated to challenging Labour in its 53 constituency seats. Naturally, there is hell to pay with the SNP which has 28 of its

35 MSPs elected as so-called "top-up" or list Members, and the Tories, all of whose 18 MSPs were elected via the lists. If Labour's idea is followed through it will certainly create a second class type of MSP which is exactly what Donald Dewar said he would not do.

To make matters worse Labour is also proposing a cut of more than 50% in the so-called "Short" money made available to Opposition MSPs to assist them in their routine work. This money is supposed to be paid under rules decided at Westminster and dreamed up years ago by Ted Short when he was Leader of the House. The SNP had calculated this might be worth up to £400,000 and is now likely to be less than half of that. Naturally, the Nationalists and Tories are up in arms and making fresh allegations of control freakery – and it is not difficult to sympathise. It does seem wrong that this money is perceived as indispensable in London but something to be tossed aside for the Opposition in Edinburgh, another argument which adds force to those who believe Labour is determined to run the Scottish Parliament as a mere adjunct of Westminster. Margo MacDonald says she will be seeking a judicial review in the Court of Session if Labour does not see reason.

I cross swords with Donald Gorrie of the LibDems on Lesley Riddoch's programme on Radio Scotland. When Lesley asks me for my views on the funding row I venture the opinion that the Labour plan smacks of a stitch-up, especially now that the LibDems are also getting their Short money despite being part of a coalition government. I tell Lesley's discussion panel that the LibDems are having it both ways by receiving ministerial salaries and the perks of office while pulling in Short money as the Opposition. "It must be great being a Liberal in Edinburgh these days," I remark. Donald Gorrie slaps me down. "No, it is not," he barks but does not get a chance to say why. He sounds fearfully annoyed. I think Donald Gorrie, who is not a supporter of the coalition and who would prefer Parliament to run the government rather than the other way round, is still determined to bring down the whole Partnership Agreement, given half a chance.

He really does believe in the supremacy of Parliament over its executive and I would not give him an argument on that score.

On a lighter note news breaks that the LibDems are being accused of control freakery of a different kind. They have been called many things since joining the coalition from Judases to traitors but never have they been charged with control freakery which is the bane of New Labour these days.

It seems that Jim Wallace is irritated by the presence behind him in the chamber of the three musketeers, as Dennis Canavan, Robin Harper and Tommy Sheridan have become known. Jim cannot communicate with his own group on the floor of the chamber because each time he looks round he finds these three in the way, we are informed. Most people suspect the truth is that the LibDems are upset by the fact that the three minority MSPs occupy centre stage in the chamber and have been lucky to catch more than their fair share of attention by the television cameras.

This is a wonderful farce in the making. Tommy threatens to organise an occupation, reminding me that he has plenty of practice in that art. "This would be the most comfortable seat I have ever had for a sit-in," he happily points out, suggesting that Jim Wallace should be the one who moves to a seat beside Donald Dewar. "You would expect the puppet to be near the puppet master," Tommy observes.

Dennis is also enjoying himself accusing Labour of encouraging the LibDems to have him moved. "Every time Donald Dewar looks up he sees me sitting there," says Dennis. "It makes him uncomfortable." Dennis also thinks Jim Wallace wants to follow the House of Commons practice of "doughnutting" whereby MPs act like cheerleaders by gathering behind a front bencher and vigorously nodding their agreement as they hang on his every word.

Harper, Canavan and Sheridan are united. They will not be moving. Harper says he will only consider doing so if he can be convinced that he is breaking rules. But there are no rules. Everyone outside the LibDem group agrees that the seating arrangements were not temporary, as claimed by the LibDem business manager, Iain Smith, and were agreed shortly after the Parliament's first session. Smith has sought the help of Sir David Steel but even he seems unable to broker agreement. There is stalemate. We now await moves to force them out of their seats and into new places which are less prominent. Some fun is in prospect.

To the official opening of the Irish consulate in Edinburgh where Dan Mulhall, the new consul general, is playing host to David Andrews, Ireland's foreign minister. Dan is in good form and we reminisce about our times in Brussels when I was European Editor of *The Herald* and he was press spokesman for the Irish Permanent Representation. Euro-nomenclature was amusing in those days. The UK Permanent Representation was known as UKrep, the Irish were referred to (by the Irish press, I should add) as MICKrep. When Robin Cook announced the setting up of a Scottish Permanent Representation it was, inevitably, known as JOCKrep. New Labour has since taken fright at the language. Scottish Permanent Representation is evidently seen as too suggestive of Scottish independence in Europe and so we shall have a prosaically named Scotland House in Brussels.

Margo MacDonald is at the party and tells me she is deadly serious about fighting Labour's funding decisions in the courts. Mike Russell, not her greatest fan, confirms that she will have party support. David McLetchie reminds me that William Hague has just received £500,000 to assist his work as Leader of the Opposition in London and complains that none of it has come north of the Border.

Joyce MacMillan expresses her disapproval of the fighting among politicians in the Scottish Parliament. She is a long-serving supporter of Home Rule and is angry that the much debated politics of consensus has broken down so soon. She is not alone. The papers are full of the same complaint. But I am enjoying it all. What are Parliaments for if not for political battle?

June 4th

They buried Kenny McIntyre today. For many years Kenny, a
latecomer to journalism, was the voice of the BBC in Scotland, not a
posh voice but a distinctively Scottish one. As a workaholic Kenny
had been told many times to slow down but at the age of 54 he was
still playing football and running and working non-stop. He died, to
the intense shock of his colleagues, after a morning run. My last
sight of him, I recall now, was a few days ago at a briefing on
procedures MSPs should follow during Scottish questions. Kenny
arrived late, as usual, and got into a terrible fankle with his recording
equipment, which was also par for his course. I noticed he was looking
pale but thought no more of it.

Everyone has a Kenny McIntyre story. My favourite was his
performance on the day Thatcher resigned. That was during a by-
election campaign in Paisley. We had gathered to listen to Iain Lawson
of the SNP at a routine party press conference when the word arrived
via the *Sun* man's mobile phone (only the *Sun* had such gizmos in
those days) that Thatcher had announced she was standing down.
We all rushed from the room leaving poor Lawson wondering if it
was something he'd said. Kenny and I drove to the Tory campaign
rooms where the hapless candidate (whose name I now forget) was
pounced on by Kenny, with tape recorder running, in a car park.

"What's your reaction?" Kenny demanded to know.
"To what?" the candidate replied.
"Thatcher has resigned," said Kenny.
"Has she?" said the candidate, adding nervously: "I think I had
better be briefed first…"

To which Kenny shouted: "This is no time for fucking niceties."
At which point he had to stop and rewind the tape.

Kenny hated being refused interviews. When John Major was
Prime Minister he was buttonholed by Kenny but refused to speak.
Major simply would not respond to repeated questions from an

increasingly frustrated Kenny. Eventually Kenny accepted defeat and
asked Major where he was going after leaving Glasgow. Major said
he was going to watch England playing cricket. "In that case I hope
your fucking team gets beat," said Kenny. Major roared with laughter

Everyone loved Kenny for his mischief and admired him for his
skills and journalistic tenacity. It was appropriate that he went to his
grave with his mobile phone and football socks. For BBC Scotland
his loss is a crisis because he was such a pivotal figure, especially
during important political times as these. The talk now is that he will
be replaced by a team, which says it all.

6

The Shape of Things to Come

8th June - 1st July

June 8th

Back to work after a week's break to find that the LibDems have brokered a compromise deal between Labour and the Opposition parties on MSPs' allowances. In effect the deal is a defeat for Labour whose miserable offer would have cost the SNP about £500,000. With the Parliament throwing out the Labour plan and adopting the LibDem proposals the Nats now lose only about £140,000 and the Tories a proportionate amount.

Knowing defeat is looming Labour decides to put up only backbenchers to argue the party's case. It does not want ministers to be seen losing votes this early on. What a mistake. The speeches are dire, especially the opener by Karen Whitefield who drones on with unswerving irrelevance about life and death in Airdrie and Shotts. She is warned repeatedly by the Presiding Officer to come to the point. None of the Labour speakers agrees to give way. The whole exercise is a depressing example of the standard of debate we might now expect. If this is the quality produced by the notorious Labour selection process which was supposed to spot only the brightest talent, then something is very wrong. The papers today are full of mickey-taking pieces, some of them quite savage. They will have their effect. Politicians don't mind being attacked for their policies and prejudices but they hate being laughed at.

June 9th

Sir David Steel is displeased, again, with the press. This time he is annoyed at us for pointing out that the first major act of MSPs is to vote themselves huge allowances. He has a point. You can't have a Parliament without paying for it and some of the coverage has been over the top. He is also annoyed at leaks about the spiralling cost of

Holyrood and stories (denied) that a series of cost-cutting measures has been approved.

Sir David summons us to explain that he has cancelled new contracts for the next 10 days but he admits that the cost for the project has gone up at the latest estimate from £90m to £109m. Donald Dewar lends his support to the Holyrood project and makes clear he has no intention of staying at the top end of the Royal Mile. He is also annoyed with the "public prints" (only Donald would use that phrase nowadays when he means newspapers).

Afterwards I ask Donald why he famously condemned Calton Hill – the most popular choice at one time for the site of the Parliament – as a "Nationalist shibboleth" and to my surprise he denies ever using the words. He ascribes them to "someone else entirely,"although he does not say who. Donald looks uncomfortable and stays silent when Alan Cochrane of the *Daily Telegraph* announces confidently that it was Brian Wilson. It does not really matter now who said it. The fact remains that Calton Hill will for ever be known as a Nationalist shibboleth – like it or not. Donald promises a free vote on the future of the Holyrood building project. My guess is that MSPs will take the chance to sound off about abandoning Calton Hill and the lack of consultation over its cancellation but in the end they will vote for Holyrood. Donald is probably wise to give them a chance to let off steam before they back down.

June 10th

European Election Day, but you would never know it. At my polling station in Milngavie there is no-one handing out party leaflets. It is quite amazing, not to say mildy worrying, how the Euro-elections have come and gone with no-one paying the slightest attention, save for a few journalists and the usual chattering classes. I know Scotland is suffering from election fatigue but this is ridiculous. None of the parties has seemed much interested. I suspect a conspiracy. The Tories hate the idea of drawing attention to Europe because of the damage it does to them at every turn, and have been almost silent. Labour is too terrified of the single currency to mention it and was determined to have a low-profile campaign. The SNP has been trying to stir up interest but doesn't have the clout of command attention on its own.

June 14th

A prize for brass neck must go to David Martin who survives as Labour's leading light from Scotland in the European Parliament. Where Labour until last week had six MEPs from Scotland it now has three. "This was a great victory for Labour," David proclaims from the Mercat Cross in Edinburgh after the declaration and he does so with a straight face. Even the passing tourists smiled.

My old school contemporary, Neil MacCormick of the SNP, at last finds himself a place in the European Parliament. Neil is a remarkable man who at the age of 58 is launching himself on a new career. At school he was always top of the class or near it, as I recall, while I was usually near the bottom. His father was "King" John MacCormick, a founder of the SNP, a gentle and courteous man who obviously imbued Neil and his older brother, Iain, with a sense of Scottish patriotism. I don't think Neil is much of a Nationalist, just a patriot. When he left school he went on to become president of the Oxford Union and later regius professor of jurisprudence at Edinburgh University. I went to count milk bottles for Stott's Dairies.

Neil's trouble is that being so bright he reached the top of his profession when he was still in his early thirties. He has been looking for some excitement ever since and now he has it. I envy him his new life in Strasbourg and Brussels where his skills as a constitutional lawyer of international standing will serve him and the SNP well. They will also worry Labour when the talk turns to the old argument about whether an independent. Scotland would have to renegotiate entry to the EU. Neil can advance a powerful case against that eventuality and there can be few people in the world more qualified to voice an opinion. I wish him well and am delighted to bequeath to him the name of my hotel in Strasbourg, a town where beds are like gold dust during Parliament week, and where I established a permanent and happy billet during my times there as European Editor. Fond memories.

The Nats have two MEPs, just being pipped for a third by the Liberal Democrats who scrape in with one despite their unpopularity over tuition fees and their troubled links with Labour in the Scottish Parliament. Most surprisingly, the Tories also take two seats and steal the show on the High Street with popping champagne corks and some studied backslapping for the cameras. Some of us remember vividly the days when they ran Scotland and enjoyed a majority from Scotland in the European Parliament. Nowadays they consider having two MEPs as a cause for jubilation. Their top-of-the-list winner is Struan Stevenson whom I used to meet frequently in Brussels in his role as a lobbyist. Until today Struan was best known for failing to win Dumfries in the General Election. The seat was his inheritance from Sir Hector Monro who reigned there for almost a quarter of a century and made the place a rock solid Tory stronghold. I can still hardly believe that my home town and county now has a Labour majority of 10,000. Struan once asked me in Brussels if I thought he would win Dumfries and I said I doubted it. He was not too pleased. The fact is he did himself no favours by blatantly ditching his long-proclaimed support for devolution in order to win the Dumfries nomination. Now he has also turned against the single currency. He will probably live to regret that, too, but at least his conscience will be soothed by the knowledge that he is en route to the good life in the opulence of the European Parliament.

David McLetchie is all smiles, boasting to me that the Scottish Tories have not the slightest difference in policy over Europe with William Hague. Oh, dear. This Tory anti-Europeanism continues to tear at the heart of the party and its support. Nothing is going to stop Europe continuing the torture of the Conservatives until the moment Britain votes to join the single currency and the matter is settled once and for all. In their hearts most Tories must yearn for the day. Only when the battle is finally lost will the party be able to regroup and revive itself as a fighting force.

June 15th

Pity the poor spin-doctor. David Whitton, who speaks for Donald Dewar, suffers at the hands of the Holyrood media pack whom he summons for the now routine Tuesday post-Cabinet briefing. Our worst fears about openness, or lack of it, in the Scottish government are confirmed as he quickly makes it obvious that the brave new world of transparency promised by the Scottish Parliament is in some trouble. David briefs us that Donald Dewar has just chaired a "hard-working" session with much discussion about his legislative statement to be delivered tomorrow.

It will cover an expected eight Bills in the coming year but no details are forthcoming from David. His explanation, delivered with some ill-concealed embarrassment, is that the First Minister must show courtesy to the Parliament by informing it first.

And that is about it. We are given no further hint of what Donald Dewar will be announcing and so the hacks decide, naturally, to shoot the messenger. Paul Gilbride of the *Daily Express* enjoys some sport by asking David: "Can you tell us about freedom of information – or is that a secret, too?"

David is decent enough to acknowledge the silliness of this so-called briefing session but is strapped by ministerial rules which appear to be out hopelessly of kilter with all the heady talk about transparency. He says rather huffily: "If you don't want these meetings we won't have them. Nothing says I have to come here and give you a story every day." He offers a final reminder that it is in the nature of governments to work behind the scenes and to say nothing until it suits them. Even going off the record – a bad old habit which some of the tabloid reporters encourage and wish to import from Westminster to Holyrood as a strict rule – fails to break the impasse.

I decide to write a little colour piece on this ridiculous state of affairs. My worry is that I might have been a touch hard on Whitton. But he's an old tabloid man himself and knows he is in a rough old trade.

June 16th

The three minority MSPs, Tommy Sheridan, Dennis Canavan and Robin Harper, complain to me bitterly that they are being denied the places they want on the Parliament's new committees. This sounds like another good Labour control-freak story. Tommy offers some useful quotes about New Labour practising exclusion when preaching the new inclusion, and Dennis, with his usual sense of mischief, attacks the Parliament's new cross-party business bureau – the sole provider of committee places – as a "politburo" and complains about Labour bullying.

Unfortunately for me, Chris Deerin of the *Daily Record* appears at my elbow just as the unhappy trio emerge from seeing the Presiding Officer and begin spilling the beans to me exclusively outside Sir David's room. They have been pleading their case before him and report that he is full of sympathy but unable to help. At the end of my interview with the three of them I am taken aside very politely by Andrew Slorance, the civil servant now in charge of media relations at the Scottish Parliament, who warns me that I must not stray into forbidden territory such as the waiting room of the Presiding Officer. Such places in the Parliament buildings are strictly out of bounds to the media. I apologise and ask Andrew if he would care to put his admonition in writing. I would like to frame it as a souvenir. Robbie holds out his hand in congratulations for my achievement in being the first journalist to be reprimanded for showing determination in pursuing a good story.

Back at the office I write some of their protests into a story by Robbie about Donald's rather dull legislative programme. The comments by Canavan and Sheridan add spice to the copy which will now be the splash. Robbie and I are just on deadline when it occurs to me that we have not asked David Whitton for his comments. We conclude that Whitton would merely brief against us and we would thereby lose our exclusive. Also, it is late and I want back to Glasgow. This emerging row makes a grand tale. There is no seat on the environment committee for Harper, the first Green parliamentarian in Britain, which is a scandal in itself, while Dennis has been knocked back in his quest for a seat on the education committee. Tommy has been refused a seat on the housing committee, which was his first choice. Dennis tells me the three were given only five minutes' notice of their exclusion before being allowed to appeal to Sir David.

They tell me they will put down emergency amendments tomorrow so that the whole house can vote on the issue. I quote Dennis complaining: "We are seeing an attempt by the governing coalition to exclude minorities. It is completely unacceptable. Decisions are being taken behind closed doors and things are being carved up in the interests of the governing parties without reference to the Scottish Parliament as a whole."

June 17th

Just as the morning debate on the troubled Holyrood project concludes, David Whitton charges into the media benches, like the bad guy in a cowboy film crashing through the saloon door looking for someone to kill. He is after me. I begin to think up a way to explain to him that my piece about his uninformative briefing was just a bit of fun and he should not take it seriously or be offended. But he's not worried about that, it seems. Far from it. In a loud voice he lets me know he has taken grave exception to our story about the three minority MSPs which appears under the headline: *Labour in bullying charge – control freaks row hits Holyrood*

I consider it rather a good headline but apparently Donald Dewar is apoplectic. Whitton's voice rises by the minute as he insists that none of it is true and that we have been sold a pup by Dennis and Tommy. My heart sinks when David tells me I am expected to explain myself to Labour's business manager, Tom McCabe, who is also said to be in a mood for murdering us. I am marched to the presence of McCabe who goes through the same story as David. I tell McCabe that I will hold up my hands, apologise and set the record straight if, as seems certain, I have blundered. I begin to regret not telephoning David Whitton on the night.

Robbie and I go for lunch to discuss how to handle this apparently sudden end to our working relationship with Whitton and our troubled dealings with his boss who has already paid one visit to the Editor to complain we are unfair to New Labour. David rubs it in a bit when he says Donald is going to complain personally to Harry – again. The First Minister's side of the story is that Labour could not make contact with Dennis to offer him a place on a committee because he could not be found at the end of a telephone. Tommy, says Whitton, was contacted several times through Hugh Kerr, the Scottish Socialist Party's Euro-candidate.

I call Dennis in his office, wondering how with one simple telephone call I can find this elusive politician when the full might of the Scottish government cannot make contact with him, despite the fact that McCabe sits a few feet away from him in the debating chamber. Dennis says there is nothing wrong with *The Herald* story and that he still has no committee place on offer, despite what Whitton says. Tommy's response is similar. Could we be right after all?

In the chamber McCabe introduces the vote on the amendments at 5pm and begins his speech with a strong attack on *The Herald*, talking of his "sense of outrage" and claiming our report is a distortion of Labour's genuine efforts to accommodate the minority Members. There is much chortling from my colleagues on the press benches, especially from Peter McMahon of the *Scotsman*. I hope he had a rocket for missing the story – because it is beginning to look as though we were right all along. I suspect Donald is primarily angered by the fact his parade was rained on by the papers generally this morning because of his unadventurous legislative programme. The committee nominations are produced for approval and, lo, the names of Harper, Canavan and Sheridan are indeed missing.

The chamber votes to give Harper his prized place on the environment committee but Tommy and Dennis are left out in the cold, apparently offered seats on committees they do not much want. The row then spills over into the black and white corridor – so-called after its marble tiles – outside the debating chamber where they convene an impromptu press conference. Farther down the corridor Dewar and Whitton are surrounded by civil servants and are trying to organise a rival briefing.

Tommy and Dennis continue to complain vociferously that they have been offered no seats, despite McCabe's comments. I report this to David Whitton who says Tommy is lying. Now things are getting heated. Donald glowers at me and I try to explain to our First Minister that I don't make up quotes for MSPs and that Canavan and Sheridan are quite unrepentant and still complaining about their rejection which is now an established fact.

Donald's anger moves to a new plateau in my experience (which is becoming considerable these days). He almost spits his contempt for Sheridan. "The man is a brazen liar," hisses Donald, not even bothering to suggest he might like not to be quoted. He insists Labour offered to give up majority votes on six committees to make way for the minority MSPs. "We bent over backwards to accommodate them," he says. But then he admits that Tommy and Dennis will not be on the committees they most want and he points out that Labour has many backbench MSPs who did not get on their preferred committees. This rather overlooks the fact that Labour has 56 MSPs, most of whom won places on their preferred committees but I am so impressed by Donald's murderous expression that I decide not to pursue the point. He walks away from me and then turns back to tell me in a raised voice: "I am surprised that a senior and experienced journalist of your standing would write a headline like that – and I shall be speaking to Harry." It is hopeless even trying to explain that I don't get to write the headlines, just the stories, but by this time the First Minister is storming off, pursued by Whitton and a crowd of civil servants all of whom look rather stunned. As Donald moves out of earshot the rest of the hacks who have witnessed this scene burst into hoots of laughter.

Back to Tommy. "Donald says you're a brazen liar," I inform him. Tommy shrugs and replies: "When Donald Dewar speaks about consensus politics he is speaking through a hole...I won't go any further." Donald, it transpires, makes three attempts to speak to Harry so he must be truly upset. After a conversation with Alf Young, an old friend, he finally reaches the Editor. Whitton tells me that our First Minister has begun to calm down a little and that the attack on me was not personal, aimed more at the fact that *The Herald* – Donald's favourite newspaper, we are always told – is being irresponsible giving such prominence to people like Canavan and Sheridan.

Harry gives me his full backing, as I expected. He thinks Donald is consumed by dislike for Dennis who humiliated Labour in the election and made him look silly in the famous handshaking incident at the inaugural meeting of the Parliament. Donald's dislike for Tommy makes Dennis seem almost like an old pal.

Some lessons should be learned from this episode. New Labour and, I'm afraid, Donald himself, truly are in danger of being seen as control freaks. It seems Donald's fury was not just at having the shine taken off his statement on the legislative programme; our real offence was to take Dennis and Tommy seriously and to give them some prominence. Yet as of today, at the end of all this fuss, our story stands. No-one has yet explained how, if Labour truly did make such huge efforts to contact Dennis and Tommy, neither of them heard from Labour officially or directly until McCabe made his statement on the floor of the chamber. Labour's handling of discussions with Sheridan and Canavan, I suspect, has been carried out at a few levels below Donald and been found wanting. Only now is Donald finding out.

I reflect on the day's events. After more than 40 years in journalism and lending editorial support to the creation of a Scottish Parliament, I am rather taken aback that one of its first acts is to denounce me and my newspaper. I have been yelled at by David Whitton, hauled before the mighty McCabe for a bollocking, attacked face-to-face in front of witnesses by the First Minister for the (alleged) inaccuracy of my reporting, and finally made the subject of a telephone call of formal complaint by the First Minister to my Editor. This is a first for any journalist in the new Scotland. No-one can deny me my place in history.

As expected our MSPs bury the tuition fees issue for several months by setting up a committee. And so the Labour-Liberal Democrat coalition government has a new lease of life as of today. The threatened LibDem rebellion amounts to no more than two recalcitrants – Jamie Stone (Caithness, Sutherland and Easter Ross) and Donald Gorrie (Central Scotland). Their party colleagues vote overwhelmingly with Labour for the promised independent inquiry rather than immediate abolition. Jim Wallace does his best to sound defiant. "We oppose fees – this remains our position," he insists, but he suffers a savaging from John Swinney. Alex Salmond also taunts Wallace by reminding him that the LibDems vowed tuition fees would be gone on the day after Labour failed to win an overall majority. "Don't you think that was wrong?" Salmond asks. Wallace waffles about the "most effective way forward." His only moment of comfort comes when he turns the tables on David McLetchie of the Tories, reminding him that the Conservatives were proposing fees of £1000 when the LibDems were campaigning for abolition.

Swinney reminds Wallace that 73 of the Parliament's 129 MSPs were elected after vowing to vote down tuition fees. "It was centre stage in the election campaign and it was not tucked away in the small print," Swinney says. "There is no earthly reason why any MSP should not vote to abolish tuition fees now."

He is right, of course. The LibDems continue to look wretched whenever they are reminded of their U-turn on fees. At moments like this the future of the coalition looks bleak.

June 21st

Sir David Steel calls us to hear the arrangements for the Royal opening (we are discouraged from calling it the State opening) of the Scottish Parliament. He tells us that a politically correct second verse of *God Save the Queen* will be sung in St Giles' Cathedral, Edinburgh, at the Kirking of the Parliament on the eve of the big event. This odd decision is Sir David's own idea, apparently, and has the approval of the Very Rev Gilleasbuig Macmillan, minister of St Giles', which means those present, including the Duke of Edinburgh, will be required to sing:

> Not on this land alone
> But be God's mercies known
> From shore to shore
> Lord make the nations see
> That men should brothers be
> And form one family
> The wide world o'er.

A search through *Herald* cuttings confirms that this verse was approved a decade ago by the Church of England's Liturgical Commission which wanted to make the sentiments of the British national anthem less belligerent. Come to think of it, the words do rather read like the work of a committee. They replace the famous second verse dating back to the Jacobite Rebellion of 1745:

> O, Lord our God arise,
> Scatter our enemies
> And make them fail;
> Confound their politics
> Frustrate their knavish tricks
> On him our hopes are fixed
> O, save us all.

The cuttings tell me a similar version to that was current in the 19th century when Britain had troubled relations with other nations:

> O, Lord our God arise
> Scatter our enemies
> And make them fail
> Confound French politics
> Frustrate all Russian tricks
> Put Yankees in a fix
> God save us all.

There is a much more contentious verse, of course. Legend has it that *God Save the King* was first sung in public at Covent Garden in Drury Lane, London, when the English heard news of Sir John's Cope's defeat by the Jacobites at Prestonpans. The occasion was reported by the *Daily Advertiser*: "On Saturday night last the audience at the Theatre Royal, Drury Lane, were agreeably surprised by the gentleman who belonged to that house performing the anthem, God save our Noble King. The universal applause it met with – being encored with repeated huzzas – sufficiently denoted in how just abhorrence they hold the arbitrary schemes of our insidious enemies and detest the despotic attempts of Papal power."

Dissident Scots love to remind the English of the verse which is seldom sung nowadays and then only to annoy them. It dates back to the Jacobite Rebellion when Marshal Wade set out for Scotland. In years past the SNP has displayed that verse in huge lettering on a banner across the platform of its annual conference.

> God grant that Marshal Wade
> May by that mighty aid
> Victory bring
> May he sedition hush
> And like a torrent rush
> Rebellious Scots to crush
> God Save the King.

Sir David informs us hastily he is not suggesting this verse is appropriate for St Giles' on June 30 but he believes the new one to be ideal because it is in keeping with the sentiments of *A Man's a Man for a' That* by Robert Burns. On several occasions, he tells us, he has heard the new second verse sung in Westminster Abbey. Oh, well, that must make it all right, then. *A Man's a Man* is to be performed the following day by folksinger Sheena Wellington in the Assembly Hall in the presence of the Queen. Whether Sheena Wellington will be allowed to sing the verse about "yon birkie ca'd a lord, wha' struts and stares and a' that..." remains to be seen.

Changed days. Some of us can remember when Hamish Henderson's revolutionary *Freedom Come All Ye* was sung at the Scottish Constitutional Convention although I don't think Donald knew then it was all about a Scottish socialist republic.

The Nats are contemptuous of the decision to sing the second verse of *God Save the Queen* and are eager to find some conspiratorial motive, ie an Establishment plot to remind us that this is to be a British as well as a Scottish occasion. Donald evidently does not wish to get involved in the debate. David Whitton tells us with a note of finality: "The opening ceremony is a matter for the Presiding Officer. It is not our responsibility."

June 23rd

Our MSPs are suffering from an unexpectedly bad press. They are back in trouble with the tabloids again after deciding to give themselves holidays which are longer than those enjoyed by MPs at Westminster. Stupidly, they also decided today to take a day off on St Andrew's Day, while the rest of the country must continue to work. This means the Scottish Parliament will not meet on November 30 but its clerks, security staff and other employees must turn up for work as usual.

The Tories make themselves look especially daft. David McLetchie complains in remarks offered just before the decision is taken without a vote that MSPs will be "skiving." This might be true

– which makes it all odder that he and his MSPs promptly vote to support the idea.

This is more ammunition for the SNP which hails the decision as a breakthrough in its campaign to make St Andrew's Day a national holiday "for showcasing Scotland to the world." Mike Russell says he wants the Scottish Parliament to do for Scotland what the Irish do for Ireland on St Patrick's Day. McLetchie is jeered by other MSPs when he attacks the Parliament's bureau – on which his own party is represented – for encouraging Members to "skive" and he complains pompously: "The last thing people in Scotland need is a holiday in the middle of the week on a dreich day in November."

Tom McCabe, in his role as Labour's business manager, protests that no-one in the bureau has been talking of MSPs skiving and he emphasises that November 30 should be recognised as the national day but not as an official holiday. MSPs fall about when he says sonorously: "The office of the clerk will remain open and MSPs will not be on holiday. They will be able to exercise a variety of functions." One backbencher shouts: "Such as breathing."

Once again Donald Dewar is anxious not to get involved and David Whitton busily briefs that the First Minister will be "speaking somewhere on St Andrew's Day and our MSPs will no doubt have constituency engagements."

Donald is plainly becoming worried at the continuing flurry of hostile headlines from the tabloids which are now deriding MSPs for their preoccupation with holidays, perks, pay, allowances and limousines. Far be it from me now to come to the rescue of McCabe and Dewar and the rest but even I think they are having an unduly rough time from some of the press. After all, you cannot elect 129 new MSPs and form a government without making arrangements for paying those involved and covering their expenses. If Scotland wants the democracy it has been shouting for over the years, it must learn that it comes at a price – in our case a very modest one compared with most. No-one in the anti-Holyrood press these days is pointing out that the Scottish Parliament is amazingly cheap at the price. How many Scottish Parliaments could be built for the price of one Millennium Dome or one Westminster extension? At current rates the Scottish Parliament could be built for the price of a couple of half decent Italian footballers.

Yet the new government is not entirely blameless. These housekeeping matters could and should have been resolved without this fuss. Ministers have allowed voters to gain a false sense of Holyrood's priorities. All the government had to do to keep the hacks at bay was throw them an occasional morsel of information on other, more important areas. But it seems no-one had the wit to think up anything which would have interested us sufficiently – or to foresee the damage which has been done with constant discussion about MSPs' pay, conditions and holidays.

June 24th

Today provides the SNP's first set-piece opportunity to shine. For the first Scottish Parliament Opposition amendment debate the Nats select the unpopular private finance initiative (PFI) as their subject, confident in the knowledge that many Labour MSPs share a dislike of the entire concept of the private sector working inside the NHS and education. But finance minister Jack McConnell promptly announces a series of apparently radical changes to the operation of PFI which knock the wind out of the SNP's sails. Even young SNP talents like Andrew Wilson, the Shadow finance minister, are left perplexed by McConnell's nifty footwork. Poor Andrew is completely unprepared for McConnell's news that future PFI buildings like hospitals and schools will return to the public sector under the terms of new contracts and that the pensions of employees transferred from the public to private sector will in future have their pensions guaranteed.

For good measure McConnell completes a disappointing day for the Nationalists by announcing out of the blue that by not collecting the Tartan Tax, the government will save £20m in administration costs. McConnell enjoys his moment of mischief by arguing with a straight face that by a coincidence the £20m saving on tax collection neatly matches the increase in costs for the new Holyrood building. Thus is an awkward problem magically solved – either by serendipity or by creative, not to say ingenious, accounting. Again the Nationalists are neatly wrongfooted. Later, in the black and white corridor, McConnell gives us an off-the-record briefing which suggests he is well on top of his new job and beginning to show cockiness for which he is famous.

June 25th
Plans for the grand Royal opening next week are beginning to look embarrassing. With the exception of Sean Connery, all the invited celebrities and famous sports personalities seem to be falling over themselves to stay away. So far those with more pressing engagements on July 1 include Sir Alex Ferguson of Manchester United, Billy Connolly (who called Holyrood a "wee pretendy parliament") Jackie Stewart, Stephen Hendry, Colin Montgomerie and many more. No fewer than four former Secretaries of State for Scotland have also remembered previous engagements. No prizes for guessing that they are all Tories (Sir Malcolm Rifkind, the soon-to-be ennobled Sir Michael Forsyth, Lord Younger and Lord Lang). All had been invited to the presence of the Prime and First Ministers in Parliament Hall and not to the Assembly Hall where the Queen will be present, and they seem to be miffed at such a slight although they are careful to deny any such thing. Still, four Tory cancellations does seem a remarkable coincidence.

I hear that Lord (Harry) Ewing, the former Scottish Office minister who was co-chairman of the Scottish Constitutional Convention, has not been invited. I give him a ring and he is his usual courteous self. Yes, it is true, he tells me, unless his invitation has been held up in the post. I remind him that he attacked the unpopular decision by Tony Blair and George Robertson (when Shadow Scottish Secretary) to hold a two-question referendum on Home Rule. Like most people, Harry thought at the time that it was unnecessary (indeed some of us thought it was a deliberate ploy to torpedo the whole devolution project). But he shrugs off the suggestion and says that he is now too old and long in the tooth to worry about such things. Yet I cannot avoid the feeling that he is rather hurt, especially because the invitations are being sent out by Sir David Steel who was Harry's co-chairman such a short time ago. Another reminder that we are a small country. Either this is an extraordinary oversight or a deliberate and rather shabby snub.

Meanwhile, Sir David Steel is putting on a brave face, protesting he is disappointed that his invitations are proving less than collectors' items. He is not surprised by the number of call-offs, he says, because the invitations went out late. It just happens that the cancellations are from the most high-profile invitees.

I never expected Connolly to appear. The wonder is he was ever invited. He has a lifelong antipathy to anything which threatens the United Kingdom and that includes the SNP for which he reserves a special loathing.

June 27th

Another attack on the SNP by Connolly is reported in the *Sunday Herald* which quotes him saying the Nationalists are racists and the cause of increased anti-Englishness in Scotland. He is speaking as an internationalist, he says. This little spat is so Scottish. It reminds us yet again that we are a wee country where differences of opinion have a tendency to explode into the open at awkward moments, rather like family feuds surfacing at funerals. This is such a moment, when the nation is nervously wondering what the implications of its decision on Home Rule might mean and where they might lead us.

Connolly's claim is easy to dismiss but I have an uneasy feeling that however wrong he might be, he speaks for a constituency, albeit a small one. Anti-Englishness, assuming it exists, has to be blamed on someone. If it exists, it does so completely outside my experience of Scotland. Anti-English government, yes; anti-English cultural domination, yes; but anti-Englishness in the purely racial or ethnic sense is something which I have never witnessed. Perhaps I move in the wrong circles.

Connolly argues that devolution is a waste of time and that no good will come of it. He believes, apparently, that proportional representation was "sneaked in" and that all we have now is another layer of government. He scorns the work of the new MSPs as "abstract" which seems an odd way to dismiss education and health. This thinking is politically illiterate. But I don't think for a moment that Connolly is alone in his opinions, however misguided they might be. He was on the Parkinson show again this week and he was hilarious. How strange that he can be so irreducibly Scottish but so contemptuous of his own country and its people, or some of them. Someone should take him aside gently and explain that the whole point of Scottish nationalism for the past decade has been to make Scotland internationalist, but on its own terms. That is what independence in Europe, the SNP's flagship policy, is all about. Politically, Connolly has never outgrown the protest movements of the 1960s when it was fashionable to be soft on totalitarian socialism abroad and when Labour in Scotland – deeply Unionist then as now, despite its claims to support Home Rule – ran terrified of rising Scottish Nationalism. In those days Labour dismissed the SNP as Tartan Tories. But who are the Tartan Tories now? Those who think like Connolly find it hard to accept that nationalism can be a force for good, witness the re-emergence of the small states of Eastern Europe from the wreckage of the Soviet Union, not to mention the conquest by nationalists and nationalism of apartheid.

June 29th

I am invited to a preview of Charlie Whelan's documentary for Scottish Television on the election. Spinners and Losers is being promoted as an insider's look at the events leading up to May 6 by "the master of the black art of spinning." In Parliament Square I meet a couple of colleagues who inform me excitedly that I have been "done" by Charlie and that I am exposed as an SNP cheerleader.

With mounting dread I make my way to the library of the Faculty of Advocates where Charlie makes his entrance in grand style, sporting that famous face-splitting grin. The PR people from Scottish Television hand out a statement quoting Charlie in his celebrated capacity as Britain's "most notorious" spin doctor. "The Scottish Parliament elections may or may not have been the most significant event in Scottish politics for 300 years but it was certainly the most stage-managed event in Scotland's political history," says the blurb. The hype is breathless: "One fact cannot be disputed. The campaign provided irrefutable proof that today politics is as much about packaging as it is about principles and it made the consultants and the special advisers key players throughout."

While this might be true it bears little relevance to the contents of the programme which turns out to be a disappointment, at least to me. Lots of shots of Charlie grinning, Charlie swigging his white wine spritzers, Charlie sprawling in armchairs in editors' offices, Charlie being bored at press conferences, Charlie looking shifty in the presence of important politicians.

Thank God he lets me off lightly. In a sequence shot in a Govan pub he suggests to Nicola Sturgeon of the SNP that I am a notorious Nationalist. Nicola replies (truthfully) that she does not know my politics. Cut to the editorial conference on the night of *The Herald* System Three poll. We are discussing my exclusive that Alex Salmond and Mike Russell are about to announce the scrapping of their daily press conferences because of the ghastly implications for the Nationalists of our *SNP in Freefall* story. I am required to explain how the SNP has found out that the poll is disastrous for the Nationalist cause. I am quoted saying I can't imagine who would tell them such a thing. At least Charlie acknowledges that my reward was a good scoop.

In truth – and in the opinion of the political press corps – the programme is good fun only for political anoraks in the parties or in the media. As for us hacks, we simply enjoy the chance to watch ourselves on the telly. For the average viewer it must be a crashing bore. In effect Spinners and Losers is an overlong obituary of the SNP's doomed campaign in Govan. Along the way Charlie completely loses the plot. There is some mention of *The Herald*'s spat with Labour over the lost advertising income and some fleeting recognition of the main issues. For me the highlight is Martin Clark, editor of the *Daily Record*, shamelessly defending his front-page story and picture of Sean Connery lunging at a photographer under the heading: So you've seen the polls then, Sean." (In fact the picture was of Connery in Los Angeles 10 days before and had nothing to do with polls in Scotland). Clark manages to keep a straight face when he says he did not seek to make any connection between Connery and the polls.

July 1st
To the Royal opening of the Scottish Parliament. Edinburgh's Royal Mile is in festive mood, thousands of curious people having turned out to watch the ceremonial. Many are tourists. It is odd to see Japanese and Americans waving the Saltire alongside Scots who have come from all over the country. To mark the great day I have a laudatory piece on Donald Dewar in *The Herald*. Harry believes it right that the First Minister should be praised for his role in bringing Home Rule to Scotland and that we should make a point of acknowledging Donald's efforts today. Many will share that view. Donald has his place in history, no question. Dennis Canavan and Tommy Sheridan poke fun at me rather publicly on the Lawnmarket pavement outside the media centre, choosing to ridicule my description of Donald as the "father of the nation," a phrase which I did not invent but which is now common currency and which I am merely quoting. When I remonstrate with Dennis I discover I am being taped by a radio reporter, causing further hilarity to the assembled hacks and curious onlookers.

Word arrives that Tony Blair has cancelled his appearance at the last minute because he is detained in Belfast by the Northern Ireland crisis. The general reaction among the hacks and some politicians is not exactly one of disappointment, perhaps relief. In Parliament Hall, where the Scottish Parliament last met in 1707, the great and the good of Scottish politics are gathered below a stunning stained-glass window by Charles Heath Wilson depicting the 1532 inauguration by King James V of the Court of Session and College of Justice. John Reid is among the guests and offers me a few kind words about my piece on the First Minister. With some relief I deduce that he has not read far enough to the part where I describe him as a "cut down Secretary of State."

There are short speeches from Sir David Steel, the four main party leaders and the Lord President, Lord Rodger, the most senior judge in Scotland. Alex Salmond makes a diplomatic job of saying today's events are just part of a continuing story. He eschews the word "independence." Donald is warmly applauded for suggesting that the best present the new Scottish Parliament could have would be peace in Northern Ireland. Jim Wallace remarks that he has been accused of being incapable of making a speech on Home Rule without mentioning Gladstone, and proceeds to talk about Gladstone. But the prize for nerve goes to David McLetchie of the Tories who says that some people in Scotland never expected to see this day, remarking with a grin: "In fact, some of us hoped we never would see this day." He reminds everyone that the Tories voted in 1707 against the Treaty of Union. "We were the Scottish Nationalists of the day."

Robbie is out to enjoy himself. He makes his entrance dressed like an extra from Brigadoon. Having been ordered by the news desk to hire a dinner suit for a function the previous night, he has held on to it for the purposes of serious celebration today. His get-up consists of revolting electric-blue trews and a Nehru-style jacket with no collar, and a shirt which is designed for no tie. He is immensely proud of his appearance which draws warm applause and jeers in equal amounts.

After the formalities in Parliament Hall I head for the press centre to watch events continuing in the Assembly Hall on a huge screen. Outside, Tommy Sheridan is addressing a rally of students protesting noisily against tuition fees. Passage to *The Herald* office in

Lawnmarket is blocked. There is nothing for it but to sit back with coffee and biscuits and be like most people: watch it all on the telly.

The Queen and her husband and eldest son make their way up the Royal Mile in the grandest ceremonial seen in Edinburgh for decades and take their seats among, not above, the MSPs. This, it has been explained to us by Sir David, is in keeping with the Scottish custom of showing respect but not deference to royalty. The so-called Honours of Scotland, the Crown which she has never worn and which was hidden away in Edinburgh Castle for much of the period after the Union of Crowns, is placed before her a few feet away and seems to fascinate her. She hardly takes her eyes off it, even while Sir David makes a point of addressing her as Queen of Scots. At least this time she is showing it more respect than she did after her Coronation when she famously turned up to be presented with the Honours while carrying a handbag when people expected her to be in full regalia. On this occasion she is wearing a dress bearing themes on the thistle. She has been listening to the right people for this occasion. Some historic damage is immediately repaired all those years later.

Sheena Wellington, the folk singer who is more famous abroad than in her native Scotland, stands in the gallery and sings, unaccompanied, *A Man's a Man, for a' That* by Robert Burns. Talk about stealing the show. I can scarcely believe what I am hearing. In the presence of the Queen, Duke of Edinburgh, Duke of Rothesay (aka the Prince of Wales) and various other Lords and Ladies she reprises Burns's quasi-revolutionary verse about rank being the guinea stamp. For good measure she sings the killer verse:

> Ye see yon birkie [fellow] ca' a lord
> Wha' struts and stares and a' that
> Though hundreds worship at his word
> He's but a coof [fool] for a' that

And, even more amazingly,

>A prince can mak a belted knight
>A marquis, duke and a' that
>But an honest man's aboon his might
>Guid faith, he mauna [must not] fa' that

To conclude this musical insurrection, Sheena Wellington invites the company – including the aforesaid dukes and prince – to join the chorus which they do, rather haltingly at first. Prince Philip and Prince Charles are suddenly glued to the words in the order of proceedings but they sing along with the entire Scottish Parliament:

>Then let us pray that come it may,
>As come it will for a' that,
>That sense and worth, o'er a' the earth
>Shall bear the gree [succeed], and a' that
>For a' that, and a' that,
>It's comin' yet for a' that,
>That Man to Man, the warld o'er
>Shall brothers be for a' that.

In the press tent and in the media gallery hardened hacks are fighting back tears. Sean Connery and other celebrities in the Assembly Hall applaud in ecstasy. This could only happen in Scotland where this extraordinary scene not only marks a political milestone but sends out an unmistakable message that our attitudes and sense of nationhood are changed for ever. Perhaps you have to be a Scot to appreciate what it means.

Donald Dewar seems inspired and makes a beautifully eloquent speech. He talks of a "moment anchored in history" and the coming of a new voice which will shape the new Scotland as surely as the echoes from the past – "the shout of the welder in the din of the great Clyde shipyards, the speak of the Mearns, with its soul in the land; the discourse of the enlightenment when Edinburgh and Glasgow were a light held to the intellectual life of Europe; the wild cry of the great pipes, and back to the distant cries of the battles of Bruce and Wallace."

This could almost be Alex Salmond talking. But there's no stopping Donald as he warms to his theme, quoting Walter Scott that only a man with soul so dead could have no sense, no feel of his native land. "For me, for any Scot, today is a proud moment: a new stage on a journey begun long ago and which has no end." He sounds even more Nationalistic, when he observes: "A Scottish Parliament – not an end, a means to greater ends." Whatever can he mean? By now fully into his patriotic stride Donald moves on to Burns who, he says, would have embraced the meaning of the engravings on the mace which the Queen has given the Parliament. It carries four words: wisdom, justice, compassion, integrity. He concludes that it is a rare privilege for an old nation to open a new Parliament.

Out in the street a strange event takes place. Thousands of people stand and cheer politicians as MSPs, MPs, and assorted other dignitaries walk up to the Royal Mile as Scottish Parliamentarians did almost 300 years ago. In the absence of a vote in those days the citizens expressed disapproval of their rulers by throwing stones at them. On this occasion Sean Connery wins an even bigger cheer than the Queen, which says something about the mood in Scotland now. Poor William Hague alone is marked out for some good-natured booing.

Concord suddenly sweeps low and deafeningly over the celebrations, attended by a guard of honour from the Red Arrows. Robbie, still dressed as a pantomime Robbie the Pict, is standing with Alan Cochrane, the notoriously hard-nosed pro-Union Scottish correspondent of the *Daily Telegraph*. Cochrane grabs Robbie's shirt where the collar should be and stabs a finger at Concord and the Red Arrows as they roar over Edinburgh Castle. "Do you know what that is?" bellows Cochrane above the din. "That's Her Britannic Majesty's Royal Air Force in action – and if your lot were in power it would be a wee hing glider!" To which Robbie responds: "Aye, but it would be oor wee hing glider."

The press corps repairs with the rest of Edinburgh for a glass of lunch, which stretches to dinner. In the Castle Bar I am inveigled into singing folksongs with Mick Broderick, a well known rascal from Arran, and some other musical celebrants. Hugh MacDonald, an old colleague and lifelong Nationalist from Islay, is in town for the day as are many others from all over the country, all wanting to say that they were there on the great day when Scotland regained its own legislature.

There is great hilarity at the antics of the *Sun*. We discover that it has sent a reporter up from London to cover the events which are considered too important to be left to its own Scottish political reporter, Andy Nicoll, who is only one of the best political journalists in Scotland. This results in the *Sun* reporting solemnly that the Scots have just abolished the Treaty of Union with England. Andy is called in to repair the damage, but too late. It is already in the paper.

History will lie as usual.

Postscript

February, 2000

The dawn of the millennium seems an appropriate moment in which to reflect on the performance of the reborn Scottish Parliament during those final days of the 20th century, now consigned to history. No-one can fail to have noticed that our young Parliament has enemies in the media, particularly among some of the more Right-wing, London-based newspapers. In Scotland itself the *Daily Record* has ridiculed it, and even the *Scotsman*'s Editor-in-Chief has launched assaults on it, most memorably in a piece in which he dismissed our MSPs as a collection of "numpties." This sort of vilification will pass as those who waged their unsuccessful campaign of resistance to Home Rule learn to enjoy the relief which comes when they stop banging their heads against the brickwork of the Scottish popular will.

Perversely, there is something peculiarly Scottish about the eagerness of a sullen minority to discredit the new order. My colleague, Iain Macwhirter, has tackled this subject, observing wisely: "The assault on the Parliament probably has something to do with latent philistinism and cretinism in the Scots character. There is a chronic lack of self-confidence in Scotland, thinly disguised by bluster and hyperbolic criticism. Yet by behaving like narrow-minded local newspapers the press are only confirming their own provincialism. In demeaning the Parliament they are demeaning themselves."

Our MSPs have learned the hard way that media attention comes most pressingly but not surprisingly when things go wrong. Many of them have complained publicly, and to journalists in private, that they feel they have been harshly treated. There is some truth in their complaints but it must also be said that our MSPs have usually been the authors of their own embarrassment. One of their first actions was to debate and establish their allowances and holidays, a decision which handed ammunition to hostile voices, and a poor impression of their sense of priorities to voters. Yet the Parliament could not have begun its work without a clear housekeeping structure. Hindsight suggests those guiding Parliamentary business in those early days were a touch hamfisted but that is just about the worst that could be said of them.

Enemies of the Parliament should reflect on the high level of interest which the people of Scotland have shown in its proceedings. On most days the public galleries are well attended, even for some of the less riveting debates. Cynicism among pundits is not necessarily shared by the people. Some of us in the Parliamentary press corps worried at one time that our paymasters would quickly grow tired of funding a major and expensive media presence, if only because the Parliament would not produce enough news. It might become a mere talking shop or engage in debates so tedious as to be unreportable. We wondered if the press presence might quickly be reduced to the status of the coterie which covered the affairs of the former Strathclyde Regional Council in its later days. This amounted to no more than a couple of staff reporters and a stringer, quite sufficient to satisfy the nation's editorial interest – not least because the nation had such little interest in its doings. In contrast, one of the Holyrood journalists' more urgent difficulties is finding workspace and time to satisfy the curiosity of newspapers and television in the Parliament's deliberations. Indeed the Scottish press's preoccupation with Holyrood has quickly become a source of growing concern to Westminster MPs who are fast becoming a lost legion in Scotland, banished to another Parliament where, they complain, their work is now ignored and their names forgotten between elections.

In contrast, MSPs have complained of having too much publicity, albeit of the wrong sort. Early strains between them and the press became so severe at one point that Sir David Steel took it upon himself to protest to the Press Complaints Commission about "bitch journalism" – a phrase since passed into common usage – after newspapers claimed MSPs were awarding themselves medals for meritorious service after only a few weeks in the job. The story had a grain of truth, but only a grain. Some anonymous civil servant had long before had the unremarkable idea of ordering the striking of an inexpensive trinket to commemorate the first elections. This harmless suggestion, about which MSPs knew nothing until they read about it in the press, became elevated to the status of scandal which it most certainly was not. But, again, it did damage the Parliament in the eyes of voters. Such innocent cock-ups are surely forgiveable in a brand new institution on a steep learning curve. The very fact that MSPs can land themselves in trouble with such cack-handed public relations should be a source of some relief. After all, the alternative is a Parliament whose every move must be vetted and choreographed by some scheming spin doctor.

Other much more significant issues have threatened the first months of the Parliament. More accurately they were a threat to the Labour-led Executive because both primarily were domestic Labour Party embarrassments. In the so-called Lobbygate affair there were no winners, only losers, after *The Observer* claimed to have exposed a cash-for-access system operating at the heart of the administration in Holyrood. It was suggested somewhat insistently by employees of Beattie Media, a successful PR company, that it enjoyed privileged access for clients to Labour Ministers. The story was given force because one of the Beattie executives, secretly filmed making his claims, was a former Labour Party HQ employee and also, more importantly, the son of Dr John Reid, Secretary of State for Scotland.

Various Ministers were implicated. Mr Dewar rode to their rescue but failed to clear them simply on the basis of their own protested innocence. To the fury of the Secretary of State, who insisted angrily that his son was innocent and was being "thrown to the wolves," Mr Dewar ordered an inquiry by the Parliament's standards committee. It concluded that no breaches of rules had been committed by Ministers. More importantly the committee set about drawing up tighter rules governing lobbying. Although Ministers were indeed vindicated, the affair suggested plausibly that a self-serving Labour nomenklatura exists in Scotland. Lobbygate also shed light on the strained relationship (much denied) between Mr Dewar and Dr Reid which became all the more obvious after they were spotted having a finger-stabbing shouting match at a Labour conference in England.

In a small country like Scotland the border between cronyism and a close but innocent working relationship among talented individuals with shared political sympathies can become blurred. Yet Lobbygate raised questions, still unanswered, about the interplay between lobbyists with strong Labour connections and the party itself, notably in the area of public service contracts. Lobbygate did the Parliament a service of sorts because it made MSPs of all parties acutely aware of the traps laid for them by the aggressive world of public relations which had cynically regarded the Scottish Parliament as just another happy hunting ground.

In the late autumn Labour suffered at its own hand again when Mr Dewar summarily dismissed his own chief of staff, John Rafferty. Mr Rafferty's arrival in the First Minister's private office – direct from his senior Labour Party job – had from the start been a source of curiosity, mainly fuelled by his appearance at the inaugural meeting of the Scottish Cabinet without his appointment even being announced. After he had been in the job for some weeks a series of odd stories began appearing in newspapers – almost always the same ones – provoking a flurry of indignant Ministerial denials. This strange process of disinformation being deliberately spread came to a head when two tabloids ran a story suggesting that Ms Susan Deacon, Minister of Health, had received death threats from anti-abortion extremists. A simple inquiry by the police, concerned for a senior public figure's personal safety, quickly established that the story was groundless. Soon afterwards Mr Rafferty was exposed as the source and to the acute embarrassment of the Labour Party he was fired by a distressed First Minister who had earlier described him as a friend of 20 years.

Rafferty's spectacular downfall was not so much a scandal as a fiasco, one which did nothing for Mr Dewar's reputation as a ditherer in a crisis. Yet in a curious way it seemed to do more harm to the Parliament itself. Mischievous pundits drew little distinction between the Parliament and its discomfited government. This tendency to blame the Parliament and devolution itself for the failings of the Executive or the embarrassments of the Labour Party became evident again with the resignation in January of Philip Chalmers, the head of Mr Dewar's strategic communications unit. He quit in a welter of lurid headlines following disclosure of his two drink-related driving offences in Glasgow's red light area. Again Mr Dewar was propelled before the Parliament to defend his most immediate circle of advisers and spin doctors. And again the usual suspects in the media gallery went into print bemoaning their inability to repeal the Scotland Act.

Lobbygate and the downfall of Mr Rafferty and Mr Chalmers were gifts to the SNP which has continued – with no great difficulty, it must be said – to live up to Alex Salmond's promise to be an effective Opposition.

The Tories, too, have made their presence felt, most effectively in the eloquent plea by Lord James Douglas Hamilton for a change to the Act of Settlement which forbids the Monarch to marry a Catholic if he or she wishes to remain on the throne. Indeed, the Tories have occasionally managed to usurp the SNP by claiming the limelight. Nationalist MSPs, jealous of their position as the official Opposition, are becoming increasingly uncomfortable with the Tories as unwanted allies in divisions, especially when the Tories scoop the publicity.

An example of this emerging strain was glimpsed after Mr Dewar made what was widely regarded as a faltering statement to the House on his reasons for dismissing John Rafferty. Custom now dictates that after debates in the chamber the press pack adjourns from the media gallery to the black and white corridor to be joined by Mr Salmond and Mr McLetchie and by Ministers or backbenchers wishing to elaborate on their arguments and to polish their soundbites.

At the conclusion of Mr Dewar's statement on the Rafferty affair, Mr McLetchie beat Mr Salmond to the corridor where he was promptly surrounded by inquisitive reporters. This led to an unseemly scene in which Michael Russell, the SNP business manager, a burly chap, took on the role of Mr Salmond's muscle. Mr Russell proceeded to collar journalists, insisting that they abandon Mr McLetchie in favour of lending an ear to the leader of the SNP. A few feet away an irritable Mr Salmond, feeling slighted and lonely, stood on his dignity, impatient to hand down his opinions in the name of the official Opposition.

A coalition of Opposition is something the SNP does not wish but sometimes cannot prevent. This attempt by the Tories to force a marriage is beginning to grate with Nationalist MSPs anxious to distance themselves from the one political party in the Scottish Parliament with which no-one will work. Quite how the SNP can shake off the attentions of their unloved partner remains to be seen.

Some Parliament-watchers have expressed puzzlement at the style of the SNP in Opposition. Nationalist MSPs have been accused of behaving out of character, which is to say that they are disciplined, organised and responsible to a degree which has surprised those who wonder whatever happened to Scottish nationalism's anarchic streak where gestures of defiance – flag burnings, street protests and rebellious conference resolutions – were once the entertaining order of the day. Mr Kenny MacAskill's arrest and brief detention without charge in London when he accompanied the Tartan Army to a football fixture against England was more in keeping with the old, defiant SNP. Sean Connery's acceptance of the previously cancelled knighthood symbolised, at least in some eyes, the new SNP. Mr Gordon Wilson, who led the party until Mr Salmond took over, has voiced disapproval of Nationalists accepting "British" honours and has articulated the fears of some in the SNP that the party is slowing being sucked into the maw of the Scottish/British Establishment.

Quite simply, the SNP appears to be growing up and biding its time as it seeks to demonstrate its fitness to be a party of government sometime in the future. This air of studied responsibility might not make for the greatest political fun but you can see why Mr Salmond is playing safe in the early life of the Parliament, the institution which is the most important of his oft-proclaimed "building blocks" to independence.

Debates in the Scottish Parliament have generally been of a reasonably high standard, after an admittedly faltering start when the press and Opposition made much of a poorly delivered speech by an inexperienced woman MSP. As is the way with politics the most important debates are sometimes the dullest, perhaps reflecting consensus on so many major issues in the new Scotland, but also meaning that in areas of the greatest relevance to the daily lives of voters – mainly health, education and justice – the level of attention by the media is at its lowest. Yet debates on these issues have produced impressive contributions from across the spectrum of the chamber.

Conversely, issues of lesser importance have sometimes attracted more attention, notably the proposed Member's Bill to ban foxhunting, and a move to soften the law which prohibits the promotion of homosexuality in schools. Though Labour might not wish to admit the fact there is evidence that on these and other issues – Motorway tolling and tobacco advertising come to mind – there is apparently a hidden hand at work in Westminster where MPs have a potentially conflicting agenda. Thus, when MSPs are blamed for a misguided sense of priority they might be merely responding to pressure from London. Many MSPs from all parties, including Labour, have looked askance at the proposal by the Chancellor, Mr Gordon Brown, that Holyrood should be represented at joint Cabinet committees. Quite apart from Mr Brown's own interest in keeping a firm grip on his power base in Scotland, this represents an anxiety in Westminster that Scotland must not be allowed to slip further, possibly beyond recall, from the grip of central government.

Most encouraging for those who wish the Scottish Parliament well is the performance of its committees which are empowered to scrutinise and introduce legislation. Not all of them carry Labour majorities. They are small but quickly proving themselves to be independently minded and efficient. Some have already shown themselves unwilling to be ciphers for the Executive. Several Ministers have wilted under the force of tough questioning, most notably Mr Jim Wallace before the Justice Committee chaired by the SNP's persistent Roseanna Cunningham. Mr Wallace had a torrid time fielding questions about emergency legislation to amend the law governing the detention of patients in the State Hospital at Carstairs – the so-called Ruddle loophole which allowed an offender to go free because he was judged to be beyond treatment for a personality disorder. These exchanges accompanied the first legislation passed by the Parliament, the Mental Health Public Safety and Appeals Scotland Act (1999).

Ms Susan Deacon (health) and Ms Rhona Brankin (sport) have also come away from committee meetings feeling bruised, and a civil servant who had just been appointed head of the prison service suffered a memorable mauling. To the annoyance of the Secretary of State for Scotland the Tory-chaired rural affairs committee backed calls for the return of 6000 square miles of North Sea fisheries to Scottish jurisdiction despite the blank refusal of the Blair Government to contemplate the idea. In doing so it reflected the will of the Parliament itself where only Labour is opposed. In this and other areas such as the Act of Settlement our MSPs are showing a willingness to debate matters which are reserved to Westminster, a sign that many Members are already impatient with the restrictions on their legislative powers.

At the start of the new millennium the progress of the Scottish Parliament is being talked about, occasionally criticised, sometimes applauded, but at least it is commanding the attention and watchful respect of most of the Scottish people. Muttering can be heard by worried Unionists that Scots electors are already showing a willingness to look to Edinburgh instead of London for leadership, in other words to regard the devolved administration almost as a sovereign legislature.

Scotland's first decentralised government, the Labour-LibDem coalition, remains a delicate flower threatened by issues including, at the time of writing, tuition fees and possible electoral reform in Westminster. All of the tensions, disputes and controversies thrown up by Home Rule in its early days are no more than the stuff of workaday politics. In other words our new Parliament is behaving just as we would expect any other Parliament to behave.

Sometime in the future, it is reasonable to predict, the Holyrood and Westminster Parliaments will be run by opposing political parties, most probably with the SNP governing Scotland. When that day comes the Scottish Parliament will have a critical influence over Scotland's and Britain's destiny, and the people who voted for Home Rule will be asked to decide in a referendum whether they want their country to remain an integral part of the United Kingdom or to reclaim its independence.

Appendix

Results of the
Scottish Parliamentary Election

May 6, 1999

In the following section the results from the 73
constituencies are given first, in area order. The
names of additional members elected by PR appear
on pages 239 – 243. The abbreviations used for the
various parties are explained on pages 243 and 244.

CENTRAL SCOTLAND

Airdrie and Shotts

Electorate. 58,481 Turnout 33,213 (56.79%)
Karen Whitefield (Lab) 18,338 (55.21%) Gil Paterson (SNP) 9,353
(28.16%) Patrick Ross-Taylor (C) 3,177 (9.57%) David Miller (LD)
2,345 (7.06%)

LAB WIN Maj. 8,985 5.19% swing from Lab to SNP

Coatbridge and Chryston

Electorate 52,178 Turnout 30,198 (57.87%)
Elaine Smith (Lab) 17,923 (59.35%) Peter Kearney (SNP) 7,519 (24.90%)
Gordon Lind (C) 2,867 (9.49%) Jane Hook (LD) 1,889 (6.26%)

LAB WIN Maj. 10,404

Cumbernauld and Kilsyth

Electorate 49,395 Turnout 30,612 (61.97%)
Cathy Craigie (Lab) 15,182 (49.59%) Andrew Wilson (SNP) 10,923
(35.68%) Hugh O'Donnell (LD) 2,029 (6.63%) Robin Slack (C) 1,362
(4.45%) Kenny McEwan (SSP) 1,116 (3.65%)

LAB WIN Maj. 4,259 8.49% swing from Lab to SNP

East Kilbride

Electorate 66,111 Turnout 41,313 (62.49%)
Andy Kerr (Lab) 19,987 (48.38%) Linda Fabiani (SNP) 13,488 (32.65%)
Craig Stevenson (C) 4,465 (10.81%) Ewan Hawthorn (LD) 3,373 (8.16%)

LAB WIN Maj. 6,499 9.95% swing from Lab to SNP

CENTRAL SCOTLAND (continued)

Falkirk East
Electorate 57,345 Turnout 35,212 (61.40%)
Cathy Peattie (Lab) 15,721 (44.65%) Keith Brown (SNP)11,582
(32.89%) Alastair Orr (C) 3,399 (9.65%) Gordon McDonald (LD) 2,509
(7.13%) Raymond Stead (Soc Lab) 1,643 (4.67%) Victor MacGrain
(SFPP) 358 (1.02%)

LAB WIN Maj. 4,139 10.21% swing from Lab to SNP

Falkirk West
Electorate 53,404 Turnout 33,667 (63.04%)
Dennis Canavan (Falkirk W) 18,511 (54.98%) Ross Martin (Lab) 6,319
(18.77%) Michael Matheson (SNP) 5,986 (17.78%) Gordon Miller (C)
1,897 (5.63%) Andrew Smith (LD) 954 (2.83%)

FALKIRK W WIN Maj. 12,192 2.02% swing from Lab to Falkirk W

Hamilton North and Bellshill
Elect. 53,992 Turnout 31,216 (57.82%)
Michael McMahon (Lab) 15,227 (48.78%) Kathleen McAlorum (SNP)
9,621 (30.82%) Stuart Thomson (C) 3,199 (10.25%) Jayne Struthers (LD)
2,105 (6.74%) Katharine McGavigan (Soc Lab) 1,064 (3.41%).

LAB WIN Maj. 5,606 13.48% swing from Lab to SNP

Hamilton South
Electorate 46,765 Turnout 25,920 (55.43%)
Tom McCabe (Lab) 14,098 (54.39%) Adam Ardrey (SNP) 6,922
(26.71%) Margaret Mitchell (C) 2,918 (11.26%) John Oswald (LD) 1,982
(7.65%)

LAB WIN Maj. 7,176 10.15% swing from Lab to SNP

CENTRAL SCOTLAND (continued)

Kilmarnock and Loudoun
Electorate 61,454 Turnout 39,349 (64.03%)
Margaret Jamieson (Lab) 17,345 (44.08%) Alex Neil (SNP) 14,585 (37.07%) Lyndsay McIntosh (C) 4,589 (11.66%) John Stewart (LD) 2,830 (7.19%)

LAB WIN Maj. 2,760   4.14% swing from Lab to SNP

Motherwell and Wishaw
Electorate 52,613 Turnout 30,364 (57.71%)
Jack McConnell (Lab) 13,955 (45.96%) Jim McGuigan (SNP) 8,879 (29.24%) William Gibson (C) 3,694 (12.17%) John Milligan (Soc Lab) 1,941 (6.39%) Rodger Spillane (LD) 1,895 (6.24%)

LAB WIN Maj. 5,076   9.10% swing from Lab to SNP

GLASGOW

Glasgow Anniesland
Electorate 54,378 Turnout 28,480 (52.37%)
Donald Dewar (Lab)16,749 (58.81%) Kaukab Stewart (SNP) 5,756 (20.21%) William Aitken (C) 3,032 (10.65%) Iain Brown (LD) 1,804 (6.33%) Ann Lynch (SSP) 1,000 (3.51%) Edward Boyd (Soc Lab) 139 (0.49%)

LAB WIN Maj.10,993 3. 07% swing from Lab to SNP

Glasgow Baillieston
Electorate 49,068 Turnout 23,709 (48.32%)
Margaret Curran (Lab) 11,289 (47.61%) Dorothy Elder (SNP) 8,217 (34.66%) James McVicar (SSP) 1,864 (7.86%) Kate Pickering (C) 1,526 (6.44%) Judith Fryer (LD) 813 (3.43%)

LAB WIN Maj. 3,072 16.82% swing from Lab to SNP

GLASGOW (continued)

Glasgow Cathcart
Electorate 51,338 Turnout 26,976 (52.55%)
Mike Watson (Lab) 12,966 (48.06%) Maire Whitehead (SNP) 7,592
(28.14%) Mary Leishman (C) 3,311 (12.27%) Callan Dick (LD) 2,187
(8.11%) Roddy Slorach (SWP) 920 (3.41%)

LAB WIN *Maj. 5,374 7.99% swing from Lab to SNP*

Glasgow Govan
Electorate 53,257 Turnout 26,373 (49.52%)
Gordon Jackson (Lab) 11,421 (43.31%) Nicola Sturgeon (SNP) 9,665
(36.65%) Tasmina Ahmed-Sheikh (C) 2,343 (8.88%) Mohammed Aslam
Khan (LD) 1,479 (5.61%) Charlie McCarthy (SSP) 1,275 (4.83%) John
Foster (Comm Brit) 190 (0.72%)

LAB WIN *Maj. 1,756 1.19% swing from Lab to SNP*

Glasgow Kelvin
Electorate 61,207 Turnout 28,362 (46.34%) Pauline McNeill (Lab)
12,711 (44.82%) Sandra White (SNP) 8,303 (29.28%) Moira Craig (LD)
3,720 (13.12%) Assad Rasul (C) 2,253 (7.94%) Heather Ritchie (SSP)
1,375 (4.85%)

LAB WIN *Maj. 4,408 7.03% swing from Lab to SNP*

Glasgow Maryhill
Electorate 56,469 Turnout 23,010 (40.75%)
Patricia Ferguson (Lab) 11,455 (49.78%) Bill Wilson (SNP) 7,129
(30.98%) Clare Hamblen (LD) 1,793 (7.79%) Gordon Scott (SSP) 1,439
(6.25%) Michael Fry (C) 1,194 (5.19%)

LAB WIN *Maj. 4326 14.59% swing from Lab to SNP*

GLASGOW (continued)

Glasgow Pollok
Electorate 47,970 Turnout 26,080 (54.37%)
Johann Lamont (Lab Co-op) 11,405 (43.73%) Kenneth Gibson (SNP) 6,763 (25.93%) Thomas Sheridan (SSP) 5,611 (21.51%) Rory O'Brien (C) 1,370 (5.25%) James King (LD) 931 (3.57%)

LAB CO-OP WIN Maj. 4,642 12.12% swing from Lab Co-op to SNP

Glasgow Rutherglen
Electorate 51,012 Turnout 29,023 (56.89%)
Janice Hughes (Lab) 13,442 (46.31%) Tom Chalmers (SNP) 6,155 (21.21%) Robert Brown (LD) 5,798 (19.98%) Iain Stewart (C) 2,315 (7.98%) William Bonnar (SSP) 832 (2.87%) James Nisbet (Soc Lab) 481 (1.66%)

LAB WIN Maj. 7,287 8.58% swing from Lab to SNP

Glasgow Shettleston
Electorate 50,592 Turnout 20,532 (40.58%)
Frank McAveety (Lab Co-op) 11,078 (53.95%) Jim Byrne (SNP) 5,611 (27.33%) Rosie Kane (SSP) 1,640 (7.99%) Colin Bain (C) 1,260 (6.14%) Laurence Clarke (LD) 943 (4.59%)

LAB CO-OP WIN Maj. 5,467 16.28% swing from Lab Co-op to SNP

Glasgow Springburn
Electorate 55,670 Turnout 24,365 (43.77%)
Paul Martin (Lab) 14,268 (58.56%) John Brady (SNP) 6,375 (26.16%) Murray Roxburgh (C) 1,293 (5.31%) Matthew Dunnigan (LD) 1,288 (5.29%) James Friel (SSP) 1,141 (4.68%)

LAB WIN Maj. 7,893 11.23% swing from Lab to SNP

HIGHLANDS AND ISLANDS

Argyll and Bute
Electorate 49,609 Turnout 32,177 (64.86%)
George Lyon (LD) 11,226 (34.89%) Duncan Hamilton (SNP)   9,169
(28.50%) Hugh Raven (Lab) 6,470 (20.11%) David Petrie (C) 5,312
(16.51%)

LD WIN Maj. 2,057 5.32% swing from LD to SNP

Caithness, Sutherland and Easter Ross
Electorate 41,581 Turnout 26,029 (62.60%)
Jamie Stone (LD) 10,691 (41.07%) James Hendry (Lab) 6,300 (24.20%)
Jean Urquhart (SNP) 6,035 (23.19%) Richard Jenkins (C) 2,167 (8.33%)
James Campbell (Ind) 554 (2.13%) Ewen Stewart (Ind) 282 (1.08%)

LD WIN Maj. 4,391 4.56% swing from Lab to LD

Inverness East, Nairn and Lochaber
Electorate 66,285 Turnout 41,824 (63.10%)
Fergus Ewing (SNP) 13,825 (33.06%) Joan Aitken (Lab) 13,384
(32.00%) Donnie Fraser (LD) 8,508 (20.34%) Mary Scanlon (C)
6,107 (14.60%)

SNP WIN Maj. 441 2.98% swing from Lab to SNP

Moray
Electorate 58,388 Turnout 33,576 (57.50%)
Margaret Ewing (SNP) 13,027 (38.80%) Ali Farquharson (Lab) 8,898
(26.50%) Andrew Findlay (C) 8,595 (25.60%) Patsy Kenton (LD) 3,056
(9.10%)

SNP WIN Maj. 4,129 4.72% swing from SNP to Lab

HIGHLANDS AND ISLANDS (continued)

Orkney
Electorate 15,658 Turnout 8,918 (56.95%)
Jim Wallace (LD) 6,010 (67.39%) Christopher Zawadzki (C) 1,391 (15.60%) John Mowat (SNP) 917 (10.28%) Angus Macleod (Lab) 600 (6.73%)

LD WIN Maj. 4,619

Ross, Skye and Inverness West
Electorate 55,845 Turnout 35,415 (63.42%)
John Farquhar Munro (LD) 11,652 (32.90%) Donnie Munro (Lab) 10,113 (28.56%) Jim Mather (SNP) 7,997 (22.58%) John Scott (C) 3,351 (9.46%) Douglas Briggs (Ind) 2,302 (6.50%)

LD WIN Maj. 1,539 2.86% swing from LD to Lab

Shetland
Electorate 16,978 Turnout 9,978 (58.77%)
Tavish Scott (LD) 5,435 (54.47%) Jonathan Wills (Lab) 2,241 (22.46%) William Ross (SNP) 1,430 (14.33%) Gary Robinson (C) 872 (8.74%)

LD WIN Maj. 3,194

Western Isles
Electorate 22,412 Turnout 13,954 (62.26%)
Alasdair Morrison (Lab) 7,248 (51.94%) Alasdair Nicholson (SNP) 5,155 (36.94%) Jamie MacGrigor (C) 1,095 (7.85%) John Horne (LD) 456 (3.27%)

LAB WIN Maj. 2,093 3.60% swing from Lab to SNP

LOTHIANS

Edinburgh Central
Electorate 65,945 Turnout 37,412 (56.73%)
Sarah Boyack (Lab) 14,224 (38.02%) Ian McKee (SNP) 9,598 (25.65%)
Andy Myles (LD) 6,187 (16.54%) Jacqui Low (C) 6,018 (16.09%) Kevin
Williamson (SSP) 830 (2.22%) Brian Allingham (Ind Dem) 364 (0.97%)
William Wallace (Braveheart) 191 (0.51%)

LAB WIN Maj. 4,626 9.46% swing from Lab to SNP

Edinburgh East and Musselburgh
Electorate 60,167 Turnout 36,989 (61.48%)
Susan Deacon (Lab) 17,086 (46.19%) Kenny MacAskill (SNP) 10,372
(28.04%) Jeremy Balfour (C) 4,600 (12.44%) Marjorie Thomas (LD) 4,100
(11.08%) Derrick White (SSP) 697 (1.88%) Michael Heavey (Ind You) 134
(0.36%)

LAB WIN Maj. 6,714 8.18% swing from Lab to SNP

Edinburgh North and Leith
Electorate 62,976 Turnout 36,646 (58.19%)
Malcolm Chisholm (Lab) 17,203 (46.94%) Anne Dana (SNP) 9,467
(25.83%) Jamie Sempill (C) 5,030 (13.73%) Sebastian Tombs (LD) 4,039
(11.02%) Ronald Brown (SSP) 907 (2.48%)

LAB WIN   Maj. 7,736 2.85% swing from Lab to SNP

Edinburgh Pentlands
Electorate 60,029 Turnout 39,600 (65.97%)
Iain Gray (Lab) 14,343 (36.22%) David McLetchie (C) 11,458 (28.93%)
Stewart Gibb (SNP) 8,770 (22.15%) Ian Gibson (LD) 5,029 (12.70%)

LAB WIN Maj. 2,885 1.67% swing from Lab to C.

LOTHIANS (continued)

Edinburgh South
Electorate 64,100 Turnout 40,135 (62.61%)
Angus MacKay (Lab) 14,869 (37.05%) Margo MacDonald (SNP) 9,445 (23.53%) Mike Pringle (LD) 8,961 (22.33%) Iain Whyte (C) 6,378 (15.89%) William Black (SWP) 482 (1.20%)

LAB WIN Maj. 5,424 10.19% swing from Lab to SNP

Edinburgh West
Electorate 61,747 Turnout 41,583 (67.34%)
Margaret Smith (LD) 15,161 (36.46%) James Douglas-Hamilton (C) 10,578 (25.44%) Carol Fox (Lab) 8,860 (21.31%) Graham Sutherland (SNP) 6,984 (16.80%)

LD WIN Maj. 4,583 2.10% swing from LD to C

Linlithgow
Electorate 54,262 Turnout 33,782 (62.26%)
Mary Mulligan (Lab) 15,247 (45.13%) Stewart Stevenson (SNP) 12,319 (36.47%) Gordon Lindhurst (C) 3,158 (9.35%) John Barrett (LD) 2,643 (7.82%) Irene Ovenstone (Ind) 415 (1.23%)

LAB WIN Maj. 2,928 9.33% swing from Lab to SNP

Livingston
Electorate 62,060 Turnout 36,570 (58.93%)
Bristow Muldoon (Lab) 17,313 (47.34%) Greg McCarra (SNP) 13,409 (36.67%) Douglas Younger (C) 3,014 (8.24%) Martin Oliver (LD) 2,834 (7.75%)

LAB WIN Maj. 3,904 8.38% swing from Lab to SNP

LOTHIANS (continued)

Midlothian
Electorate 48,374 Turnout 29,755 (61.51%)
Rhona Brankin (Lab Co-op) 14,467 (48.62%) Angus Robertson (SNP) 8,942 (30.05%) John Elder (LD) 3,184 (10.70%) George Turnbull (C) 2,544 (8.55%)Douglas Pryde (Ind) 618 (2.08%)

LAB CO-OP WIN *Maj. 5,525 4.71% swing from Lab Co-op to SNP*

MID SCOTLAND AND FIFE

Dunfermline East
Electorate 52,087 Turnout 29,659 (56.94%)
Helen Eadie (Lab Co-op) 16,576 (55.89%) David McCarthy (SNP) 7,877 (26.56%) Carrie Ruxton (C) 2,931 (9.88%) Fred Lawson (LD) 2,275 (7.67%)

LAB CO-OP WIN *Maj. 8,699 10.96% swing from Lab Co-op to SNP*

Dunfermline West
Electorate 53,112 Turnout 30,671 (57.75%)
Scott Barrie (Lab) 13,560 (44.21%) Douglas Chapman (SNP) 8,539 (27.84%) Elizabeth Harris (LD) 5,591 (18.23%) James Mackie (C) 2,981 (9.72%)

LAB WIN *Maj. 5,021 8.77% swing from Lab to SNP*

Fife Central
Electorate 58,850 Turnout 32,852 (55.82%)
Henry McLeish (Lab) 18,828 (57.31%) Tricia Marwick (SNP) 10,153 (30.91%) Jane Ann Liston (LD) 1,953 (5.94%) Keith Harding (C) 1,918 (5.84%).

LAB WIN *Maj. 8,6753.62% swing from Lab to SNP*

MID SCOTLAND AND FIFE (continued)

Fife North East
Electorate 60,886 Turnout 35,941 (59.03%)
Iain Smith (LD) 13,590 (37.81%) Edward Brocklebank (C) 8,526
(23.72%) Colin Welsh (SNP) 6,373 (17.73%) Charles Milne (Lab) 5,175
(14.40%) Donald Macgregor (Ind) 1,540 (4.28%) Robert Beveridge (Ind)
737 (2.05%)

LD WIN Maj. 5,064 5.33% swing from LD to C

Kirkcaldy
Electorate 51,640 Turnout 28,342 (54.88%)
Marilyn Livingstone (Lab Co-op) 13,645 (48.14%) Stewart Hosie (SNP)
9,170 (32.35%) Michael Scott-Hayward (C) 2,907 (10.26%) John
Mainland (LD) 2,620 (9.24%)

LAB CO-OP WIN Maj. 4,475 7.42% swing from Lab Co-op to SNP

Ochil
Electorate 57,083 Turnout 36,867 (64.58%)
Richard Simpson (Lab) 15,385 (41.73%) George Reid (SNP) 14,082
(38.20%) Nicholas Johnston (C) 4,151 (11.26%) Jamie Mar and Kellie
(LD) 3,249 (8.81%)

LAB WIN Maj. 1,303 3.55% swing from Lab to SNP

Perth
Electorate 61,034 Turnout 37,396 (61.27%)
Roseanna Cunningham (SNP) 13,570 (36.29%) Ian Stevenson (C) 11,543
(30.87%) Jillian Richards (Lab) 8,725 (23.33%) Chic Brodie (LD) 3,558
(9.51%)

SNP WIN Maj. 2,027 0.82% swing from SNP to C

MID SCOTLAND AND FIFE (continued)

Stirling
Electorate 52,904 Turnout 35,805 (67.68%)
Sylvia Jackson (Lab) 13,533 (37.80%) Annabelle Ewing (SNP) 9,552
(26.68%) Brian Monteith (C) 9,158 (25.58%) Iain Macfarlane (LD) 3,407
(9.52%) Simon Kilgour (Ind)155 (0.43%)

LAB WIN Maj. 3,981 11.47% swing from Lab to SNP

Tayside North
Electorate 61,795 Turnout 38,055 (61.58%)
John Swinney (SNP) 16,786 (44.11%) Murdo Fraser (C) 12,594
(33.09%) Marion Dingwall (Lab) 5,727 (15.05%) Peter Regent (LD)
2,948 (7.75%)

SNP WIN Maj. 4,192 0.94% swing from C to SNP

NORTH EAST SCOTLAND

Aberdeen Central
Electorate 52,715 Turnout 26,495 (50.26%)
Lewis Macdonald (Lab) 10,305 (38.89%) Richard Lochhead (SNP) 7,609
(28.72%) Eleanor Anderson (LD) 4,403 (16.62%) Tom Mason (C) 3,655
(13.80%) Andrew Cumbers (SSP) 523 (1.97%)

LAB WIN Maj. 2,696 11.73% swing from Lab to SNP

Aberdeen North
Electorate 54,553 Turnout 27,821 (51.00%)
Elaine Thomson (Lab) 10,340 (37.17%) Brian Adam (SNP) 9,942
(35.74%) James Donaldson (LD) 4,767 (17.13%) Iain Haughie (C) 2,772
(9.96%)

LAB WIN Maj. 398 12.31% swing from Lab to SNP

NORTH EAST SCOTLAND

Aberdeen South
Electorate 60,579 Turnout 34,690 (57.26%)
Nicol Stephen (LD) 11,300 (32.57%) Mike Elrick (Lab) 9,540 (27.50%)
Nanette Milne (C) 6,993 (20.16%) Irene McGugan (SNP) 6,651 (19.17%)
Scott Sutherland (SWP) 206 (0.59%)

LD WIN Maj. 1,760 6.36% swing from Lab to LD

Aberdeenshire West and Kincardine
Electorate 60,702 Turnout 35,736 (58.87%)
Mike Rumbles (LD) 12,838 (35.92%) Ben Wallace (C) 10,549 (29.52%)
Maureen Watt (SNP) 7,699 (21.54%) Gordon Guthrie (Lab) 4,650
(13.01%)

LD WIN Maj. 2,2890.12% swing from C to LD

Angus
Electorate 59,891 Turnout 34,536 (57.66%)
Andrew Welsh (SNP) 16,055 (46.49%) Ron Harris (C) 7,154 (20.71%)
Ian McFatridge (Lab) 6,914 (20.02%) Dick Speirs (LD) 4,413 (12.78%)

SNP WIN Maj. 8,901 1.06% swing from C to SNP

Banff and Buchan
Electorate 57,639 Turnout 31,734 (55.06%)
Alex Salmond (SNP) 16,695 (52.61%) David Davidson (C) 5,403
(17.03%) Maitland Mackie (LD) 5,315 (16.75%) Megan Harris (Lab)
4,321 (13.62%)

SNP WIN Maj.11,292 1.80% swing from C to SNP

NORTH EAST SCOTLAND (continued)

Dundee East
Electorate 57,222 Turnout 31,663 (55.33%)
John McAllion (Lab) 13,703 (43.28%) Shona Robison (SNP) 10,849
(34.26%) Iain Mitchell (C) 4,428 (13.98%) Raymond Lawrie (LD) 2,153
(6.80%) Harvey Duke (SSP) 530 (1.67%)

LAB WIN Maj. 2854 7.78% swing from Lab to SNP

Dundee West
Electorate 55,725 Turnout 29,082 (52.19%)
Kate MacLean (Lab) 10,925 (37.57%) Calum Cashley (SNP) 10,804
(37.15%) Gordon Buchan (C) 3,345 (11.50%) Elizabeth Dick (LD) 2,998
(10.31%) James McFarlane (SSP) 1,010 (3.47%)

LAB WIN Maj. 121 15.07% swing from Lab to SNP

Gordon
Electorate 59,497 Turnout 33,622 (56.51%)
Nora Radcliffe (LD) 12,353 (36.74%) Sandy Stronach (SNP) 8,158
(24.26%) Alex Johnstone (C) 6,602 (19.64%) Gillian Carlin-Kulwicki
(Lab) 3,950 (11.75%) Hamish Watt (Ind) 2,559 (7.61%)

LD WIN Maj. 4,195 5.08% swing from LD to SNP

SOUTH OF SCOTLAND

Ayr
Electorate 56,338 Turnout 37,454 (66.48%)
Ian Welsh (Lab) 14,263 (38.08%) Phil Gallie (C) 14,238 (38.01%) Roger
Mullin (SNP) 7,291 (19.47%) Elaine Morris (LD) 1,662 (4.44%)

LAB WIN Maj. 25 7.27% swing from Lab to C

SOUTH OF SCOTLAND (continued)

Carrick, Cumnock and Doon Valley
Electorate 65,580 Turnout 41,095 (62.66%)
Cathy Jamieson (Lab Co-op) 19,667 (47.86%) Adam Ingram (SNP) 10,864 (26.44%) John Scott (C) 8,123 (19.77%) David Hannay (LD) 2,441 (5.94%)

LAB CO-OP WIN Maj. 8,803 10.86% swing from Lab Co-op to SNP

Clydesdale
Electorate 64,262 Turnout 38,947 (60.61%)
Karen Turnbull (Lab) 16,755 (43.02%) Ann Winning (SNP) 12,875 (33.06%) Charles Cormack (C) 5,814 (14.93%) Sandra Grieve (LD) 3,503 (8.99%)

LAB WIN Maj. 3,880 10.22% swing from Lab to SNP

Cunninghame South
Electorate 50,443 Turnout 28,277 (56.06%)
Irene Oldfather (Lab) 14,936 (52.82%) Michael Russell (SNP) 8,395 (29.69%) Murray Tosh (C) 3,229 (11.42%) Stuart Ritchie (LD) 1,717 (6.07%)

LAB WIN Maj. 6,541 9.41% swing from Lab to SNP

Dumfries
Electorate 63,162 Turnout 38,482 (60.93%)
Elaine Murray (Lab) 14,101 (36.64%) David Mundell (C) 10,447 (27.15%) Stephen Norris (SNP) 7,625 (19.81%) Neil Wallace (LD) 6,309 (16.39%)

LAB WIN Maj. 3,654 4.99% swing from Lab to C

SOUTH OF SCOTLAND (continued)

East Lothian
Electorate 58,579 Turnout 35,582 (60.74%)
John Home Robertson (Lab) 19,220 (54.02%) Calum Miller (SNP) 8,274 (23.25%) Christine Richard (C) 5,941 (16.70%) Judy Hayman (LD) 2,147 (6.03%)

LAB WIN Maj. 10,946 3.10% swing from Lab to SNP

Galloway and Upper Nithsdale
Electorate 53,057 Turnout 35,316 (66.56%)
Alasdair Morgan (SNP13,873 (39.28%) Alex Fergusson (C) 10,672 (30.22%) Jim Stevens (Lab) 7,209 (20.41%) Joan Mitchell (LD) 3,562 (10.09%)

SNP WIN Maj. 3201 2.16% swing from SNP to C

Roxburgh and Berwickshire
Electorate 47,639 Turnout 27,876 (58.52%)
Euan Robson (LD) 11,320 (40.61%) Alasdair Hutton (C) 7,735 (27.75%) Stuart Crawford (SNP) 4,719 (16.93%) Suzanne McLeod (Lab) 4,102 (14.72%)

LD WIN Maj. 3,585 4.88% swing from LD to C

Tweeddale, Ettrick and Lauderdale
Electorate 51,577 Turnout 33,715 (65.37%)
Ian Jenkins (LD) 12,078 (35.82%) Christine Creech (SNP) 7,600 (22.54%) George McGregor (Lab) 7,546 (22.38%) John Campbell (C) 6,491 (19.25%)

LD WIN Maj. 4,478 0.42% swing from LD to SNP

WEST OF SCOTLAND

Clydebank & Milngavie
Electorate 52,461 Turnout 33,337 (63.55%)
Des McNulty (Lab) 15,105 (45.31%) Jim Yuill (SNP) 10,395 (31.18%)
Rod Ackland (LD) 4,149 (12.45%) Dorothy Luckhurst (C) 3,688
(11.06%)

LAB WIN Maj. 4,710 9.97% swing from Lab to SNP

Cunninghame North
Electorate 55,867 Turnout 33,491 (59.95%) Lab win
Allan Wilson (Lab) 14,369 (42.90%) Kay Ullrich (SNP) 9,573 (28.58%)
Mike Johnston (C) 6,649 (19.85%) Calum Irving (LD) 2,900 (8.66%)

LAB WIN Maj. 4,796 8.77% swing from Lab to SNP

Dumbarton
Electorate 56,090 Turnout 34,699 (61.86%)
Jackie Baillie (Lab) 15,181 (43.75%) Lloyd Quinan (SNP) 10,423
(30.04%) Donald Reece (C) 5,060 (14.58%) Paul Coleshill (LD)
4,035 (11.63%)

LAB WIN Maj. 4,758 6.33% swing from Lab to SNP

Eastwood
Electorate 67,248 Turnout 45,396 (67.51%)
Ken Macintosh (Lab) 16,970 (37.38%) John Young (C) 14,845 (32.70%)
Rachel Findlay (SNP) 8,760 (19.30%) Anna McCurley (LD) 4,472
(9.85%) Manar Tayan (Ind) 349 (0.77%)

LAB WIN Maj. 2,125 0.75% swing from Lab to C

WEST OF SCOTLAND (continued)

Greenock & Inverclyde
Electorate 48,584 Turnout 28,639 (58.95%)
Duncan McNeil (Lab) 11,817 (41.26%) Ross Finnie (LD) 7,504 (26.20%)
Ian Hamilton (SNP) 6,762 (23.61%) Richard Wilkinson (C) 1,699
(5.93%) David Landels (SSP) 857 (2.99%)

LAB WIN Maj. 4,313 13.64% swing from Lab to LD

Paisley North
Electorate 49,020 Turnout 27,750 (56.61%)
Wendy Alexander (Lab) 13,492 (48.62%) Ian Mackay (SNP) 8,876
(31.99%) Peter Ramsay (C) 2,242 (8.08%) Tamsin Mayberry (LD) 2,133
(7.69%) Fiona Macdonald (SSP) 1,007 (3.63%)

LAB WIN Maj. 4,616 10.46% swing from Lab to SNP

Paisley South
Electorate 53,637 Turnout 30,656 (57.15%)
Hugh Henry (Lab) 13,899 (45.34%) Bill Martin (SNP) 9,404 (30.68%)
Stuart Callison (LD) 2,974 (9.70%) Sheila Laidlaw (C) 2,433 (7.94%)
Paul Mack (Ind) 1,273 (4.15%) Jackie Forrest (SWP) 673 (2.20%)

LAB WIN Maj. 4,495 9.73% swing from Lab to SNP

Renfrewshire West
Electorate 52,452 Turnout 34,037 (64.89%)
Patricia Godman (Lab) 12,708 (37.34%) Colin Campbell (SNP) 9,815
(28.84%) Annabel Goldie (C) 7,243 (21.28%) Neal Ascherson (LD)
2,659 (7.81%) Allan McGraw (Ind) 1,136 (3.34%) Patrick Clark (SWP)
476 (1.40%)

LAB WIN Maj. 2,893 5.77% swing from Lab to SNP

WEST OF SCOTLAND (continued)

Strathkelvin and Bearsden
Electorate 63,111 Turnout 42,390 (67.17%)
Sam Galbraith (Lab) 21,505 (50.73%) Fiona McLeod (SNP) 9,384 (22.14%) Charles Ferguson (C) 6,934 (16.36%) Anne Howarth (LD) 4,144 (9.78%) Maxi Richards (Anti-Drug) 423 (1.00%)

LAB WIN Maj. 12,121 3.98% swing from Lab to SNP

Additional Members Elected by Proportional Representation

CENTRAL SCOTLAND
Electorate 551,733

Members Elected
Lyndsay McIntosh (C) Donald Gorrie (LD) Alex Neil (SNP) Michael Matheson (SNP) Linda Fabiani (SNP) Andrew Wilson (SNP) Gil Paterson (SNP)

Party Share
Lab 129,822 (39.28%); SNP 91,802 (27.78%); C 30,243 (9.15%); Falkirk W 27,700 (8.38%); LD 20,505 (6.20%); Soc Lab 10,956 (3.32%); Green 5,926 (1.79%); SSP 5,739 (1.74%); SUP 2,886 (0.87%); ProLife 2,567 (0.78%); SFPP 1,373 (0.42%); NLP 719 (0.22%); Ind Prog 248 (0.08%).

GLASGOW
Electorate 531,956

Members Elected
William Aitken(C) Robert Brown (LD) Dorothy Elder (SNP) Sandra White (SNP) Nicola Sturgeon (SNP) Kenneth Gibson (SNP) Tommy Sheridan (SSP)

Party Share
Lab 112,588 (43.92%); SNP 65,360 (25.50%); C 20,239 (7.90%); SSP 18,581 (7.25%); LD 18,473 (7.21%); Green 10,159 (3.96%); SocLab 4,391 (1.71%); ProLife 2,357 (0.92%); SUP 2,283 (0.89%); Comm Brit 521 (0.20%); Humanist 447 (0.17%); NLP 419 (0.16%); SPGB 309 (0.12%); Choice 221 (0.09%).

HIGHLANDS AND ISLANDS
Electorate 326,553

Members Elected
Jamie MacGrigor (C) Mary Scanlon (C) Maureen MacMillan (Lab) Peter Peacock (Lab) Rhoda Grant (Lab) Winnie Ewing (SNP) Duncan Hamilton (SNP)

Party Share
SNP 55,933 (27.73%); Lab 51,371 (25.47%); LD 43,226 (21.43%); C 30,122 (14.94%); Green 7,560 (3.75%); Ind Noble 3,522 (1.75%); Soc Lab 2,808 (1.39%); Highlands 2,607 (1.29%); SSP 1,770 (0.88%); Mission 1,151 (0.57%); Int Ind 712 (0.35%); NLP 536 (0.27%); Ind R 354 (0.18%).

LOTHIANS
Electorate 539,656

Members Elected
James Douglas-Hamilton (C) David McLetchie (C) David Steel (LD) Kenny MacAskill (SNP) Margo MacDonald (SNP) Fiona Hyslop (SNP) Robin Harper (Green)

Party Share
Lab 99,908 (30.23%); SNP 85,085 (25.74%); C 52,067 (15.75%); LD 47,565 (14.39%); Green 22,848 (6.91%); Soc Lab 10,895 (3.30%) SSP 5,237 (1.58%); Lib 2,056 (0.62%); Witchery 1,184 (0.36%); ProLife 898 (0.27%); Rights 806 (0.24%); NLP 564 (0.17%); Braveheart 557 (0.17%); SPGB 388 (0.12%); Ind Voice 256 (0.08%); Ind Ind 145 (0.04%); Anti-Corr 54 (0.02%).

MID SCOTLAND AND FIFE
Electorate 509,387

Members Elected
Nicholas Johnston (C) Brian Monteith (C) Keith Harding (C) Keith Raffan (LD) Bruce Crawford (SNP) George Reid (SNP) Tricia Marwick (SNP)

Party Share
Lab 101,964 (33.36%); SNP 87,659 (28.68%); C 56,719 (18.56%); LD 38,896 (12.73%); Green 11,821 (3.87%); SocLab 4,266 (1.40%); SSP 3,044 (1.00%); ProLife 735 (0.24%); NLP 558 (0.18%).

NORTH OF SCOTLAND
Electorate 518,521

Members Elected

David Davidson (C) Alex Johnstone (C) Ben Wallace (C) Richard Lochhead (SNP) Shona Robison (SNP) Brian Adam (SNP) Irene McGugan (SNP)

Party Share

SNP 92,329 (32.35%); Lab 72,666 (25.46%); C 52,149 (18.27%); LD 49,843 (17.46%); Green 8,067 (2.83%); Soc Lab 3,557 (1.25%); SSP 3,016 (1.06%); Ind Watt 2,303 (0.81%); Ind SB 770 (0.27%); NLP 746 (0.26%).

SOUTH OF SCOTLAND
Electorate 510,634

Members Elected

Phil Gallie (C) David Mundell (C) Murray Tosh (C) Alex Fergusson (C) Michael Russell (SNP) Adam Ingram (SNP) Christine Creech (SNP)

Party Share

Lab 98,836 (31.04%); SNP 80,059 (25.15%); C 68,904 (21.64%); LD 38,157 (11.99%); Soc Lab 13,887 (4.36%); Green 9,468 (2.97%); Lib 3,478 (1.09%); SSP 3,304 (1.04%); UK Ind 1,502 (0.47%); NLP 775 (0.24%).

WEST OF SCOTLAND
Electorate 498,466

Members Elected
Annabel Goldie (C) John Young (C) Ross Finnie (LD) Lloyd
Quinan (SNP) Fiona McLeod (SNP) Kay Ullrich (SNP) Colin
Campbell(SNP)

Party Share
Lab 119,663 (38.55%); SNP 80,417 (25.91%); C 48,666 (15.68%);
LD 34,095 (10.98%); Green 8,175 (2.63%); SSP 5,944 (1.91%);
Soc Lab 4,472 (1.44%); ProLife 3,227 (1.04%) Individual 2,761
(0.89%); SUP 1,840 (0.59%); NLP 589 (0.19%); Ind Water 565
(0.18%).

Abbreviations used in these Listings

Conservative **C**
Labour **Lab**
Liberal Democrat **LD**
Scottish National Party **SNP**
Green Party **Green**
Anti-Corruption, Mobile Home Scandal, Roads **Anti-Corr**
Independent Anti-Drug Party **Anti-Drug**
Anti-Sleaze Labour **AS**
British National Party **BNP**
Braveheart **Braveheart**
Christian Unity **Ch U**
Communist Party of Britain **Comm Brit**
People's Choice **Choice**
Democratic Nationalist **Dem Nat**
Highlands and Islands Alliance **Highlands**
Humanist Party **Humanist**
MP for Falkirk West **Falkirk W**

Independent **Ind**
Independent Democrat **Ind Dem**
Independent Independent **Ind Ind**
Independent Labour **Ind Lab**
Independent Noble **Ind Noble**
Independent Progressive **Ind Prog**
Independent Robertson **Ind R**
Independent Sleaze-Buster **Ind SB**
Independent Voice for Scottish Parliament **Ind Voice**
Independent Labour Keep Scottish Water Public **Ind Water**
Independent Watt **Ind Watt**
Independent for You **Ind You**
Independent Individual **Individual**
International Independent **Int Ind**
Liberal Party **Liberal**
Scottish People's Mission **Mission**
Natural Law Party **NLP**
ProLife Alliance **ProLife**
Referendum Party **Ref**
Civil Rights Movement **Rights**
Scottish Conservative Unofficial **SCU**
Scottish Families and Pensioners Party **SFPP**
Scottish Labour Independent **SLI**
Scottish Labour Unofficial **SLU**
Scottish Socialist Alliance **SSA**
Scottish Socialist Party **SSP**
Scottish Unionist Party **SUP**
Socialist Labour Party **Soc Lab**
Socialist Party of Great Britain **SPGB**
Socialist Workers Party **SWP**
UK Independence Party **UK Ind**
Value Party **Value**
Witchery Tour Party **Witchery**

Other Saltire Publications

About the Saltire Society

The Saltire Society was founded in 1936 at a time when many of the distinctive features of Scotland's culture seemed in jeopardy. Over the years its members, who have included many of Scotland's most distinguished scholars and creative artists, have fought to preserve and present our cultural heritage so that Scotland might once again be a creative force in European civilisation. As well as publishing books the Society makes a number of national awards for excellence in fields as diverse as housing design, historical publication and scientific research. The Society has no political affiliation and welcomes as members all who share its aims. Further information from The Saltire Society, 9 Fountain Close, 22 High Street, Edinburgh. EH1 1TF Telephone 0131 556 1836. FAX 0131 557 1675 email saltire@saltire.org.uk Web Site: http://www.saltire-society.demon.co.uk